Soldiers of the Legion: a tale of the Carlist war.

Herbert Hayens

Soldiers of the Legion: a tale of the Carlist war.
Hayens, Herbert
British Library, Historical Print Editions
British Library
1898 [1897]
413 p. ; 8°.

SOLDIERS OF THE LEGION

By the same Author.

SOLDIERS OF THE LEGION. Price 3s. 6d.

AN EMPEROR'S DOOM. Price 5s.

CLEVELY SAHIB. Price 5s.

UNDER THE LONE STAR. Price 6s.

T. NELSON AND SONS,

London, Edinburgh, and New York.

Soldiers of the Legion

A Tale of the Carlist War

By

HERBERT HAYENS

Author of "Under the Lone Star," "Clevely Sahib,"
"An Emperor's Doom,"
&c. &c.

T. NELSON AND SONS

London, Edinburgh, and New York

1898

CONTENTS.

LIST OF ILLUSTRATIONS.

SOLDIERS OF THE LEGION.

CHAPTER I.

A TASTE OF CIVIL WAR.

"ARE you dead, Mr. Powell ?"

I recognized the voice, but the oddity of the question in itself would have revealed the speaker's identity.

The night was so dark that I could not see even the man against whose body my head rested, but a pair of strong arms encircled me, as if to prevent my being snatched away.

Just at first it was difficult to realize clearly aught of that which had happened, and I lay speculating in a dreamy manner on my novel and decidedly uncomfortable position.

I was cold and wet; my limbs felt like leaden weights, my head was dizzy and ached with a throbbing pain. A furious rain beat down upon my upturned face, while from below came a sound as of angry waters thundering against a barrier of rock.

Once or twice I endeavoured to make my voice heard,

but the words were drowned in the tumult, and my comrade, placing his lips to my ear, shouted, "Easy all, Mr. Powell; now that I know you are alive, we can wait for the rest. But you lay so plaguy still that I was frightened."

Then I resumed the interrupted reverie, and wondered curiously why I did not go to my cabin.

And where was Pym Forrester? Had he turned in?

This thought unlocked the flood-gates, as it were, and memory came flowing in with a rush.

I once more stood at Pym's side on the deck of his yacht, while the heaving billows flung themselves savagely upon us, straining the timbers from stem to stern, and tossing the little craft about like a cockle-shell.

I could still feel the grip of his hand, and hear his cheery voice shouting, "It's all over, Arthur," as a gigantic wave, lifting the frail boat clean out of the water, sent it with a crash against some jagged rocks.

At that point all recollection ceased. Between that event and the question which begins this chapter lay a wide gap, impossible for me to bridge.

By some marvellous chance I had escaped an almost certain death; but of the others, save Dick Truscott, the man who held me, there was no sign.

Again I questioned myself concerning Pym. Was it possible that Dick and I were the sole survivors from the wreck?

Stricken with horror, I stretched forth my hands in the darkness, and called wildly upon my lost friend.

"Steady, sir," cried Truscott; "another jerk like that one, and we shall both be at the bottom of the Bay of Biscay."

Until then I did not know how dangerous was our situation, but at his words I lay passive, waiting with aching heart for the coming of the dawn.

It came at length, cold and cheerless; and as the sullen clouds rolled slowly back, I was more than ever amazed at our providential escape.

We lay on a narrow ledge of rock, to the very edge of which the hungry waves flung themselves, hissing and foaming, as if engaged in a desperate attempt to sweep us from our precarious refuge.

Then, too, I gathered a true perception of the service which Dick had rendered me. Throughout the weary hours he had held me firmly in a close embrace, knowing well that one instant's loosening of those friendly arms would have precipitated me headlong into the raging waters.

I began to thank him, but he checked me.

"No need of thanks, Mr. Powell; I was only too glad of the chance of dragging you out. But how I managed to get here in the dark is more than I can tell."

I turned and gazed at the waste of waters, as if, by dint of straining, my sight would force into being some vision of the wrecked yacht and my vanished friend.

Alas! over all that sullen, wide expanse nothing living moved.

Above our heads a few birds, uttering discordant cries,

wheeled in irregular flight; and below, the seething billows made a moaning sound, as if in despair at their failure to engulf us.

But of the hapless vessel and her gallant crew not a trace remained.

We looked in vain for a spar, the plank of a boat, the cap of some drowned mariner. Nothing rewarded our gaze, save the still angry waves.

"No good staying longer, sir," said Dick; "Mr. Forrester hasn't come ashore here at all events."

"Nor anywhere else," I answered mournfully, striving to rise.

"That's as may be," Dick responded, not cheerfully nor hopefully, but in a quiet, even tone, which jarred terribly upon my unstrung nerves; "it's no good cudgelling our brains; we might aim a hundred shots and never hit the mark. What we have to think of now is to get out of this place. Cling to that piece of rock and try to stand."

I did as he bade me, but without his support I must have tumbled from the ledge; my legs were devoid of power, and wholly useless.

"Raise one foot at a time and stamp on the ground—not too hard at first; the muscles are all tied up in knots."

I made a wry face, and Dick, who was rubbing his own limbs, exclaimed encouragingly, "Ah! that's right. That's what folks call 'pins and needles,' but I expect it feels more like red-hot iron skewers just now. Keep on with it, sir."

The pain was in truth very great, and more than once

nearly wrung from me a cry of agony; but I persevered, and at length had the satisfaction of being able to stand upright.

"That's better," my companion remarked; "and now we will make a move."

This was a very good suggestion, but how to put it into practice I could not well conceive. At our feet rolled the sullen waters, above our heads towered menacingly the huge rocks.

Up these we must perforce climb; and Dick, whom nothing ever disturbed, methodically began the perilous ascent.

"Take your time, and don't trust your weight on any stone before trying if it is firm," he said. "Some of them are very deceiving.—Ah, there goes one!" and a big boulder which had appeared to be firmly embedded went spinning and crashing into the sea.

Painfully and laboriously we toiled upwards, dragging ourselves from ledge to ledge, from rock to rock, now hanging over the precipice with only the support afforded by our hands, now pausing a moment on some narrow foothold in order to recover breath.

During one of these halts, I was gazing in despair at the distance yet to be traversed, when Dick said brusquely, "Don't look up, Mr. Powell, or down, but keep your eyes on the work in hand. Time enough to stare at those rocks when we reach them. One step at a time—that's the way to get on. Now, are you ready? I'm going to steer to the right; it seems easier on that side."

Again we moved forward, and surely, if slowly, won our way.

About three-quarters of the course had been successfully negotiated, when we struck into a narrow defile lying between two upright cliffs. Here a more rapid rate of progression became feasible, and as the danger of being precipitated over the rocks had practically ceased, I followed Dick with a lighter heart.

By this time it was broad daylight, and both of us were spent with our exertions and famishing from lack of food.

There was certainly much cause for thankfulness in having so wonderfully escaped a violent death, yet the situation was far from pleasant.

We had been cast ashore at some point on the north coast of Spain, and stood wet, hungry, and exhausted, without money, and possessed only of the clothes which we were wearing.

Even under ordinary circumstances such a position must have proved very disagreeable; but it was the autumn of 1835, and the north of Spain was convulsed by a cruel and devastating civil war.

Fire and sword, pillage and murder, racked the unhappy land. Life and property were alike insecure, and the flames of burning villages attested the fury of the strife.

What chance then had we, unarmed and penniless, of gaining a place of safety?

I was brooding over this question, when my comrade, who had pushed on ahead, halted and made signs for me to approach.

"Here is a beaten track which no doubt leads to the nearest village," he said; "we will follow it."

"What are your plans?" I asked.

"I have only one, and that is to secure a good breakfast."

"Have you considered the danger? Suppose we fall into the hands of the Carlists."

"Well," he said inquiringly; "what would be the result?"

"Simply that we should have no further need of breakfast; they would destroy our appetite by a dose of lead."

"Then we must go to work cautiously, for although we can do without the bullets, the breakfast must be had."

This could not be denied, yet it was with extreme reluctance that I continued along the track which Dick had discovered.

My anxiety increased when we entered a small wood, through the middle of which the path ran, and I scanned every tree with a nervous dread.

Grief at the loss of a stanch friend, the night's exposure, acute pain from a wound in the head, caused by being dashed against the rocks, and hunger, all combined to make me feel low-spirited, and unconsciously perhaps to exaggerate the peril.

For nearly a mile we continued the march, and then the trees, all of which were small in size, suddenly ceased.

We were on a plain, which appeared to be the summit of a gentle hill.

Dick, still going first, reached the edge and peered over.

"Smoke," he said shortly, "and therefore fire. We shall find a village in the valley, somewhat to the left."

While traversing the wood we had each obtained possession of a stout stick, and gripping these tightly we began the descent.

The side of the hill was clothed with brushwood, and at one part it dipped abruptly, preventing us from perceiving, until quite close, a large house that stood in the hollow.

Lying flat behind one of the low bushes, Dick stretched out his hand and whispered, "Here is our opportunity, sir. Breakfast or lead! we shall soon know which it is to be. You stay here, while I skirmish round a bit."

Without giving me time to answer, he moved away, and I waited, half dead with misery and fatigue.

No smoke rose from the one chimney within my view; not a sound reached me from the courtyard of the dwelling.

I was too fatigued to reason clearly, yet the silence impressed me by its strangeness, and filled me with a dim foreboding of evil.

The sight of my comrade's face as he returned deepened the misgiving into certainty.

Truscott was one of those men whose features rarely betray the workings of their minds. He may have felt deeply—indeed a later experience showed conclusively that he did—but the results were not manifest to the spectator. I had known him several months, and twice during that time he had been within an ace of death without exhibiting a trace of discomposure. Pym Forrester called him the "Cast-iron man," and the term seemed aptly to describe him.

When, therefore, he crept back, his face bloodless, and his

eyes staring with horror, no words were needed to inform me that he had met with an adventure far beyond the ordinary.

He flung himself down at my side, and lay still, save that the fingers of one hand alternately unclosed and closed themselves round his staff.

"Well!" I exclaimed, finding that he did not speak; "what about the breakfast?"

He gazed at me curiously, as if only half understanding.

"Ah!" he answered, after a pause, "I had forgotten. The sight yonder," and he pointed towards the house, "has made me feel silly."

Then in an undertone he added, "And this is called a Christian land."

"What is it?" I asked impatiently; "what have you seen?"

"Enough to make my blood run cold. But come and judge for yourself."

With increasing wonder at his strange mood, I crept behind him, and we descended cautiously to the rear of the building, which evidently belonged to a person of wealth and position.

Nothing living made its appearance at our approach; we heard not the bark of a dog, nor the neigh of a horse.

My comrade led me to the front, and here visible tokens of something unusual presented themselves.

The stable was open and empty, the door of the house was smashed, a clot of blood reddened the step.

Without uttering a word, Dick guided me to a long

low-roofed room on the right, and then, halting, placed a finger on my lips as if enforcing silence.

Well was it that he used the precaution. Even in spite of the admonition I could barely repress a cry of horror at the spectacle.

On a couch at the left side of the room lay a woman, partly dressed, encircling with either arm the body of a little child. The light of day played upon their features, and showed us that they slept peacefully—the last sleep of death.

Before the group, in an attitude of indescribable mournfulness, stood a man of middle age, tall, muscular, and with limbs well knit. His hands were red, and the same dye stained the sleeves and breast of his doublet. He uttered no sound, and his eyes were unmoistened by tears, but his hopeless grief was terrible to look upon.

I touched Truscott, intending to draw him away, and at the instant the Spaniard turned swiftly.

Whether the movement was due to chance or otherwise, I could not determine; but he faced us, and I marvelled greatly at the sudden change which his features had undergone.

The grief-stricken man was transformed into a wild animal. His eyes blazed with a savage ferocity, holding me in thrall.

With a lightning-like rapidity he levelled a pistol and took aim, while I, spell-bound, continued to watch him.

Dick, ever prompt in presence of danger, seizing my arm, threw me forcibly on the ground, and the bullet sped harmlessly over our heads.

"The poor fellow will work us mischief," my comrade said; "he is half crazy with grief."

"He thinks we are his enemies; leave him to me." And before he had time to reload I sprang to my feet, and approached the window.

"Pardon our intrusion, señor," I said, addressing him in Spanish; "we are English sailors—shipwrecked—cast ashore in last night's storm. A little while ago we were bemoaning our own misery, now we stand abashed in the presence of yours."

"I accorded you but poor hospitality, Señor Inglese," he responded gravely. "I took you to be one of those accursed bandits whose handiwork you perceive. This is a house of mourning, and a sad heart makes an indifferent host. But if it please you, enter."

"If we can be of any service—or, shall we fetch assistance from the village?"

Again the Spaniard's features were convulsed with rage, and, turning in the direction of the neighbouring houses, he cried passionately, "The people there are all Carlists; they would murder both you and me, did they know we were here."

"But you must do something," and I motioned significantly towards the couch.

His hand stole to his side, and his fingers gripped firmly over the hilt of a long rapier.

But although his speech was yet laboured, he had mastered his emotions, and replied to my remark with a certain grave courtesy.

"I will dig my dear ones a grave," he said, "and then join the troops of the queen. After that, may my sight be keen and my wrist steady."

I begged that he would allow us to help him, and further suggested that we might then undertake the proposed journey in company.

"I thank you," he replied, "and accept the offer gratefully. But you are faint, and require food. Alas! I do not know if these brigands have left aught in my dwelling. Enter, señors, and search."

To me the idea of eating and drinking in the presence of such a tragedy was strongly repellant; but Truscott, to whom I translated the conversation, brushed aside my scruples.

"The Don has common-sense on his side," he declared. "What aid can we give in our weak state? You cannot handle a spade, and I am little better. I will go on a prospecting tour."

"Make haste then; I have no mind to be trapped in this place."

"No, it would prove awkward, seeing that we are unarmed. Maybe the Don has a stock of weapons on hand."

While Dick was foraging for food, I explained to the Spaniard, who was plainly a man of importance, that we lacked arms, and were, therefore, practically useless in case of an attack.

"That is bad," he said, "as no doubt the wolves will soon be upon my track. But I can furnish you with swords and a couple of muskets. Your comrade looks as if he could use his weapons."

"He is an old soldier, and true as steel."

"And stout-hearted. Ah, you English are brave. My father fought under your great Wellington. But you are hurt; your head is cut!"

"It is a trifle; my companion will attend to it."

From a recess the Spaniard brought forth the weapons, which had been carefully concealed, and laden with these I staggered towards the adjoining room, where Dick was setting out the provisions which he had discovered.

"That's better," he said cheerfully, coming forward to relieve me of my burden. "With a bit of trusty steel, and full stomach, we need not fear any number of Carlists. Take a draught of this red wine, and then I'll bathe that wound for you."

"Thanks," I said, when he had made me more comfortable; "now we will sit down to our long-waited-for meal."

The provisions consisted of bread, a few eggs, and some dried fruits, which we devoured greedily, washing the food down with the strong wine of the country.

When we could eat no more, Dick suggested that we should help our host, and then get away as quickly as possible.

The Spaniard approving the proposal, we set to work at once, and in a secluded spot on the hillside dug a deep grave.

The task presented little difficulty, owing to the lightness of the soil, and in a short time a rude resting-place for the hapless woman and her little ones had been hollowed out.

Then we carried them to their narrow bed, and Dick and I turned aside to avoid witnessing our host's pathetic grief.

Not until the last did he break down, and even then he

exhibited but a momentary discomposure. The tears welled up in his eyes and overflowed, but he brushed them aside impatiently, as if scorning such womanish weakness. He kissed his wife for the last time, and strained the dead children to his breast.

Then he turned to us, saying, "Now, señors, I am ready."

Simple words, simply spoken, destitute alike of bravado and weakness; yet they came from a broken heart.

Very tenderly, and with great reverence, we laid these innocent victims of a cruel war to rest, the children in their mother's arms.

The picture is present to me now, inexpressibly sad and pathetic.

The dark clouds of the preceding night had rolled away; the sun beat upon our heads with a fierce power. Behind us rose the walls of the deserted building, in front the brush-covered hill, at our feet the open grave. Dick and I, wet with perspiration, leaned upon our spades; the strong man at our side stood as if cut from stone by the cunning art of the sculptor.

Presently his lips moved; he uttered a short prayer, and then, by a gesture, motioned us to proceed.

My hand trembled as I lifted the implement, and I laboured with half-averted gaze.

When the last sod was replaced, the Spaniard drew a small crucifix from his pocket, kissed it, and placed it at the grave-head.

Dick cast a glance at the beaten soil, and with a heart-felt "God have mercy upon you," turned away.

I followed slowly, feeling no shame at the tears which wet my cheeks, and in the courtyard of the house we were joined by our host. He spoke no word concerning the strange rite in which we had just borne part, but walked with unfaltering steps into the house.

I pressed upon him the advisability of taking food, but he repelled me with a gentle courtesy.

"Perhaps to-morrow, señor," he said, "but not now; the bread would choke me," and the break in his voice revealed how terribly he suffered.

Dick advised making preparations for the journey, and when I repeated his remark to our host, the latter promptly acquiesced.

"The distance is short, but the dangers are many," he said. "I will lead you from here to a hiding-place in the hills where we must lie till dusk."

With the readiness of an old campaigner, Dick speedily collected a store of provisions, and urged us to make an immediate start.

At the last moment, however, the Spaniard raised an unexpected objection.

"I have considered the matter afresh, señor," he announced, "and honour forbids me to avail myself of your company. Alone it is possible for you to pass safely through the country. Against you the Carlists bear no animosity, and it may chance that they will let you go free. I, on the contrary, am a marked man, a known supporter of the government, and they would shoot me without hesitation. Why should I drag you into peril?

Señor, it must not be. I will wage my fight unaided. Once you were suspected of bearing friendship towards Philip d'Acaya, the order for your death would go forth."

I translated this speech to Dick, whose answer was just what might have been expected.

"Tell the Don he's a fine fellow, and I'm proud to be his friend," he said. "As for his precious scheme, it's all nonsense and out of reason. He can wait for the Carlists here, or on the hillside, but while he is in danger, Dick Truscott stands by his side—and Mr. Powell, too, I'm thinking."

"Most certainly, Dick;" and well pleased, I repeated to the Spaniard my comrade's remarks.

Admirably schooled as his features were, he could not wholly conceal his gratification, nor did he attempt seriously to combat the decision to which we had come.

"I have warned you of the peril," he said; "but you are brave men, and belong to a nation that holds danger in light esteem. So be it. I accept your aid, and you shall find me stanch as one of your own compatriots."

"Of that there can be no question," I responded; "and now that the business has been settled, let us hasten."

Don Philip, making for the hillside, led the way, while we followed closely in his wake.

At one point he paused, and turned to take a farewell view of his ruined home. For a few minutes he stood silent, gazing fixedly at the deserted house, then with an abrupt movement he resumed the journey, and we were fairly adrift in Spain.

CHAPTER II.

A NARROW ESCAPE.

UNDER the guidance of Don Philip, who appeared to know every foot of the ground, we made rapid progress; but it was not his intention to proceed far, and soon abandoning the open country, he struck southwards amongst a chain of rocky hills.

Entering a narrow gorge, he led the way cautiously, warning us to preserve the strictest silence. In single file we crept along, clambering over the boulders, toiling painfully upwards, until finally our guide made a welcome halt.

"Here is safety," he whispered, pointing to a hole in the rock so small that Dick found great difficulty in squeezing through.

A few yards inside the ground dipped abruptly, and we let ourselves down into a rocky apartment, the confines of which could not be perceived because of the gloom.

The Spaniard informed us, however, that the extent was small, and led the way to a recess on the farther side.

Dick laid down the stock of provisions, and placed his gun handy, in case of an attack; but Don Philip expressed the opinion that we were not likely to be disturbed.

"Nevertheless," he added, "I will keep watch while you sleep."

"How long shall we stay here?" Dick asked, through me.

"Five hours, or perhaps six."

"Then we will take turn and turn about, Mr. Powell, and the Don shall have the first watch. Ask him to waken me at the end of two hours."

Our guide readily agreed to this proposal, and very shortly Dick and I were sleeping soundly.

I do not know whether the Spaniard slept at all, but he was wide awake and pacing the cave restlessly when the time came for me to relieve Dick.

The latter, instead of resuming his nap, unfastened the packages of provisions, and I earnestly entreated Don Philip to join us.

This he did with extreme reluctance, eating and drinking very sparingly, as though the action caused him actual physical pain.

While the meal proceeded, I questioned him as to his plans; for beyond the fact that the country was in a state of anarchy, I knew little.

"At present," he answered, "we are in the neighbourhood of Caboda, and as soon as night falls, I purpose journeying towards Vitoria. At that place I expect to find General Cordova, who has just been appointed to the command of the army."

"When do you reckon to arrive?"

"That is hard to tell. The difficulties are numerous; the

Carlists have posts established everywhere; their spies are in every village; probably we shall be compelled to make a wide sweep. But, as our proverb has it, 'Better go about than fall into the ditch.'"

"A capital maxim, and one to be commended. But your speech makes it appear that the Carlists are gaining ground. I always imagined the insurrection to be a trifling one."

"Are you talking about the Carlists?" Dick interrupted. "I remember seeing Don Carlos in London. Trying to make himself king of Spain, isn't he?"

"Yes; and this part of the country is almost wholly in his favour."

"But his claim isn't good?"

"That depends on the view you take. His brother Ferdinand left no son, and, according to the Salic law, his daughter Isabella could not reign. Consequently Don Carlos was the next heir; and although the king repealed the law, I believe that his brother never acknowledged his power to do so."

"Then it is simply a question of Isabella or Carlos."

"Not exactly. It is rather a struggle between the new and the old—between Isabella governing as a constitutional queen, and Carlos as an absolute king."

"Yet this Don has a strong following?"

"Yes; the priests are on his side because he is a rigid Catholic. In addition, the Basques, a hardy race who inhabit these northern provinces, are ready to die in his service."

I could scarcely forbear smiling at Dick's next question, it threw such a flood of light upon one side of his character.

"What will they get out of it?" he asked.

"The inquiry would take us a long way back into ancient history," I said; "but the explanation is simple. These Basques are distinct from the Spaniards, and have always enjoyed special privileges, which they call *fueros*. Now it is considered likely that the queen's party will abolish these privileges, while, on the other hand, Don Carlos has sworn most solemnly to maintain them."

"Then, instead of being Carlists, these Basques are really Fuerists."

"I believe you have hit the mark—but our companion is ready to start."

Twice during this conversation the Spaniard had left the cave to peer into the night, and now he approached us.

"Señor," he said, "the time has arrived. Yet before we venture forth, I pray that you will reconsider your decision. You have still an opportunity of leaving me, and I repeat that it is your wisest course."

"And break our compact? Fie! Don Philip. You do not place much trust in an Englishman's pledge."

"Pardon, señor, but we are almost strangers to each other, and you are about to risk your lives on my behalf."

"We shall face the danger in the company of a brave man," I replied, bowing.

"'It avails little to the unfortunate to be brave,'" he returned gloomily, "and I have realized the significance of the saying. However, it would be churlish to offer further opposition; perhaps time will afford me an opportunity of repaying this act of generous friendship towards a lonely and sorrowful man."

One by one we drew ourselves up from the cave, and, passing through the small opening, stood on the hillside.

Night had fallen, but the darkness was not sufficiently great to stop our advance, and the Spaniard led us straight through the narrow gorge without mishap.

By a beaten track we climbed the opposite hill, and from its summit were enabled to distinguish the flickering lights from various scattered villages, and what we judged to be the watch-fires of Carlist encampments.

Almost without hesitation Don Philip selected his line of march, and, keeping close together, we descended the slope.

Avoiding the highroad, and steering clear of the houses, we made our way across cultivated fields and desolate heath-land—at one time wading through a shallow brook, at another tearing our flesh amongst thorny bushes. Still we pushed on resolutely, until Don Philip called a halt at the foot of a range of hills.

"Here," he said, "we must act with the utmost caution. Two days ago, these heights were occupied by the Carlists; but whether the rebels have since been withdrawn I am uncertain."

"Could we not work round either to the right or left?"

"It would take hours, and the difficulty would still confront us. We are as likely to encounter the Carlists at the base as on the summit."

I explained the dilemma to Dick, who voted for keeping straight on.

"Better to be attacked on the hills than down here in the open," he remarked.

Accordingly, we began to move forward slowly, following close behind Don Philip, and taking especial pains not to dislodge any loose stones.

We had scaled perhaps half the height, when Dick pulled my sleeve.

"Danger," he whispered laconically; "we are being pursued."

I informed the Spaniard, and we all stopped, listening with strained ears. Whatever doubts we may have entertained were speedily put to flight.

We could hear distinctly the footsteps and the voices of a number of men who were ascending the path in our rear. They were talking loudly and boisterously, making no secret of their presence, and from this fact I derived a little comfort.

"They are not tracking us," I said in Spanish; "so much is certain. If we push on swiftly we shall gain the top."

"And fall into the hands of their comrades. The main body are on the ridge. This is but a small detachment returning from some special errand."

I turned to Dick and informed him of this surmise.

"Just so," he assented coolly; "no doubt the Don is right. We are in a trap, and must cut a way out. If we could clamber up these rocks we might hide for a spell, but that is out of the question. Stand by for a rush.

There is a bend just below. Directly they turn the corner, at them with the steel; don't bother about the guns. Tell the Don to take the right hand, and no shouting. They will be more frightened by the silence."

Our scanty preparations were quickly made, and we stood shoulder to shoulder peering into the gloom.

Once Don Philip's arm touched mine, and I could feel that he was quivering with excitement.

Nearer and nearer the men came, so that we could hear their speech plainly. Their expedition had evidently proved a success, for they were in the highest spirits, and sang snatches of stirring war-songs.

One circumstance struck me as being strange. Although the oncomers were undoubtedly Spanish, I could yet understand little of their language, which sounded harsh and strident.

I did not then know how far the speech of the Basque peasants differed from that of the ordinary Spaniards.

As the soldiers approached the bend, Dick laid his open hand twice upon mine, and then two fingers, from which by-play I inferred that our opponents were twelve in number.

These odds were great; but we held the advantage in position, and in the knowledge of our adversaries' presence.

The darkness, too, favoured us, as it served to conceal our scanty numbers, and would, if we once forced a passage, militate strongly against pursuit.

Suddenly two shadowy figures took dim shape in the gloom, and were quickly followed by three or four more.

We waited no longer, but with the noiseless spring of mountain cats leaped into their midst.

The effect was tremendous. The Carlists, overwhelmed by surprise, offered no resistance, but fell back in headlong flight upon their comrades in the rear.

Wishful to avoid bloodshed, Dick and I only tried to force a passage, but Don Philip fought for all three. The swift circlings of his sword were like flashes of lightning darting in all directions. Man after man went down; the thirsty sword drank blood at every stroke. It seemed as if his arm would never tire in the fell work.

But at last we were through, and racing down the narrow path, increasing at every second the distance from the scene of conflict.

The Carlists, recovering from their stupor, very soon began firing at random, and several bullets struck the rocks unpleasantly close to us. Then, gaining courage, our opponents began to pursue; and before we reached the bottom, the noise behind made it plain that they had been largely reinforced.

"The Don was right," said Dick, glancing around; "we were making straight for a hornet's nest. We have given them a pretty scare, anyhow."

Along the summit of the hills, for a considerable distance, a line of fire now shot out, showing that the Carlists were on the alert; and indeed we could see their dusky figures flitting to and fro, as the glare of the fires fell upon them.

"What on earth are they up to?" I asked in surprise, as the roar of a big gun boomed out.

Dick chuckled quietly. "They are paying us a mighty compliment," he said; "they are afraid of a night attack. The notion will hold them in check long enough for us to get away."

In the open Don Philip resumed the lead, and still keeping near the foot of the hills, hurried us in a south-westerly direction.

On the heights the enemy continued to display great activity, and it was patent that they were thoroughly alarmed.

As Dick had predicted, this favoured our immediate escape, since the men already in pursuit were recalled in order to guard against the expected attack.

This left our course free, and we made the most of the opportunity.

I had always considered myself a good walker, but before long I trailed after Don Philip like a tired child, and even the redoubtable Dick began to show symptoms of fatigue.

Our guide, on the other hand, marched along with a dogged perseverance which I afterwards discovered to be characteristic of Spanish soldiers.

Left to myself, I should have lain down in a ditch, but this a certain pride of race forbade; it should not be said that an English lad failed where a Spaniard succeeded.

Therefore I struggled on, with every joint in my body aching, yet possessed, nevertheless, with a firm determination to keep up.

Much to my secret gratification, it shortly became

apparent that we must soon seek the shelter of some friendly hiding-place, unless we were prepared to brave the dangers of travelling in the light of day. Already the grey dawn was stealing into the face of the eastern sky, and a considerable distance remained to be traversed before we could turn the Carlist position. But Don Philip was leading, and until he spoke, I did not care to offer any suggestion.

Dick, however, had no such scruples; and as the day perceptibly broadened, he turned to me, saying, "Unless we intend walking into the arms of these Carlists, it is high time that we cast about for a hiding-place. Ask the Don what his plans are."

"Your comrade is right, señor," our guide made answer to my inquiry; "we must seek shelter. And yet it is a great pity. We shall have to lie idle a whole day. However, there is no help for it; we must bow to the inevitable. If I have brought you aright, we shall shortly come to a thick wood, in which we can easily conceal ourselves."

This speech pleased me, and I stepped out with fresh ardour.

The night was drawing to an end when we reached the wood, and the surrounding objects were rapidly becoming distinctly visible.

"Nothing much to spare," said Dick; "but the Don rattled us along in fine style. He's a splendid chap for a foreigner. I believe he could do another march without breaking down. And did you take notice of his sword-play in the pass? I fancy he did pretty well, for a first instalment, in squaring up accounts with the Carlists."

Don Philip richly deserved Dick's encomiums. His features, grave and impassive, exhibited no signs of weariness; his head erect, his back straight, he walked with an even tread, as if the journey had but just begun.

I complimented him upon his extraordinary vigour, but he turned the compliment aside.

"No, no, señor," he exclaimed; "we are not fairly matched. I am a younger man than your comrade, and older than you. I am in the prime of life, when my physique is at its best. Besides, the ground is familiar to me, and that counts largely in my favour. However, let us set about finding a hiding-place."

The wood, although small in extent, was thickly studded with trees, and, once away from the outskirts, we found little difficulty in concealing ourselves.

Don Philip selected the spot—a hollow in the midst of a cluster of trees—and here we sat down.

"Now," said Dick, "first we will have something to eat, and then two of us can sleep; the third must watch."

As before, our guide undertook the first watch, which suited me admirably, as I could barely keep awake, even during the meal.

"Have no misgivings, señor," Don Philip said; "none are likely to discover our retreat."

Personally I was far too fatigued to concern myself about the Carlists; and having heaped together some dead leaves to serve as a pillow, I lay down, and passed at a bound into the realm of slumber.

When Dick awakened me, I was glad to see that at last our ally slept, and thus, for a brief time at least, was enabled to forget the tragedy which had made a wreck of his life.

Although still feeling stiff and sore, I was in much better trim, and was able to look forward cheerfully to resuming the journey.

At the end of a couple of hours the others sat up, and we began to consider our future proceedings.

One disagreeable fact stared us in the face—we had consumed all the provisions which Dick had brought, and this threatened largely to augment our difficulties.

"We cannot march all night without food," Dick declared; "I am hungry now before the start."

"To enter a town will be running grave risks," I observed; "I will ask Don Philip his opinion."

Here again the Spaniard afforded proof of his wonderful stamina, making light of our distress at the lack of provisions.

"But," he added, "if the señor wishes, we can procure food on the other side of the hills. There is a little village which boasts a *venta*—the lowest kind of inn. The accommodation is rough, the fare coarse, and the company undesirable."

"And the danger?" I asked.

His lip curled in a fine scorn, and he tapped the hilt of his sword significantly.

"If it is our pleasure to stay at the venta," he said, "we shall not be deterred by the idea of danger."

As my opinion entirely coincided with that of Dick's, it was finally resolved that we should make for the village of which the Spaniard spoke; and, in order to lose no more time than was really unavoidable, we immediately started for the edge of the wood. Here we waited until dusk, and then resumed the journey.

Whether the Carlists had abandoned the heights we could not conjecture, but they did not show themselves; and indeed for two hours we travelled without meeting a single human being.

We had now flanked the hills, and having proceeded some distance to the south, turned eastward.

The end of another hour's brisk walking brought us to the village—a narrow, straggling street, with pools of dirty water, heaps of manure, and all manner of offal, which smelled most offensively.

There were no people stirring, and the houses were in darkness; but judging from what could be made out, they were wretched, tumble-down tenements.

Don Philip strode on in advance, heedless of danger, while Dick and I followed, having our guns ready in case of need.

At the last house our guide stopped, and indicated that we had reached the venta.

From the outside, it was certainly an uninviting-looking building; but it was too late to draw back, and pressing closely upon the Spaniard's heels, we entered an apartment, the door of which stood open.

Don Philip had made three assertions concerning the venta, and two of them were at once amply verified.

The accommodation was rough, the company undesirable; what the fare would be like remained to be seen.

The room in which we now were contained no window, but had various little slits in the wall. From the floor to the ceiling, the place was enveloped in a thick smoke, which caught my breath and set me coughing violently. A huge wood fire burned on some stone slabs in the centre of the kitchen, and the smoke, or more strictly a small portion of it, found its way slowly through a hole in the roof.

Round the fire, a motley crowd of perhaps twenty men had gathered. Most of them were drinking and smoking, some were cooking, while two or three groups were engaged in an outlandish game with greasy cards.

"A rough crew," commented Dick, in a whisper; "we are likely to have trouble, if they become suspicious. However, we must see it through now. Look at the Don; not much fear about him, anyway."

Our Spanish comrade, as calmly as if in the house of friends, was calling for the landlord, who came up slowly—a short, fat man, with hairy arms and a neck like a bull's.

I had heard much of the dignity and stateliness of Spanish manners, but on the present occasion they were sadly lacking.

The landlord peered into our faces with an inquisitive rudeness far from reassuring, and insolently demanded our business.

Don Philip acted as spokesman, while we stood at attention, prepared for any emergency.

"A room and a supper," he said haughtily; "and see to it that we are served at once. A noble of Spain does not brook waiting."

"'Better to go to bed supperless than get up in debt,'" returned the innkeeper, with a cunning leer, and a glance towards his associates.

I thought the Don would have struck him to the earth, but in spite of the insult he controlled his temper.

Carelessly tossing the man a piece of silver, he said, "Enough of words; show us a room, and bring the best your house affords."

"This way, most illustrious," the landlord responded, with thinly-veiled sarcasm; "you shall be served fully as well as in your own lordly mansion."

By this time the other occupants of the apartment had closed round, and from one or two quarters I heard a muttered "Christinos—foreign devils!" but these remarks I, of course, ignored.

We pushed with little ceremony through the group of scowling men, and followed the surly host up a wide but dark and evil-smelling staircase.

At the end of a short passage, which contained a recess on either side, he threw open a door, and bowing with feigned politeness, bade us enter.

The chamber was small, and the space still further confined, as one part formed an alcove, in which stood a dingy-looking bedstead.

A square table, a couple of chairs, and a stout chest, comprised the furniture; the walls were bare, and the floor uncarpeted.

The landlord placed a rickety lamp upon the table, and withdrew to prepare the meal.

Dick's first action, when we were left alone, was highly significant. Having carefully examined his gun, he placed it, together with his sword, within easy reach.

"I can't make much of these foreigners' lingo," he exclaimed; "but, from their faces, I should judge we are as likely to get bullets as bread."

"More than likely, Dick; but perhaps they will give us both," I answered, having seen to my weapons.

Don Philip, who had been pacing the room, now turned to me and said, "Señor, we must be prepared for a fight; the people below are all Carlists."

The entrance of the landlord, and a slovenly-dressed woman bearing the meal, prevented a reply.

I fancy that the sight of our weapons gave him rather a shock; but he offered no remark, and the insolence of his demeanour was somewhat lessened.

The supper proved better than the appearance of the place warranted us in expecting. It consisted of eggs poached in oil, some passable cheese, a pile of white bread, and red wine.

One little circumstance struck me as being peculiar, and its explanation did not tend to increase my feeling of security.

As the landlord turned to leave the room, Don Philip called him back.

Pouring out a bumper of the liquor, he said sternly, "Drink, and do not be ashamed of your company."

The innkeeper took the vessel and drained it to the bottom; then, setting the cup on the table, he went out.

Noting my look of surprise, Don Philip said, "Now we may drink in safety; our fat friend would not have poisoned himself knowingly."

I stared at him aghast, unable to speak.

"Poisoned wine is not altogether unknown in these parts," he explained; "but we can venture to drink this."

Dick had already begun an attack on the provisions, and despite my horror at the Spaniard's statement, I speedily followed suit.

Don Philip ate more sparingly, but between us the eatables soon vanished; and I was just pouring out a last draught of wine, when Dick rose from the chest which had served him for a seat, and at one bound sprang across the room.

The door had been pushed slightly ajar from the outside, and the next instant Dick dragged into the middle of the chamber a little weazened old man, whose face was white as bleached linen, and whose legs tottered under him.

"Mercy, señors, mercy!" he sputtered. "For the love of the Virgin, spare me! I am a friend; I came to warn you. Quick! they will murder us all."

"Unhand him, Dick," I said quietly; "he brings news. —Now, old man, what is it? Speak without fear."

"They are going to kill you," he gasped. "The Carlists have a post close at hand, and messengers have been sent to them. I am a Christino; my son serves in the army of the queen; that is why I tell you."

"Can we get out?" I inquired, and the old man shook his head.

"The house is surrounded," he answered; "the men are in hiding, and they have guns."

Don Philip gave him a gold coin, and advised him to steal away while there was yet time; then, as the door silently closed, we stood gazing into each other's faces.

CHAPTER III.

THE FIGHT IN THE VENTA.

DICK was the first to speak.

"It's easy to see that the little man brought bad news," he said; "but you forget that I didn't understand a word of his jabber."

I rapidly explained what had been taking place, and invited his opinion as to the best course to be pursued.

His reply was prompt, and, to my thinking, unanswerable.

"Make a bolt," he said emphatically, "and cut our way through. Once outside, they will lose us in the darkness. To stay here is to be killed. But what does the Don say?"

I put the question to the Spaniard, and his answer was not at all to my taste.

"It is of little moment," he remarked calmly; "death is certain, here or there—we cannot escape. The exit is guarded; the men are hidden and out of danger. They will shoot us down like tame pigs, and we shall not see even the hands which direct the bullets. Now, in this room we can fight, and sell our lives dearly. Therefore I shall stay here—it will form an admirable citadel;" and he glanced complacently round the little apartment.

"The Don is an old mule," Dick declared, when informed of his resolve; "but as we dragged him into the scrape, we must stand by him;" and without more ado, the sturdy fellow began to make arrangements for the defence.

It was difficult for me, young and hot-blooded, to wait quietly in what common-sense told me was simply a death-trap; yet I could leave neither the Spaniard nor Dick. Indeed, the latter's behaviour would have shamed the most cowardly into a semblance of bravery. I knew quite well that he regarded each moment passed in the room as bringing us a step nearer to death, that he indulged no hope of ultimate safety, and looked upon our fate as being practically sealed.

At the same time, he had in view the chance which a bold dash might have afforded us; but after his first impatient exclamation, no murmur of complaint passed his lips.

He felt that indirectly we were responsible for the situation, and were in honour compelled to abide by the Spaniard's decision.

Now, just at first, I could hardly acquit Don Philip of exhibiting a certain inconsiderate selfishness in thus exposing us to a peril of such magnitude.

His case differed from ours very materially. Life for him possessed little value; its joys were over; the future offered him only hopeless misery. His breast was animated by but one desire; one idea dominated him to the exclusion of all else.

Proud, haughty, and passionate, he burned to avenge the

grievous wrong which had been done him, and would welcome death if his sword were but red with the blood of his foes.

And a more fitting opportunity could never offer than this. This small room should be made memorable as the scene of a struggle the noise of which should spread throughout the land. People from far and near should speak with whispering breath of his mighty prowess, and tell of his vengeance.

On the other hand, his reasoning may have been perfectly sound. The men outside had doubtless hidden themselves securely, and were prepared to shoot us down the instant that we came within range.

However, in either case the die was cast. We had elected to remain, and it behoved us to meet our fate like men.

Before proceeding to barricade the door, I crept into the passage and listened. All was silent; not a sound came from below; we might have been the sole inmates of the house.

"As I told you," Don Philip remarked; "every man has received instructions and is in his place."

Without undue noise, we carried the various articles of furniture to the door, and fixed them in such a position as to form an efficient barricade.

"Shall I put out the light?" I asked softly.

"When the attack begins," Dick said, and he placed it at the foot of the alcove. "They will send a scout or two in advance, and the darkness would make them suspicious.

Stand clear of the door, sir; it will soon be riddled by bullets."

Don Philip now directed my attention to a noise outside, which sounded like the uniform tramp of feet.

"The detachment of Carlists," he said quietly, and his face shone with eager anticipation.

Now, strange as the assertion may appear, it is none the less true that I received this announcement with a feeling of positive relief. The few minutes of inaction had told upon me heavily; my nerves were unstrung, and the beating of my heart was painfully rapid.

Since that day, I have looked more than once into the face of Death; but to wait passively, as I did then, for his slow yet certain oncoming, is sufficient to awe all but the very stoutest.

And in justice to my comrades, but more especially to Dick Truscott, I must set down here that they stood the test bravely.

Of the Spaniard this was to be expected, since it was of his choosing, and all the strongest passions known to the human race were enlisted in his behalf.

But Dick, who had no interest in the stranger's quarrel, who had no wrongs to avenge, to whom life was a precious gift not lightly to be cast away, proved himself equally courageous, and from time to time I gazed across the darkened chamber at his resolute features with the highest admiration.

Only once did he make any allusion to the coming encounter, and that was after the arrival of the Carlists.

"Good-bye, sir," he said, grasping my hand warmly; "we shall soon join Mr. Forrester. Tell the Don I'm sorry to have led him into this mess, but it's useless crying over spilt milk."

Don Philip listened to the translation of this speech with a proud smile.

"Let not your brave comrade be downcast on my account," he exclaimed; "I am well satisfied. My sole regret is at having involved you in my fate."

Twice during the interval of waiting we heard a sound as of creaking stairs, and then again all was still.

With my whole heart I longed for the coming of the enemy, but encouraged by Dick's example, I concealed my tremors, and tried to preserve a calm demeanour.

"Don't throw a shot away," was Dick's advice; "send every bullet home."

"They are coming, señors," whispered the Spaniard; "I hear their feet on the stairway; they hope to take us by surprise."

"Put out the light, Mr. Powell," Dick cried, as with a rush the Carlists swept along the passage, and flung themselves against the door.

Darting swiftly across the room, I blew the light out and returned to my place.

So violent had the concussion been, that I fully expected the door to come in with a crash; but the timbers held bravely.

From outside came a babel of voices, and one, high above all the rest, I heard without understanding. Don Philip, however, in a running commentary, made me acquainted with the meaning.

"That is a Basque officer," he said; "he is urging his men to batter down the door, and to shoot both the foreigners and the Christino. They are to give no quarter."

The unexpected check appeared to excite our opponents to a kind of frenzy. The shouts and blows were redoubled, and it was evident that the door could not much longer resist the strain.

Still we remained silent, crouched behind the improvized barricade.

Even in the midst of the din, I noted how differently the attack affected my two comrades. The Spaniard had lost his calm air; his eyes blazed with passion, the hot blood crimsoned his cheeks, he was devoured by a reckless impatience. I could hardly have wondered had he assisted in breaking down the door, so eager was he for the fray. Dick, on the contrary, retained his composure, and well merited poor Pym Forrester's description as the "Cast-iron man."

"They have brought choppers," he said coolly; "now we shall see the splinters fly."

"Why don't they fire?" I asked.

"Too crowded; all huddled round the door. It's a great mistake, and will cost them three lives at the start."

"The Basque officer is wondering if we could have escaped by another exit," whispered Don Philip; "the silence makes him uneasy."

"He will soon learn," I replied, as an axe came crashing through one of the panels.

The Carlists yelled with delight, but still we kept quiet.

Three or four well-directed blows in succession now widened the gap, and soon only the furniture intervened between us and the Carlists.

Unhappily for them, two of the men carried torches, which enabled us to take good aim.

"Cover your nearest man," said Dick; "now!" and a simultaneous report from three guns rang out.

The cry of triumph ceased; the soldiers, startled at the swift death of their three comrades, fell back a few paces, and we hastily reloaded.

Then from the darkness they poured in a straggling and ineffectual fire, which we left unanswered.

"First blood to us," said Dick, during an interval of quiet; "that volley has taught them caution."

"Yet it is hardly needed," I remarked; "one good rush, and the business would be settled."

"Ah, you are a young hand, Mr. Powell, or you would know that very few men care to run upon certain death. Ah! look out."

A number of bullets whistled harmlessly over our heads, and with an inspiriting shout of "*Viva el Rey!*" the soldiers dashed at the barrier.

Once again our guns carried death into their ranks; but although the men wavered and finally broke, the Basque officer, with a gallant daring that excited my warm admiration, came right at the obstacle.

With a marvellous agility he sprang on the table, and waving his naked sword, repeated his battle-cry, "*Viva el Rey!*"

The words still rang on the air, when Don Philip, with a fierce lunge, passed his sword through our adversary's body, and the unfortunate officer fell, either dead or badly wounded.

Amongst the Carlists, confusion now reigned supreme. Although terribly angry, it was plain that their losses disheartened them, and they betrayed little inclination to renew the attack.

"The Don has saved us for a time," Dick said; "the fall of their officer has left them like a ship without a rudder."

"Still it can only end one way," I observed, and my comrade assented.

Two further attacks, however, we repulsed without damage to ourselves, and then we waited for the final act.

Our stock of ammunition, scanty in the beginning, was exhausted; and we had only the cold steel upon which to depend.

It could not be said that we gave way to despair, since all along we had fought, well knowing the hopeless nature of the struggle; yet, perchance, until that moment, we had never fully realized the significance of our hapless plight.

All this time the Carlists kept up a desultory firing, and now we heard them stealing along the narrow passage, closely hugging the walls.

"They will be fierce enough when they find that we are

out of ammunition," Dick said; "but, Mr. Powell, I've been thinking that you may yet have a chance to get away. The Don and I can find them plenty of work for a few minutes. Now, if you stood on that side, close to the door, you might manage to slip into the passage. There is a risk, of course; but the darkness would—"

"No, no, Dick," I interrupted; "we came together and will go together, or not at all. I am not a rat to desert the sinking ship."

"Good lad," he said; "have your own way. Thank God, we can meet death with a clear conscience. That's everything, to my thinking."

I could hear the Spaniard humming to himself in a sort of joyous cadence. For him the supreme moment was swiftly approaching. No particle of fear found lodging in his breast; he was revelling in the anticipation of the coming struggle.

The firing ceased, a short pause ensued; then an order was issued, and a close volley was poured into the dark chamber.

We could dimly discern the figures of our foes as they swarmed towards the dismantled doorway, and alas! we were powerless to keep them at a distance.

As if an inkling of the truth had reached them, they threw off their fear and advanced with a bold rush, amidst renewed shouts of "*Viva el Rey.*" Upon our poor barricade they leaped, and sprang to the floor with fierce cries.

Unable to stem the fierce onslaught, we promptly wheeled to the left and placed our backs against the wall.

The instant that they perceived us, they surged forward tumultuously. One, a big, burly man, who brandished aloft a heavy sword, led the attack.

"*Viva el Rey!*" he cried furiously, "*Viva el Rey!*"

"*Viva la Reina!*" responded Don Philip, and darting to the front, with a lightning-like celerity, he pierced the Carlist leader through the heart.

The man fell without even a groan, and his nearest follower, tripping over the body, was immediately dispatched by Dick.

The crowd recoiled, and with a sudden spring Don Philip was again amongst them, his blade plying on all sides.

A dozen times he might have been slain, as he offered no guard, but simply cut and thrust with such rapidity, that it was difficult for the eye to follow the course of his sword.

The next instant we were all three shoulder to shoulder, and for a moment it really seemed as if we should gain the upper hand.

The uproar now became deafening, and while the Carlists pealed forth their war-cry, Don Philip's "*Viva la Reina!*" rang like a trumpet-blast high above it all.

The odds, however, were too great. Foot by foot the enemy forced us back to our original position, and there we continued the desperate struggle.

Twice the steel point pricked my sword arm, drawing blood, and had it not been for Don Philip's adroitness, I must have been killed outright.

But our Spanish ally fought with what can only be described as a superb recklessness. His defence lay in the swiftness and strength of his blows. Not a weapon touched him, while his own sword seemed to point at every foe in the same instant.

Nevertheless the continual exertion began perceptibly to tell upon us. My arm ached, my head was dizzy. Dick, who stood on the Spaniard's right, still laid about him lustily, but with less vigour than at first, while even Don Philip's arm showed signs of tiring.

Suddenly, to my extreme amazement, the last named, as if filled with new life, darted to the front, and "*Viva la Reina!*" once more echoed through the room.

"Courage, señors!" he cried; "we are saved. The Christinos are coming. *Viva la Reina! Viva la Reina!* Down with the Carlist dogs!"

Inspirited by his example, we dashed at the Carlists, and in another minute there was borne to our ears the sound of footsteps hurrying along the passage.

The Spaniard's words revealed to me the truth—the Carlists were caught in their own trap.

With a cry of rage they burst towards the doorway, and uttering frantic shouts, cut a way for themselves through a body of troops who endeavoured to bar their path.

"Another five minutes and they would have been too late," observed Dick tranquilly.

He did not attempt to pursue the retreating Carlists, neither did I; but the vengeance of Don Philip was far from sated, and he rushed with the crowd into the corridor.

Out there in the darkness the two factions fought with a savage ferocity, but gradually the cry of "*Viva el Rey!*" became less frequent, and finally ceased.

Our position now was somewhat awkward, as the Christinos, returning, might attack us in mistake; but happily our suspense was ended by the sound of Don Philip hailing us from the passage.

"You are alive, señor!" he said, "and your comrade! It is a miracle; the saints fight for us. Descend with me into the street. The Christinos are bringing torches, but the sight is an unpleasant one. Many men have fallen."

"Some of them still live," I remarked; "who will see to the wounded?"

"We shall carry off our injured; our friends occupy a post at a short distance. But time presses; the Carlists who have escaped will return with reinforcements."

We traversed the corridor softly, avoiding with the utmost care the bodies of those who had been hurt.

In front of the house, a singular spectacle presented itself. The Christino commander, evidently a man of promptitude and dispatch, had secured a primitive-looking cart and two half-starved horses. On this old-world vehicle a part of his men were placing their wounded comrades; while the remainder had formed up in readiness to repel any attack which the Carlists might make.

A couple of oil lamps and the same number of torches threw a fitful light over the darkness, making the scene strangely weird and impressive.

Everything was done without noise or confusion, and

though the men worked with amazing swiftness, yet, as far as I could judge, they performed their task in a very workman-like manner.

When all was arranged, we set out, the soldiers being formed in a hollow square, having the cart in the midst.

Dick and I marched in the rear with Don Philip, who, in rather extravagant language, introduced us to the nearest Christinos as valiant Englishmen, who had fought stoutly for the queen.

As yet we had not spoken to the leader of the little force, and we could only guess at the happy chance to which our rescue might be ascribed.

At present, however, the main object was to reach the Christino post, which lay amongst the hills about three miles to the south-east.

From a few words, uttered now and again in an undertone, I gathered that the majority of the Carlists had escaped, and there existed every probability of a sudden and determined attack.

The road was wretched in the extreme, and it was only with the greatest difficulty that the half-starved beasts managed to drag the cart along.

The sufferings of the injured must have been excruciating, but beyond an occasional involuntary moan, the patient fellows uttered no cry, bearing their pain with an astonishing fortitude.

Arrived at the foot of the hills, a few men were sent to give warning of our coming, and to bring back stretchers, since it was wholly out of the question that the cart should traverse the rocky defiles.

Here, then, we halted until the messengers returned, when a part of the force instantly began the work of carrying the wounded to the summit.

"If the señors approve, we will remain with the rear," Don Philip said; "it is just possible that the Carlists may yet come up."

"As you please," I responded, and translated the remark to Dick, who was preparing to help in the removal of the wounded.

"The Don must be a perfect glutton at fighting," that worthy said, but nevertheless he took his place by my side.

The operations, however, were concluded without interruption, and finally we had the satisfaction of reaching the Christino post.

Don Philip now introduced us to Colonel Qualeda, our rescuer, who, discovering that I could speak Spanish, warmly thanked me for the assistance which Dick and I had rendered his compatriot.

"Yet it was only your opportune aid which prevented us from being overcome," I observed; "and that reminds me we are still ignorant to what chance we owe your assistance."

"A mere accident, señor. One of my band, returning from an errand, called at a house in the village where he has friends. While there, he heard that three strangers were supping in the venta, and that the landlord had sent word of their presence to the Carlists. Thinking the news might prove important, he hurried with all speed to me. That is the story, señor; and I rejoice that my brave fellows arrived in time."

"You have placed us under a lasting obligation, colonel," I said; "we owe our lives to you."

"They were jeopardized in the defence of my friend," he returned, bowing courteously; "so in reality I but cancelled a debt."

"And the soldier! is he here? Would that it were in my power adequately to reward him; but alas! the waves swallowed up all my possessions and left me destitute."

"You forget, señor," interposed Don Philip, "I am equally indebted to the brave soldier, and my purse is not so light but that it can pay for all."

"Then as it must needs be so, perhaps the colonel will allow the man to be brought to us," I said, unwilling that a feeling of false shame on my part should prevent the worthy fellow from receiving a suitable reward.

He was quite young, being little more indeed than a lad, and slightly built; but his frame was muscular, his movements active, while his whole bearing testified to his military training.

He blushed with gratified pride at our praise, and declined firmly, but with the utmost respect, to receive the proffered money.

"It would spoil all my pleasure, señors," he said. "You have given me thanks, my chief has commended me; I am more than content."

"A gallant answer, Juan," exclaimed his colonel; "I will

take care that your service shall be properly recognized. —And now, señors," he exclaimed, as Juan saluted and withdrew, "what are your plans? In what way can I assist you?"

"I am on my way to Vitoria," Don Philip replied; "and these brave Englishmen volunteered to accompany me until I reached the queen's army. Now, however, I presume that there is little likelihood of encountering further danger."

"Ah, you scarcely realize the terrible condition of the country! We are not safe even here on this rock. The Carlists display a most marvellous activity. Repulsed in front, they attack us from the rear; beaten at one spot, they rally in another; they are everywhere. Each village is filled with their spies, who report all our doings and intentions, so that the enemy can take measures accordingly."

"But surely you are in touch with the main body of troops," I observed.

"Only in an indirect manner, by means of detached posts like this one."

"Then why do not the Carlists crush you in detail?"

"Their army is too far off. In this district they have only small bands, too weak for carrying a fortified position. But have you supped? Ah, yes! and I am glad of it. Our stock of provisions is scanty, consisting only of a little bread and a few skins of wine. But perhaps you smoke? No! Does your comrade?"

Dick, as I have stated, was ignorant of Spanish;

but he understood the offer of a good cigar, and was speedily enjoying the luxury of which lately he had been deprived.

"These Dons are not half bad fellows," he said gravely, blowing a puff of smoke into the air, "and first-class judges of tobacco."

Colonel Qualeda reverted to the subject of our plans, and a casual remark decided me to go on with Don Philip to Vitoria.

"There is an English officer with our general," the colonel said, "who has been sent from England to try to secure better treatment for the wounded on both sides."

"That will answer our purpose admirably," I observed; "we can tell him our story, and throw ourselves upon his protection. At the same time, we shall be able to keep with Don Philip."

Dick fully agreed with my proposal, and it was resolved that, after an hour's sleep, we should set forth, escorted for the first few miles by a detachment of soldiers that the colonel kindly offered to lend us.

Further, he insisted upon our sleeping in his tent, which, with the exception of that devoted to the use of the wounded, appeared to be the only one in the place, nor would he take any notice of my protest against depriving him of his quarters.

CHAPTER IV.

WE ARRIVE AT VITORIA.

I HAD feared lest the excitement aroused by the recent fight would keep me awake, but as soon as I lay down I lost all consciousness, and knew nothing further until Don Philip bade me rise.

"You slept so peacefully, señor," he said, "that I was reluctant to rouse you; but our time is up."

The speaker showed no symptom of fatigue, nor did Dick, and having given myself a vigorous shake, I followed them out of the tent.

The Christinos, with the exception of a dozen men who were breakfasting, already stood at their posts, this being the hour most favoured by the enemy for delivering an unexpected attack.

Colonel Qualeda at once joined us, and with profuse apologies for the meagreness of the fare, invited us to partake of the morning meal.

"We are expecting fresh provisions before nightfall," he said; "but at present I can offer you only a little bread and wine."

The bread was dark-coloured and slightly sour, but it

was rather the deficiency in quantity than in quality that particularly troubled us.

However, we finished the breakfast, such as it was, and prepared to start.

The colonel now furnished us with a fresh supply of ammunition, and added to his kindness by giving Dick half a dozen cigars, one of which that inveterate smoker instantly lit.

Then Lieutenant Delgado, the officer in command of the escort, was introduced to us; and having bidden our kindly host adieu, we began to descend the mountain side.

The lieutenant proved an intelligent young man, and perceiving me to be on friendly terms with Don Philip, whom he knew by repute, chatted unreservedly concerning the state of the country.

"Of course," he said, with a charming frankness, "I am not competent to criticize the conduct of our generals, but every one acknowledges that affairs are drifting into a critical condition. The country is torn asunder by endless divisions. No one places the slightest confidence in any of our public men. Governments come and go, and outside Madrid all interest in their composition is dead. The big towns make laws for themselves, and every province is independent of its neighbour. Our soldiers are serving without pay, and living upon scanty rations. There are no stores, and but little ammunition. Don Carlos is at Orduna, General Ituralde at Puente la Reyna, while we lie idle."

"Now that General Cordova is in command, we shall see an alteration for the better," Don Philip interposed.

"If it rested with him, but it does not. What can he do without money or food or ammunition? And there is not a peseta in the treasury!"

"Then you think that Don Carlos will be victorious?"

"Not at all! the country will have none of him. Don Carlos on the throne means an absolute monarchy, the rule of the priests, and the revival of the Inquisition. Spain has had enough of these institutions."

"Then how do you account for the number of his partisans?" I asked.

"Well, first, there is the natural sympathy accorded to a man who has scarcely been treated with strict justice. Although I fight for the queen, I admit that, by right of descent, Carlos should be king. Had there been any chance of his governing in a constitutional manner, my sword would have been at his service. As it is, I fight for the liberties of the people."

"The situation appears to me parallel with our own Stuart times," I observed thoughtfully. "It is with you a question of Don Carlos or the freedom of a nation."

"That is so, señor; and although, in a way, I am sorry for Don Carlos, yet the claims of one man cannot be balanced against the progress of a whole land. And what a land, señor! Think of its history. Once we Spaniards led the world. Our flag waved over every sea; east and west the waters swarmed with our ships. The flag of St. James swelled to the breeze in far distant countries. The brightness of the Crescent waned before the lustre of the Cross. Throughout the civilized world our kings held the keys of peace and war. Powerful rulers trembled at their nod, and served them on bended knee. And the arts flourished. We possess a roll of names famed in painting and sculpture, music and literature. Ah, señor, it was with pride then that one could say, 'I am a Spaniard!' Alas! our glories faded long ago. To-day, what is Spain? Amongst the nations it is a cipher. Foreigners extend to us their sneers or their pity. Can you wonder, señor, that our young men smart with wounded pride—that they look forward with eagerness to the dawning of a brighter era? Spain is not dead, señor, and the day is at hand when it will once more take its rightful station amongst the foremost nations of the earth. That is why I, and thousands more like-minded, are prepared to pour out our blood in defence of the little Isabella."

"May your hopes be realized," I said; "but if all Spaniards were animated by your feelings, this unnatural war would speedily cease."

"Ah!" he responded with a sigh, "had our rulers exercised ordinary precautions the war would not have begun. The Basques care little for Don Carlos, but are passionately attached to their ancient privileges. It was because these were threatened that the revolt spread."

By this time we had left the hills some distance in our rear, and were marching along a country road. Across the fields to the right and left an occasional house appeared in sight; but of the inhabitants, we saw only women and children.

At the end of four miles the lieutenant halted his men

and bade us farewell, having first informed Don Philip of the best route which led to the next Christino post.

"The danger is slight now," he observed finally; "but perhaps it would be well to avoid the village on your left, just as you enter the hills."

We thanked him cordially, and stood for a few minutes watching his small band begin the return journey.

"The men cover the ground well," Dick said, as we turned away, "but they want dash. Don't get enough to eat, I suppose. They should have a beef-steak each in the mornings—that would set them up."

If Dick held one opinion more firmly than any other, it was that beef ruled the world. With him it was an article of faith not to be questioned that England owed her supremacy to the ox.

I heard him once, in a discussion on the battle of Waterloo, explaining the superiority of Englishmen over all other peoples on this very ground.

"Of course we won," he said dogmatically; "we were bound to. The French fought well, I don't deny; but they can't stay like our men. And why? The reason is plain: they don't get enough meat. Why, most of their food is broth, and made out of vegetables. And is it likely that cabbage and beans can stand up against beef? Ask your common-sense. Of course it isn't. And that's how it is that we are bound to whip the foreigner every time."

Thus this present remark concerning the Spaniards did not surprise me, and I must confess that just then I would willingly have played my part as Dick's typical Englishman, had the means been forthcoming.

As it was, however, I walked on after Don Philip, and tried hard to forget that I possessed an appetite.

After leaving the lieutenant the journey was uneventful, until, having passed the village of which he warned us, we entered the hills.

"This would make a splendid place for an ambush," Dick remarked, as we clambered up a steep and narrow path; "a hundred resolute men could hold this post against an army."

"Then we three would stand a poor chance," I answered; "but, fortunately, there are no Carlists near at hand."

"So much the better—but what is the Don about?"

Our guide had come to a halt, and was making a warning gesture.

"Be steady, señors," he whispered, as we reached him. "I thought I detected a movement behind the rocks above us. Perhaps it was fancy."

"Or our Christino friends of the next post," I suggested. "However, we will advance with caution," and I passed on the warning to Dick.

The path which we traversed exhibited the greatest irregularity with regard to both slope and breadth. Some portions would have presented little difficulty to a laden wagon; at others, again, we barely found room to walk all three abreast.

As Dick had remarked, it formed a grand position for an ambush, and more than once I caught myself speculating upon what would happen if the Carlists were in possession.

However, we kept on cautiously, looking keenly to right and left, and ready at an instant's notice to make use of our muskets.

Don Philip, who, being acquainted with the country, went first, did not stop again till he came to the entrance of a narrow gorge—the narrowest and steepest that we had yet seen.

No words were needed on his part to point out the necessity for the utmost vigilance. If an enemy lay behind those rocks which towered skyward on either side of us, then was our doom indeed sealed.

We stopped a full minute, listening for any chance sound that should indicate the presence of unseen watchers, and then began the ascent of the gorge.

Had I been leading, I should have quickened the pace considerably, but Don Philip advanced as unconcernedly as if our safety was assured.

Doubtless this was the correct attitude to assume, as, once inside the ravine, the question of escape or destruction was taken out of our hands. If those rocks sheltered a lurking foe, we were lost; and perhaps it was well to confront our fate, whatever it might be, with a manly dignity.

Nevertheless, I will not attempt to disguise the fact that I most earnestly wished our guide would take matters a little less coolly.

And this desire of mine was increased, rather than

lessened, when a clear and menacing "*Quien viva!*" rang out from an undetected spot.

Mechanically I raised my gun and glanced around. Not a person was in sight, but from the rocks on each side of the ravine there peeped out the gleaming barrels of a score of rifles.

Without a word I grounded my weapon and stood still.

"No getting out of this, Mr. Powell," Dick said; "they have the whip-hand, and no mistake."

I looked at Don Philip, and, engrossed as I was by my own fears, found time to admire his gallant bearing.

"Friends!" he answered calmly, in reply to the challenge; "on the way to Vitoria."

On our right hand, and a little in advance, there seemed to be a hurried consultation; and then a red flag was hoisted—the Carlist signal denoting "no quarter!"

The spectacle filled me with a mortal dread. Hitherto I had clung to the hope that the challengers formed a portion of the Christino force which we were seeking, but that hope was now dispelled.

Dick had also caught sight of the flag, and instantly realized its significance.

"Hope they will shoot straight," he said philosophically.

From the direction of the flag some one now raised the cry, "*Viva Carlos Quinto!*" and the guns held by unseen hands were brought to bear more directly upon our little group.

"Stand firm, sir," said Dick; "better get it over at once;" and I tried hard to conquer the trembling in my limbs.

When the cheer died away, Don Philip spoke again.

"Hold your fire one moment," he said; "I have a boon to ask, not for myself, but for my two comrades. They are English sailors, shipwrecked and adrift in a strange country. Our quarrel is naught to them. Therefore grant them their lives, if you possess a spark of honour."

Then, smiling proudly, he cried aloud, "*Viva Isabella Segunda!*" and before any one could guess his intention, he levelled his gun and sent a bullet straight through the red banner.

"Faith, Mr. Powell," said Dick, "we shall die in good company; the Don is a bold customer."

I scarcely heard these words, being lost in amazement at the Spaniard's act. He stood now, erect and fearless, gazing scornfully towards the torn flag. But no answering shower of bullets greeted this unprecedented outrage.

For a little while ensued an intense silence, and then, as if animated by a common impulse, the men behind the rocks sprang to their feet and responded with a vigorous cheer.

From the throats of all thrilled the cry, "*Viva Isabella Segunda!*" and one man, whose uniform proclaimed him an officer, came scrambling over the rocks to where we stood.

Making his way to Don Philip, he said, "Pardon our stratagem, señor; but the Carlists have played us some scurvy tricks lately. Only yesterday, one, dressed as a Christino officer, slipped through our fingers. He answered all my questions, and produced a pass signed by General Espartero; yet the rogue, notwithstanding, was simply a spy in disguise. But, señor, permit me to remark that I am still ignorant of your name."

"Don Philip d'Acaya," our guide replied. "My comrades, as I have told you, are English sailors. They are proceeding in my company to Vitoria, and have already rendered me good service."

"They are brave men," was the answer, "and"—with a low bow—"worthy comrades of a brave man. But let us proceed. I will accompany you as far as the hilltop, and send a couple of men to escort you to our colonel's quarters."

Giving an order to a subordinate, he led the way with Don Philip, while Dick and I walked behind, even yet scarcely crediting our good fortune.

"That was a queer dodge," my comrade remarked, as we toiled along, "and a good thing for us that the Don kept his nerve."

"Just at present Spain does not seem the safest place to travel in," I answered; "but I fancy the worst is over, and that we really shall arrive at Vitoria after all."

"I'll give my opinion when we get there," Dick responded; "then it is more likely to be right," and I was forced to own that he had wisdom on his side.

On the summit of the hill the young officer took his leave, having first ordered two of his men to guide us to Colonel Lorenzo, who, with a body of troops, occupied the opposite heights.

"Now, señor, we can breathe freely; our difficulties are at an end," Don Philip said, as we descended the slope.

"This Colonel Lorenzo is a friend of mine, and will aid us to the best of his ability."

That the Spaniard spoke with authority we received abundant proof as soon as the Christino camp was reached.

The colonel accorded his friend a hearty greeting, and, after a short conversation, bade one of his officers take Dick and myself aside and find us something to eat.

The fact that a flat rock served as a table did not particularly trouble us, nor did we repine at having to dispense with several articles which usually adorn the dinner-table in civilized life.

A soldier-servant brought some bread, a piece of meat—from what animal remained a mystery—and a fair quantity of the inevitable red wine. With these provisions we made a substantial meal, after which Dick lit a fresh cigar in tranquil mood.

Don Philip now came over, and begged that we would pardon him for having left us alone.

"The colonel is an old friend," he explained, "and we had many private matters to talk over."

I checked him smilingly, and said, "Do not be uneasy concerning us; we have fared well, and are content to await your pleasure."

"In that case," he rejoined, "we will remain with these good friends until to-morrow. I have learned that a strong detachment, escorting some provision-wagons, will pass within a few miles of this post. Under its protection we can resume the journey in safety. As this is only a temporary post, there is little in the way of comfort; but the officers have had a wooden building erected, and this is at your service. Now I will bid you adieu until the morning."

"Well," exclaimed Dick inquiringly, as the Don withdrew, "what is the next move?"

"The next move is to stay still. Don Philip has arranged to proceed in the morning with a convoy of provisions."

"A very sensible plan, too," interposed my comrade.

"Therefore we must pass the intervening time as comfortably as possible. There is a shed yonder in which we can sleep."

"After supper?"

"If these good folks indulge in that luxury, which I doubt. However, we may as well make a little tour."

"The Dons look very sulky," Dick remarked. "Are they afraid that we shall eat up all their provisions?"

"No, they are friendly enough, but reserved. The average Spaniard is not a hail-fellow-well-met individual, and it takes time to get on intimate terms with him. Now, these men know nothing of us; we are strangers and aliens; for aught we can tell, they may regard us as secret enemies. Nevertheless, they will treat us with perfect courtesy and civility."

This statement of mine was fully borne out, as our new companions, without unbending from their haughty demeanour, showed us real kindness.

At dusk we were provided with another meal, and then one of the officers pointed out the warmest corner of the shed, and brought a couple of greatcoats, in which we wrapped ourselves.

Dick, in whom a life of adventure had deepened a certain trait of suspicion, placed both sword and musket within easy reach, and I felt well assured that the slightest noise would waken him.

Personally I experienced no distrust, and, almost as soon as the officer departed, fell asleep.

The sun shone high in the heavens when the sound of voices aroused me, and looking up I perceived my comrade and Don Philip, who were endeavouring to carry on a conversation in the most comical broken English, mixed with a few Spanish words.

Hearing me move, Dick said, "We are having a famous talk, Mr. Powell. The Don has given me a lot of interesting news. I don't know what it's all about, but he seems wonderfully pleased."

"Good-morning, señor," Don Philip said; "I have been telling your comrade that we have just time for breakfast, and then we must start. The colonel has received information that the convoy is approaching."

"Breakfast, Dick," I said; "and then *en route* for Vitoria."

"With all my heart, sir," he answered, and together we went into the open.

At the conclusion of the meal we were joined by the colonel, who attended us into the plain, there to await the convoy.

It was a glorious morning, but the wind blew keenly, and I was not sorry at hearing the beat of horses' hoofs.

A bend in the road concealed the oncomers, but before long a dozen cavalry men cantered into view.

At sight of the colonel, the leader reined in his horse and saluted, while the former asked a few questions. The officer replied in a low tone, and then the little troop rode past, to be succeeded shortly by the main body.

First appeared a train of heavily-laden mules accompanied by the muleteers, who were cracking their whips and shouting with considerable gusto.

Half a dozen bullock-carts, which came next, excited Dick's interest, and, I fear it must be added, contempt.

They were certainly primitive-looking objects, in shape somewhat like ancient Roman chariots, and of the most ponderous build. The wheels were simply massive circles of wood and iron, with three stout cross-bars; and the noise produced by their action on the axles was, to put it mildly, far from musical.

A number of soldiers marched on either side of the wagons, and a third body brought up the rear.

The officer in command was, we learned, a Captain Serrano, to whose care the colonel confided us; and after an interchange of courtesies, we set out in the company of our new acquaintances.

I do not propose dwelling upon this portion of the journey, more especially as little happened worthy of being chronicled.

As was perhaps natural, Don Philip passed most of the time with Captain Serrano, leaving Dick and me to entertain each other.

In the neighbourhood of Vitoria ample proofs of the military occupation of the district presented themselves, and the town itself had the appearance of a camp.

Once inside the gates, we took leave of Captain Serrano, and went with Don Philip to the general's quarters.

At that place the first disappointment awaited us. General Cordova was absent, and not expected until the next day: while we could glean only the vaguest and most shadowy information respecting the British officer who was attached to the Spanish army.

"It is unfortunate, señor; but the evil can soon be remedied," said Don Philip graciously. "To-night I will find you a bed in one of the inns, and the morrow will, doubtless, bring better news."

I did not much like this arrangement, my experience of Spanish inns having been the reverse of pleasant, and my apprehensions were rather increased by his next words.

"Perhaps it will be as well," he resumed, "to keep within doors. At present my countrymen are unduly excited, and they might imagine you to be other than you really are. I have many things to arrange, but I will return in the morning, and then we will see what can be done."

I bowed but did not reply, being, in truth, dubious what answer to frame.

Crossing the open space in which we stood, he led us through a series of side streets in the old part of the town, and finally halted in front of a fairly decent inn.

"Here you will be comfortable," he said. "The people

are old acquaintances of mine, and will willingly oblige me.—Ah, Mateo," he broke off, as a thin, cadaverous-looking man came forward, "how are you? These gentlemen are my friends, whom I have brought to stay for the night. Can you find them a room?"

"Certainly, señor; my house and all it contains is at your service."

"Then lodge them quickly; they are fatigued, and want rest."

We now bade Don Philip adieu, and followed Mateo up the dirty staircase, along a still dirtier corridor, and so into a large room, half bare and wholly cheerless.

"Well, Dick," I said, when our host had departed to get some supper, "we are safely in port at last;" in answer to which my comrade laid down his gun carefully and whistled.

CHAPTER V.

WE LEAVE VITORIA.

IN spite of Dick's undisguised suspicion, I could not think that we were in any real danger. To our swords Don Philip owed his life, and this formed a bond between us not easily severed. But even if he were not the honourable man I judged him, he could gain nothing by playing us false.

"Oh, I have no ill thoughts of the Don," Dick said, when I pointed this out, "none whatever. He's a fine fellow, and we could trust him with our lives a thousand times over. But, you see, our safety does not depend upon him. Here we are, a couple of strangers in a fortified town. The streets are filled with soldiers, and in war time they don't stop to ask many questions. Now this landlord may be honest as day, but he has a tongue. In an hour, every one who passes this way will know of our being here. That is odd to begin with, and all sorts of stories will soon be flying about."

"But we are friends!"

"Ay, just so, friends to one party; that's the mischief of it. However, there's little sense in meeting trouble half-way, though it's just as well to be ready."

With this sentiment I was entirely in harmony; but the landlord, coming in with supper, interrupted the conversation, and it was not resumed.

Before settling down for the night, however, Dick secured the fastenings of the door and window, which was a difficult task, more especially with regard to the door.

As I anticipated, the night passed without incident; and after breakfast, in the morning, I felt tempted to smile at Dick's notion of danger.

"At what time is the Don likely to come?" my comrade asked, as a neighbouring clock struck eleven.

"I expected him before this; perhaps he is waiting to see General Cordova. I hope he will come soon; it is tedious staying here with nothing to do."

Nevertheless I had to control my impatience, as it was nearly five o'clock when Don Philip arrived.

"I trust that you will pardon me, señor," he said politely; "but it was impossible to come sooner, and even now I have failed in my errand. The British officer, Colonel Wylde, is at San Sebastian, and General Cordova has not returned."

"Then what are we to do?"

"Remain here until I have seen the general. There is one piece of news, however, which will interest you. Your fellow-countryman, General Evans, is at San Sebastian."

I looked at him in amazement. "Do you mean with a British army?"

"Not exactly. I believe your government refused to aid us with regular soldiers, but has permitted the voluntary enlistment of several thousand men. They are to be known as the British Legion, and will form a part of the Spanish army."

"To assist in putting down the insurrection?"

"Yes."

"In that case there is no further need of caution on our part, for which I am glad. It is terribly fatiguing to stay indoors."

"Yet I must beg that you will continue to do so. The sentiment is perhaps absurd, but my countrymen are very vexed about the matter, and the alliance is far from popular."

"Wounded vanity!" I remarked.

"It is certainly lowering to the national honour, and in that light the people in general regard it."

"That is, they will accept our help and detest us for giving it."

"You phrase it strongly, señor, yet there is truth in your words. But the feeling of irritation will lessen, and soon we shall work in a friendly spirit by the side of your countrymen."

"Meantime my comrade and I are placed in a very inconvenient position. What of the people in this house? Are they to be trusted?"

"Have no uneasiness, señor; they would die in my service. Besides, the delay cannot be long. The general must soon return; very likely he is back now. I am going straight to his quarters."

He bowed courteously to each of us and withdrew, promising to return the next day.

Left alone with Dick, I related what had passed, and told him of Don Philip's wish that we should not venture into the street.

Ignoring the latter part, my comrade began talking about the British Legion.

"Now, that's the kind of thing," he said, "that a plain man like myself can't understand. If the government wish to help in putting down Don Carlos, why don't they send out a proper army? This half-and-half business is no good to anybody. They should either do the thing thoroughly, or let it alone."

"They seem 'willing to wound and yet afraid to strike,'" I quoted.

"It's worse cowardice than running away from a battle-field," Dick went on. "But anyway the Legion has a good leader; that is, if General Evans be Lacy Evans."

"Have you met him?" I inquired.

"Met him! Why, I served with him at Waterloo. He's a sterling soldier, and if the Dons give him a free hand, Don Carlos is as good as defeated. He served in the Peninsular campaign, fought in Canada, and came back in time for Waterloo. Oh, he's a downright fighting man, every inch of him."

"One would fancy that the Spaniards would receive him with open arms."

"I don't know," responded Dick philosophically. "If you have a job on hand that beats you, you don't always feel grateful to the man who comes and does it for you. I've often heard old soldiers say that the Dons never forgave them for beating the French. I suppose that seeing another do what you can't manage yourself makes you feel small."

"There's a good deal in that, Dick," I said; "it must be galling."

Having nothing else to do, we sat chatting until bed-time, and my comrade made the hours pass pleasantly enough with graphic descriptions of the many adventures he had met with during his earlier years.

True to his word, Don Philip came the next morning, but unfortunately he brought little fresh news. General Cordova had returned to Vitoria, but was so busy that our friend could not find an opportunity of bringing our circumstances to his notice.

Several days, in fact, passed without anything definite being done, and I was proposing to Dick that we should make a start on our own account, when late one night Don Philip paid us a further visit.

At first we chatted upon indifferent topics, but I could tell by the Spaniard's face that he had something important to communicate.

"I have seen the general," he said, after a while, "and am the bearer of a proposal from him."

"To us?"

"Yes. Your comrade is of course included, but it is you to whom I am particularly to address myself. I told General Cordova the story of our adventures, and the gallant part which you played. The general desires me to compliment you upon your courage."

"I appreciate the honour," I returned, bowing low; "but it would have been more fittingly bestowed upon my brave comrade."

"The remark is just what I should have expected from you," he said politely. "But I grow tedious in unfolding the object of my visit. It is connected with the British Legion, concerning which I have already spoken. The general wishes to send by the hands of a trusty messenger a letter of extreme importance to the leader of the Legion. My description of your exploits, señor, has led him to fix upon yourself as a suitable agent. May I inform him that you will undertake the task?"

Now, I will confess without reserve that this request coming from the commander-in-chief of the Spanish armies gratified my youthful vanity; yet I possessed sufficient common-sense to know that the undertaking was full of danger.

My one qualification was a fair knowledge of the Spanish tongue, but the difficulties were numerous, and some of them I proceeded to set forth.

"I am willing to justify your general's confidence, señor," I began; "but it would give small proof of ability to rush blindly into such an enterprise. In the first place, I have no money; and again, my attire would excite suspicion in the mind of every passer-by. I should be attacked by Christino and Carlist alike."

"Each of those points has been considered. With regard to the first, the general will not send you out penniless. The second will be left to your discretion. You can go in disguise, or as a Christino officer."

"Then the country is strange to me; I am ignorant of the route."

"The general has selected a trusty soldier who will act both as guide and servant."

"And what of my comrade?"

"He will go with you."

Turning to Dick, I told him of the proposal, and asked his advice.

"Accept," he said unhesitatingly; "it will be better than staying cooped up here."

"When does the general wish us to start?" I asked.

"In the early morning. I myself will ride with you a little way from the city."

"And you will make the necessary arrangements?"

"Assuredly, señor; all may safely be left in my hands."

"Then you may tell the general that I consent."

"We had better get a few hours' sleep," Dick said, when our visitor had gone; "who knows when we shall have another chance," and he began to undress.

It was still dark when the landlord, knocking at the door, announced that Don Philip was below, adding that he had brought the articles of which the señor had spoken.

Unfastening the door, I admitted the long-visaged Mateo, who placed two bundles on the floor.

"The señor has sent these," he explained; "and as soon as you are dressed, breakfast will be ready downstairs."

Having lit the lamp and washed ourselves, we put on the Spanish uniforms, and leaving the old garments, descended to the lower room.

Don Philip was seated at a well-laid table, amply furnished with meat and bread, poached eggs, and cups of steaming chocolate.

He saluted us affably, and while we breakfasted, gave me my final instructions.

"Remember," he said, "that your object is to reach General Evans as soon as possible. As far as we know, he is still at San Sebastian, but it is not certain. That, however, you will ascertain on the journey, and regulate your movements accordingly. This purse contains sufficient money to cover your expenses; the horses you will retain as a present from General Cordova. You may place implicit confidence in the soldier, Pedro Gamboa, and be guided by him."

"Where is he?" I inquired.

"He will be here immediately with the horses.—Mateo, see if the soldier has come."

The landlord went out and soon returned, bringing with him the man, at whom I looked with interest.

Whether he was a young man or an old I could not well determine, but his features expressed both honesty and shrewdness. He was tall and broad-shouldered, but he did not carry a superabundance of flesh; and, unlike most of the Spaniards we had yet met, his eyes twinkled with a droll humour.

Don Philip pointed to me and said, "This is Don Arturo

Powell, the señor whom General Cordova has commanded you to serve. You will obey him as you would the colonel of your regiment."

The soldier saluted with military precision, and I suggested that while we were examining the horses, he should have some breakfast, at which, poor fellow, his face brightened up wonderfully.

Don Philip now gave me the letter, and we moved out to the court-yard. The horses were sorry-looking nags; but not to do the gallant animals an injustice, I hasten to add that their performance was far better than their woe-begone appearance led me to expect.

"I have taken care to stock you with provisions," Don Philip said, as we mounted, "so that you need not enter a Carlist village in order to dine," and he glanced in rather a comical manner at Dick.

We rode slowly through the still sleeping town to the gate, where, on the production by Don Philip of an order from General Cordova, we were permitted to pass.

The dawn was beginning to break; the clouds showed grey, the wind blew chill, and I was glad when the Don allowed his horse to canter.

A few miles out we met several bullock-carts laden with provisions lumbering city-ward.

We had ridden perhaps eight miles, when Don Philip reined in his horse.

"Here, señor," he said, "I must bid you and your brave comrade good-bye. It is unlikely that we shall ever meet again, but I shall remember you for all time. Upon the subject of my grief I care not to dilate, but I am not unmindful of your delicate sympathy and loyal comradeship. What the future holds in store we cannot tell; but if my wishes avail aught, happiness and prosperity lie before you."

"Farewell, señor," I replied; "I take leave of you with regret, and so does my comrade, who, like myself, looks upon you as a brave and honourable gentleman."

He shook each of us by the hand, and Dick said, "Good-bye, Don; you're one of the right sort anyhow."

Don Philip repeated his adieus, spoke a few words to Pedro, and then, turning his horse's head, rode back towards Vitoria.

"Now, Pedro," I said to the servant, "let us get forward as quickly as may be. But, first, are we wise in continuing on the main road?"

"Until within a few miles of Vergara we can safely venture, señor. At that place the Carlists have a strong force."

"We must keep out of their way; I do not wish to be stopped on the road."

Pedro crossed himself solemnly. "The saints forbid, señor," he said, "that you should fall into the hands of the Carlists. Have you not heard of the Durango decree?"

"No! What is that?"

"A proclamation in which Don Carlos commands his supporters not to give quarter to any foreigner found bearing arms against him. All such are to be shot without mercy."

"Impossible!" I cried; "such barbarity is unheard of."

"It is true all the same, señor; you may be certain of that. This is a cruel war. Each side takes for its motto, '*Guerra a cuchillo.*'"

"War to the knife," I echoed thoughtfully, and turning to Dick, told him of the discovery I had just made.

"The knowledge will make us fight all the harder, sir, if it comes to fighting," he replied calmly. "It is a cruel law, and one which will do no good. No men fight so desperately as those who have a halter round their neck."

This assertion was doubtless correct, but it yielded me little comfort, and for a time I rode forward rather dejectedly.

It was not exactly that I feared death; it was the manner of it. The idea of being taken and shot like a common brigand was intensely disagreeable; but gradually the buoyancy of youth recovered its ascendency, and I banished the unpleasant subject from my mind.

The morning was fine; I had money in my pocket, a horse under me, and a trusty comrade at my side, so that the situation was not devoid of pleasure.

"Dick," I said, "how poor Mr. Forrester would have revelled in an adventure of this kind, had he lived! I can just imagine with what glee he would have donned his Spanish uniform this morning at the old inn."

"Ah!" responded Dick, "a commission in the Legion would have suited him well. Plenty of harum-scarum youngsters have come out from England, I'll be bound, and amongst them Mr. Forrester would have been in his element. However, it was not to be."

"No," I said sadly, and relapsed into silence.

Soon after this I observed Pedro, who had gone in front, engaged in conversation with a muleteer; and hastening up, I was in time to hear, though not to understand, the stranger's last remark.

"Who is that, Pedro?" I asked suspiciously, as, at my approach, the man moved off.

"A Carlist spy, señor, who has for once overshot his mark."

"I recognized that he was a Basque."

"Ah, by his speech, señor. It is a difficult language for strangers. They tell a story in Biscay, that the devil once spent seven years amongst the mountaineers trying to learn it, and then gave up in despair."

"A comical story, Pedro; but what made you suspect the man of being a spy?"

"He was too friendly, señor; but, 'He that will deceive the fox must rise betimes.' Yonder Basque is a poor bungler, and will not thrive at his trade."

"He may be more cunning than you think," I observed.

"Not he, señor. As my countrymen say, 'He's not worth his ears full of water.' But in order to make quite sure, we will leave the road a little farther on, and make across the country for a point beyond Vergara."

Accordingly, we rode on a distance of half a mile, and then turned to the right down a narrow lane, and so into the open country.

We had reached the brow of a gentle eminence, when

Pedro, pausing, pointed out the muleteer whom we had left on the main road.

"Quickly, señor," the soldier said, "down the hill; we must not let the spy catch sight of us. He is pushing on with all speed to Vergara."

Putting our horses to the gallop, we raced down the slope and across the adjoining plain.

"You were right, señor," Pedro said, drawing rein at the foot of the opposite hills; "the rascal was craftier than I expected. However, I think we are out of danger now. They of Vergara will search for us towards Durango, while we are quietly journeying in the direction of Tolosa. It would be well to get down here, señor, and lead the animals over the hill. On the other side we shall find a good road."

Acting upon his advice, we began the ascent of a narrow pass, which Pedro assured me was practicable for the horses.

"Indeed, they would carry us easily enough, señor, but it is as well to husband their strength," he added.

The incident of the spy was on the whole, perhaps, a fortunate one, as it made us more cautious, and caused us to advance with greater vigilance.

Half-way down the slope on the opposite side, Dick, who was on my right, suddenly stopped and held up a finger in warning.

"Listen," he whispered; "what is that noise beneath us?"

"Stay with Pedro and the horses behind that rock while

I find out," I answered; "it sounds like a body of troops on the march."

"Have a care, señor," said Pedro; "if they spy you out we are lost."

Gliding lightly and with the utmost circumspection from one point to another, I came finally to a spot from which the road could be seen winding round the base of the hills.

As I conjectured, the sound which Dick's keen hearing had caught was made by the march of a body of troops, and a glance showed me that they did not belong to the Spanish army.

They numbered, as nearly as I could judge, about five hundred bayonets, and marched in very loose order, but with a light, swinging, and buoyant step.

Lying flat on the ground, I watched them with interest; it was my first view of these warlike mountaineers.

Strong, robust men they seemed, and active withal; well-made, and in much better condition than the Spanish soldiers we had seen at Vitoria.

Their uniform was simple but effective. Instead of a helmet, the head-dress was a light, round, cloth cap, which I afterwards learned was called a *boina;* a grey cloth frock-coat with plain metal buttons, linen trousers, and string-made sandals, completed the costume.

Each man was armed with a musket, and round his waist his *canana,* or cartridge-pouch, was fixed by means of a strap, in which the bayonet was stuck.

Formidable enemies these, I thought, knowing every foot of the ground, acquainted with every path and defile in the mountains; and I hardly wondered that the Christinos should despair of subjugating them.

I waited until the last files passed my post of observation, and then rejoining my companions, reported what I had witnessed.

"They must be moving from Arrioa," said Pedro, in perplexity; "it is strange. Perhaps there is some affair going on at Orduna, and they have been summoned to assist Don Carlos. This is awkward for us, señor, since others may be travelling to the same place. We must take double care."

We led the horses very cautiously down the remainder of the path, and, finding that the Carlists had disappeared, we mounted and rode off at full speed.

Instead of keeping to the road, however, Pedro led us through little-used lanes, and over desolate fields, across the country.

"We lose time this way, señor, but it is safer," he explained. "If the Carlists are moving to any particular spot, they will march by the roads, and I feel sure that something is on foot."

"Can we not seek information at one of the cottages?" I asked.

"No, señor, the risk is too great; the peasants about here are nearly all Carlists."

"Still we must obtain news somehow. I do not wish to reach San Sebastian and find that we have passed the Legion on the road."

"I have a plan, señor; it is this. Some of my friends

live at Tolosa—the town where we are going now. I propose that while you stay outside in some safe place, I shall steal into the town and pick up all the information I can."

"But I understood that Tolosa was occupied by the Carlists!"

"What of that? Something must be risked, and the danger is small. It will be a dark night, and the Carlist sentries are not expecting an attack."

I volunteered to accompany him, but he scouted the suggestion.

"It would be madness, señor—downright madness," he cried. "By myself, I can go and return in safety; but with you—pardon me, señor—the result would be different."

He appeared to have such implicit confidence in his ability to conduct the enterprise successfully, that I was induced to yield, although with a certain amount of reluctance.

It was already dusk when about half a mile eastward of Tolosa we came to a disused building, lying back some distance from the road; and here it was resolved that Dick and I should stay, while Pedro went on his dangerous quest.

"If I do not come back within three hours, señor," he said, "you will know that the little queen numbers one soldier less in her ranks. In that case, push on with all speed to San Sebastian."

Having led his horse into the hovel, which had been

used originally as a cowshed, he bade us adieu, and crossing the field towards the town, was soon swallowed up in the darkness.

"We may as well put our animals inside," Dick said; "it will be warmer for them."

This we did, and having given them a little of the corn which Don Philip had thoughtfully provided, took up our own places just within the doorway.

CHAPTER VI.

AN ADVENTUROUS RIDE.

IT was dreary work waiting there in the deepening darkness, and about the end of the second hour I began to be oppressed by a feeling of dread that we had seen the last of Pedro.

As is frequently the case during a period of suspense, the dangers multiplied themselves indefinitely, and it seemed to me almost certain that our faithful comrade could not escape them.

By degrees, too, the peril of our own situation became in my excited mind more alarming. I strained my eyes until they ached, watching the imaginary movements of phantom enemies. Every night-sound—the cry of a bird, the sough of the wind through the branches, the snapping of a twig, the tick of an insect in the grass—made me start, and twenty times my fingers stole to the trigger of my musket.

The horses, having eaten their corn, stood enjoying the halt; and occasionally Dick spoke to them in a low voice, in order to accustom them to our presence.

"Time is nearly up, Mr. Powell," my comrade whispered,

at the end of another half-hour. "I'm beginning to think that the Spaniard has run his head into a noose. If so we shall have plenty of work to get away. Do you know which course to steer?"

"Not in the least, except that San Sebastian lies to the north. If it were a clear night the stars would help us."

"Quite as well as it is," Dick responded; "the light would be of more use to the Carlists than to us."

We once more relapsed into silence, which was suddenly broken by the sounds of firing.

The shots came from the highroad, and at some distance to our left. I clutched Dick's arm nervously, but he remained cool and collected.

"Listen," I whispered; "what do you make of that?"

"We might make twenty guesses and miss every time," he said. "Perhaps the Carlists are after our friend Pedro."

"In that case we are lost; he will make straight for us."

"I'm not so sure of that; he seems to me rather a crafty fox."

"Had we not better get the horses out in readiness?"

"It would save time, certainly; but, on the other hand, they might do us more harm than good. No, I think we will let them stay. The firing has stopped."

"Then we may say good-bye to Pedro."

"Prophesying is a bad habit to take up, Mr. Powell, it so often works out wrong."

For another ten minutes we stood listening and peering into the darkness. The noise had died away, and we were once more wrapped in the silence of night.

"Poor Pedro!" I exclaimed sadly; "I wish I had forbidden his going. It was a foolhardy enterprise."

"Hist!" whispered Dick, "don't move; there is something living close at hand. I heard those bushes yonder crack."

It was fortunate that Dick uttered his warning, as in my excitement I should most assuredly have committed some foolish act, for now I could distinctly hear the crackle of branches.

"Friend or foe? Pedro or the Carlists?"

The answer to the unspoken question speedily came.

"Make no noise, señor—it is I, Pedro; the Carlists are out."

The next moment he raised himself from the ground almost at my feet.

"Are you hurt?" I inquired. "We heard the sounds of the firing."

"No, señor, these Carlists are bunglers; I have put them on the wrong track," and he laughed softly.

"You have been in Tolosa?"

"Yes, señor, and bring back ill news. I scarcely know what advice to give. The Carlists are swarming in all directions. It is said that they have fought a battle at Los Arcos under General Ituralde, and been beaten, which has made them very savage."

"But we are not near Los Arcos?"

"No, señor, that place is close to Estella; but the defeat makes a great difference in the movements of the Carlists here."

"Did you learn anything of General Evans?"

"The brave English have thrown themselves into Bilbao, and the Carlists have raised the siege."

"Bravo!" I cried; "that is a good beginning."

"But not for us, señor; it makes our task all the harder. Now, we cannot travel on any road without the fear of meeting bands of Carlists marching from one post to another. My friends tell me that they are everywhere."

"Well, Pedro, we will take our chance. Carlists or no Carlists, General Cordova's orders must be obeyed."

"Good, señor. 'He who rides behind another does not travel when he pleases.' Are we to make for Bilbao or San Sebastian? The dangers are equal either way."

"We will go straight to Bilbao, where you say the Legion is."

We brought out the horses very quietly, and still leading them, stole along in single file by the side of the hedge.

For more than a mile we journeyed in this wretched manner, keeping parallel with the highway as nearly as the nature of the ground would admit.

Then I ventured to suggest that we should regain the road, and Pedro reluctantly consented.

All through the night we rode and walked alternately, sometimes cantering gaily over a stretch of level ground, at others leading our horses through narrow defiles, picking our way carefully amongst rocky boulders, making, as Dick described it, one step forward and two backward.

Nevertheless, we continued, under Pedro's guidance, to make fair progress, and only once did he lead us into danger.

It happened in this wise. We had just emerged from the narrow outlet of a deep valley, when we were confronted by a glare of fire, which showed us that we had stumbled into the street of a straggling village.

At the farther end we saw numerous men lying round the watch-fires, and several others, as if on guard, walking to and fro.

"A Carlist post, señor," whispered Pedro; "shall we turn back?"

"Too late, my friend; they have seen us. Ride on coolly, answer their challenge, and then make a dash for it.—Dick, keep an eye on their guns."

We cantered on as unconcernedly as if in the midst of friends, but before the fires were reached, a dozen men sprang from the ground and a commanding "*Quien viva?*" rang out.

It was a critical moment, but none of us flinched, and before the challenge was repeated we were close upon the group of soldiers.

Then Pedro, with the greatest effrontery, answered "*Viva Carlos Quinto!*" and made as if he would pull up.

At the same instant a lynx-eyed Carlist dashed at his horse, shouting, "They are Christinos—look at their uniforms! Kill the Christinos!"

The cry was taken up by his comrades, and the street echoed with shouts of "Kill the Christinos!"

Rising in his stirrups, Pedro responded with a gallant "*Viva Isabella Segunda!*" and then like a flash we swept past them.

Too late came the shower of bullets; we had turned the corner, and were speeding away in safety.

"A close shave that," Dick remarked when we slackened rein. "I am afraid that one fellow got under my horse's feet. What a queer place to choose for a village!"

This adventure had the effect of rendering us more careful, such close quarters to the Carlists being far from desirable.

"Are you quite sure of your road, Pedro?" I asked.

"I think so, señor; that is to say, we are going in the right direction. When the dawn breaks we will find an old peasant and ask."

The horses now began to exhibit symptoms of weariness, and, indeed, I had expected them to break down long before this.

However, we pushed on steadily, being anxious to cover as much ground as possible before we were brought to a compulsory halt.

All this time the clouds had been gradually lifting, and now the peaks in our rear were bathed in the golden rays of the rising sun.

Pedro gazed about him, his features betraying an unusual indecision.

"Señor," he said frankly, "I do not recognize this place. Will you take my horse and ride on slowly, while I go to the farm-house on yonder hill? I do not like asking for information, but it would be foolish to go further in what may prove to be a wrong direction. The people at the farm cannot see you, if you rein up behind that hedge."

Proceeding on foot, he approached the building by a circuitous route, and observed a similar precaution on the return journey.

"It is all right, señor; we are half-way between the towns of Elgoibar and Marquina. If the roads were clear we could eat our dinners in Bilbao."

"Why not as it is? There can be little danger now that the Carlists have abandoned their posts."

"The Carlists have gone away, señor, it is true, but not far. From the talk of the old man yonder, I gathered that several fresh battalions have been brought up from a distance."

"Then what is to be done?"

"Have patience, señor, and wait for the dusk."

This advice vexed me—I could ill brook further delay; and yet, perchance, Pedro's counsel was sound.

I put the matter to Dick, and he sided with the Spaniard.

"Three men, however brave they may be, can't make much headway against a hundred," he said; "and if these places are in the hands of the Carlists, I don't see how we are to get through in broad daylight. It's a nuisance, of course; but if Pedro can find a decent hiding-place, I vote for a halt."

Both my comrades would have pushed on had I given the order, but I did not care to disregard their counsel; and accordingly, a few hundred yards further on, we turned aside into the recesses of a thick forest.

Here we tethered the horses, and having eaten a portion

of the provisions which Don Philip had supplied, made ourselves comfortable.

Pedro, who, like Don Philip, appeared able to do without sleep, took the first watch, while Dick and I, having full confidence in his vigilance, lay down on a bed of leaves.

Directly evening approached, we unfastened the horses, and, leading them out, once more gained the road.

"Now," I exclaimed joyously, "no more vexatious delays. Hurrah for Bilbao and General Evans!"

We cantered off in good spirits, rejoiced to find ourselves in action, and within measurable distance of completing the journey.

Avoiding the town, or rather village, of Marquina, Pedro took us by some cross-ways lying to the north of it.

The few houses that we passed were in darkness, and the inmates had apparently retired for the night.

The horses, fresh from their long rest, went along merrily, and though the rain began to fall, we scarcely heeded the discomfort, in looking forward to the speedy termination of our labours.

From Guernica a comparatively straight road runs to Bilbao, and this we struck a little westward of the former place.

I rallied Pedro upon his fears, remarking that, as yet, our ride had proved quite a pleasant little expedition.

"May it so continue, señor," he answered; "but there is plenty of time still in which to meet a Carlist bullet."

"But we have passed the worst dangers," I urged.

"If it please the Virgin and the saints, señor. For my part, I shall feel safe only when we are in Bilbao. I have fought these Carlists, and there is a saying in our tongue, 'Whom a serpent has bitten, a lizard alarms.'"

In my ignorance I rather smiled at the deep respect in which Pedro held the prowess of his Carlist adversaries, but later I learned to acknowledge the justice of his sentiments.

Their valour was certainly disgraced by acts of the most barbarous cruelty; but of their fighting qualities there could be no question.

At the moment, however, I made Pedro some jesting reply, and urged my horse to a quicker pace.

Bilbao lay before us, and now that the goal was so close at hand I was all on fire to meet it.

Suddenly we were startled by the sight of a red, quivering flame which shot high into the heavens from the midst of the wooded slope on our right.

"Push on, señor," Pedro cried. "The Carlists are at work there; that flame comes from a burning house."

I stopped my horse, and sat gazing in consternation at the red glow.

"Can we do nothing?" I asked; "there may be people in the house."

Pedro made a gesture of impatience. "Fly, señor," he said, "while there is still time. We can do no good. We shall only make three more for the Carlists to kill."

"Nevertheless I am going," I answered doggedly. —"Dick, will you come with me?"

"That will I," he said, and we made for the bank.

"'He who is well and seeks ill, if it comes, God help him,'" muttered Pedro resignedly; but, none the less, the brave fellow followed us.

The road on our right was bounded by a high but sloping bank, and we were endeavouring to find foothold for the horses, when a black object loomed up in front of us, and rushed furiously down the slope.

"A horse and a rider," cried Dick, reining in his own frightened animal.

"And they are down. Quick! take the reins."

I sprang to the ground and ran towards the fallen animal; it lay motionless and dead.

Then I made an unexpected discovery—the rider was a girl.

I raised her head in my arms, and while Pedro guarded the horses, Dick brought some wine which we had saved for emergencies.

"The heart still beats," I said; "she is not dead."

We forced a little of the wine between her teeth, and bathed her forehead with the water from a tiny rill which ran by us.

In a few minutes she gave a deep groan, and then in tones of mingled anger and terror cried, "Rubio! Rubio!"

"For the love of the Virgin, señor, let us get her away," exclaimed Pedro. "Dominic Rubio is the most bloodthirsty bandit in all Spain. He is the terror of the mountains."

BRITISH
10 NO 97
MUSEUM

"It's time to be moving," Dick said quietly; "there's a search-party out;" and looking up, I beheld a score of torches between us and Bilbao.

"Lift her on my horse, Dick, and hold her so while I mount. Now, I am ready. Don't spare any of those rascals; they are not worth pity."

Keeping well abreast of each other, we rode towards the advancing torch-bearers, who, on observing us, uttered a yell of satisfaction.

But their joy was ill-timed and did not last long.

Pedro, rendered desperate by the fear of a cruel death, dashed at them like a madman; while Dick, on the other side of me, delivered his blows with the skill of a practised swordsman.

The light from the torches revealed the girl in my arms, and the robbers made frantic but fruitless efforts to reach her.

Gradually we drew clear of the bandits; but the shouts and yells, the groans of the fallen, the fierce oaths of the survivors, raised up fresh enemies, and it needed not Pedro's sudden exclamation to warn me that a body of horsemen rode hard on our track.

"We shall enter Bilbao in fine style," panted Dick, as the horses struggled gamely on. "Bend low; they are beginning to fire."

We could hear the clatter of hoofs in the rear, and it seemed as if our pursuers were gaining on us, when Pedro called out that a second band of Carlists blocked the road.

Dick also saw them, and without hesitation wheeled to

the right, spurring his horse up the bank, and shouting for us to follow.

Personally my one chance of safety lay in flight, as, encumbered by the girl's dead weight, I could not strike a blow in self-defence.

However, I resolved that she should not fall into the hands of her foes, and, setting my teeth firmly, rode hard.

The confusion was now at its height. Rubio and his gang had apparently withdrawn, but the Carlists, horse and foot, kept up the chase. Bullet after bullet came singing in our wake or whistling overhead, and to this music must be added the cries of the Carlists, the *vivas* of Pedro, and our own hurrahs.

Where we were riding I knew not, nor how any of us kept our seats.

Twice my horse stumbled and would have fallen, had it not been for Dick's ready arm, but we managed somehow to keep going.

A few of the Carlist infantry, making use of a short cut, threw themselves boldly across our path, but failed to stop us.

Then, without warning, the terrified horses went with a bound into a river, and as the waters rose above my feet I gave myself up for lost.

I heard Dick giving me directions, but could not understand his words; my arms, numbed by the girl's weight, seemed useless, and I expected every moment that she would slip into the stream.

The Carlists, too, lined the bank which we had just quitted, and their bullets cut up the water around us.

But it was fated that they should not have all the fun. To our unbounded surprise, a telling volley was poured amongst them from the opposite bank, and we heard the joyous sound of a British cheer.

"Hurrah for the Legion!" cried Dick, in stentorian tones. "Keep up, Mr. Powell; we shall beat the Dons yet."

Then the shouting was redoubled; the men had caught sight of us, and a dozen of the brave fellows dashed into the water to our assistance.

The aid was rendered just in time; my arms could no longer hold their burden, and when the girl was taken from me, they hung limp and useless at my side.

"Be careful, men," I said; "the lady is badly hurt."

"Run for a litter, some of you," exclaimed some one whom I took to be an officer; and addressing me, he added pleasantly, "You have chosen a queer way of entering Bilbao."

"Blame the Carlists," I answered; "they determined upon introducing us with *éclat*. But am I speaking to an officer of the British Legion?"

"Yes, I am Captain Adyce."

"My name is Powell. I am seeking General de Lacy Evans. My comrades and I have ridden from Vitoria with dispatches."

"And the lady?"

"No, we picked her up on the road. I fancy she was escaping from a band of brigands. I suppose I shall be able to find some sort of accommodation for her?"

"The town is very full," Captain Adyce responded dubiously.

I called Pedro, and asked him if he knew any one in Bilbao.

"Yes, señor," he replied; "I have a friend to whom we can take the poor lady."

"That is well; you shall guide these soldiers to the house."

The men now came with the litter, and we marched into Bilbao, escorted by a sergeant whom Captain Adyce instructed to conduct me to General Evans.

The noise of the firing had caused a commotion in the town, and quite a crowd of sight-seers assembled to witness our entry.

All kinds of remarks were indulged in at our expense, some merry, others commiserating, and a few sarcastic.

I was rather puzzled at this free expression of opinions until I bethought myself of our Spanish costumes, and realized that the soldiers of the Legion mistook us for natives.

This perhaps they were the more encouraged to do through hearing me address Pedro in the Spanish language.

"Faith!" exclaimed one little man, "it's the Spanish army. There's been a big battle somewhere, I'll wager. They're bringing in their wounded."

"That's the army," said another—"the wooden man riding with the ambulance. The tall chap is a brigadier-general, I should say, and the other is the commander-in-chief."

"The war won't last long now," added the first speaker; "we shall be home again at Christmas."

"Wonder where they got their horses."

"It's a special breed that the Dons keep for themselves."

"Pure Arabs, and full of blood; look how they prance!"

Purposely raising my voice, I said, "Dick, there's a good judge of horse-flesh; he must be a stable-boy out of work."

At these words the crowd became silent, and many of the men had the grace to look ashamed.

"Faith, Charlie," cried the little man who started the ball, "that's the biter bit, and no mistake; shure, the gintleman is as English as meself," which raised another laugh, as the speaker was unmistakably a son of the Emerald Isle.

The house to which Pedro led us was situated in a side street, so narrow that the tops of the opposite buildings almost touched each other.

The inmates had gone to bed, but after repeated knockings, and a conversation carried on in low tones between our guide and an unseen person in an upper story, the door was thrown open, and Pedro entered by himself.

In a few minutes he came out accompanied by a buxom woman, who superintended the removal of the injured girl into the house.

As General Cordova's money had not been drawn upon, I was able to reward the bearers of the litter with a trifling gift, and they took their departure well satisfied.

Pedro meanwhile had gone in search of a Spanish physician, and anxious to learn his opinion, I requested the English sergeant to wait a little while.

To this he readily consented, and we passed the time chatting about the doings of the British Legion.

"We are far from being in good trim yet," he said, and I thought his manner a trifle despondent; "the men are brave enough, and will uphold the honour of the old flag later on, but bless you, sir, three-fourths of them have never handled a musket in their lives. They couldn't hit a haystack, much less a Carlist. But there, I'm an old soldier myself, and that makes a wonderful difference."

"Here is another," I said, pointing to Dick—"a Waterloo veteran."

The sergeant grasped Dick by the hand and wrung it warmly.

"We ought to be friends," he said; "I was at Waterloo. Are you going to join the Legion? General Evans will be glad to get the help of an old campaigner."

Dick's reply was prevented by the return of Pedro with the physician, to whom I briefly recounted the nature of the señorita's accident.

"Poor child," he said softly; "I will do what I can. But first, señor, permit me to thank you for a kindly act towards one of my countrywomen."

"I shall be amply repaid by her recovery," I answered, with a low bow, and stood aside to let him pass.

Pedro now undertook to find shelter for the horses, and he also informed me that we might all three lie at the house of his friend during the night.

This was good news, as the hour was growing late,

and I should have found much difficulty in procuring a suitable lodging.

A few minutes later, the doctor called me within. His features were grave, and their expression prepared me for an adverse report.

"Señor," he began, "I grieve to tell you that the señorita whom you so courageously befriended is very ill. I do not think that she will die, but it may be months before she is well enough to be moved."

"She will be safe here," I answered, "and, as far as my means go, she shall be no expense to the people of the house."

I drew out General Cordova's purse, and emptied its contents on the table.

"Ah, señor, the English are truly called a generous people," he cried. "For myself, I require nothing; my services shall be given freely. But the woman of the house is poor, and the señorita will need nourishing things."

"Let her have them," I answered. "I make you guardian of the purse, and if there is sufficient to pay the woman for her trouble, so much the better. Now I must go; I have much to do."

"But you will return?"

"Yes, to-night I shall sleep here; the future is uncertain."

He paid me a score of compliments, and I believe he was sincere; but time was speeding, and it behoved me to seek General Evans. I bade him farewell a second time, and accompanied by Dick and the sergeant, set off in the direction of the general's quarters.

CHAPTER VII.

DAVID AND JONATHAN.

BY this time the streets were quiet, and for the most part deserted, so that we had little trouble in making our way to the building in which the leader of the Legion was temporarily lodged.

Taking leave of the sergeant, I explained my errand to an officer, and was immediately shown with Dick into an empty room. Here we were joined by the general, who greeted us in the most kindly manner.

I looked at him with interest, and will at once admit that his appearance greatly prepossessed me in his favour.

He was a tall, well-proportioned man, bordering on fifty years of age, dark complexioned, and with dark moustache, which gave him a somewhat Spanish aspect.

His face wore an anxious, troubled expression, but this gloom vanished when he smiled.

I had written my name on a piece of paper, which he now held in his hand.

"Mr. Powell?" he said inquiringly.

"I am Arthur Powell; my comrade is Richard Truscott. Have I the honour of addressing General Evans?"

"I am he," was the smiling answer.

"Then, general, this letter is for you. I have brought it from General Cordova."

What the contents were I cannot say, but judging by the transitory frown which clouded the reader's brow, they were not of a pleasing nature.

The next instant, however, he smiled again, and glancing at his watch, bade us be seated.

"I must steal a few minutes from my work," he said, 'to hear your story. You are both English, I perceive, yet you wear Spanish uniforms, and come from Vitoria."

"The circumstances readily admit of explanation," I answered, "and the narrative need not detain you long."

Thereupon, beginning with the wreck of the yacht, I related the various incidents which had taken place—the meeting with Don Philip, the adventurous journey to Vitoria, and the successful carrying out of General Cordova's orders.

"You cannot justly complain of monotony during the last week or two," he said, when I had finished; "you seem to have enjoyed a fair share of excitement. By the way, you mentioned a Mr. Forrester. Did he come from Devonshire?"

"Yes, he was the son of Sir Nicholas Forrester," and my heart grew heavy at the recollection of poor Pym's tragic fate.

"You two were greatly attached to each other," the general went on musingly—"a modern David and Jonathan friendship."

"We were more than brothers," I said curtly, wondering at the remark.

Seeing that he had hurt my feelings, the general changed the subject by inquiring what my comrade and I intended to do.

"That is a question which must soon be answered," I replied; "but as yet we have not talked about it."

"Well," he said, "come and see me in the morning at ten o'clock. I suppose you have found a lodging. I shall not forget your gallant ride, if it is in my power to serve you."

We took leave of him and passed into the street, where Pedro was waiting for us.

"Pardon me, señor," said my trusty follower, "but I feared you might miss your way."

"And so came to guide us. You are a good fellow, Pedro. I hope some day to be able to reward you."

"I do not need that, señor; it is a pleasure to serve you," and so saying he walked on, bidding us follow.

In the room which had been set apart for our use were two curtained recesses facing each other, and each containing a bed.

Pedro having brought a light, left us, and we, being thoroughly worn out, undressed without delay and were soon asleep.

When I awoke, Dick was already stirring, and soon afterwards Pedro came in with some breakfast, consisting of eggs poached in oil, bread, butter, and chocolate.

As yet Pedro had not reported himself to the Spanish

general in Bilbao, and I counselled him to wait until our return before doing so.

"By the way, I have not asked after the señorita," I said, as we were starting. "Is she better?"

He shook his head, saying, "No, señor: she is still insensible."

This was not a very encouraging sign, and I began to fear that the poor girl was beyond the physician's skill.

I strove hard, however, to banish this apprehension, and the endeavour was materially aided by the novel sights and sounds which met me at every step.

The town was alive with unwonted bustle and activity. Crowds of people patrolled the streets, and their varied costumes formed a bright and pleasing picture.

The Scottish bonnets and tartans of the Legion's Highlanders; the red *boinas* of the Chapelgorris—Spanish irregulars; the sober green of the rifle corps; the red coats and white trousers of the infantry, contrasted with the quieter dress of numerous civilians, both Spanish and British, who mingled with the soldiers. But, in view of the appointment with the general, we could not stand to watch the ever-shifting panorama, so, rather reluctantly, we kept on our way.

A soldier ushered us into the little room where the interview of the preceding night had taken place, and here we awaited the general's coming.

In a short time the door was again opened, and an officer of the Legion entered.

Seeing that the new-comer was not General Evans, I

was about to withdraw my cursory glance, when a word from Dick held me spell-bound.

"If you are not Mr. Forrester," he said calmly, "you're either his ghost or his double, and you don't look like a ghost."

At these astonishing words the officer took a step forward and cried, "Dick! Dick Truscott, alive, and turned into a Spanish soldier! What does it mean? I thought no one but myself was saved from the wreck. How did you escape, and what are you doing here? Did you see anything of Mr. Powell when the yacht went down?"

Now it so chanced that I stood in a somewhat retired position, and was partly hidden by Dick, so that the speaker could only catch a glimpse of my uniform, and naturally took me to be a Spanish officer.

At this question, however, I could no longer remain a passive spectator, but came to the front, where the daylight fell upon my features, and the dear fellow was almost overcome by his strong emotions.

"Arthur!" he gasped. "Am I dreaming? Are we all ghosts? Speak, my dear boy; let me hear your voice."

We were both trembling violently, the surprise was so great, the meeting so unexpected. Each of us had believed so implicitly in the other's death that it was hard to realize the glad truth.

I tried to speak, but could not, and sitting down by the table, wept like a child.

Pym still lived! it was too wonderful. To me it was as if the sea had literally given up its dead. Often since the fatal night of the wreck I had pictured him lying on the bed of the cruel ocean, and mourned in secret over his unhappy fate.

And now he stood before me, his features sparkling with life and health, handsome and debonair as ever.

Let me endeavour to give, in a few words, a sketch of the man whom I loved more than any one on earth.

He was tall and powerfully built, with muscular limbs, broad shoulders, and deep chest. His complexion was strikingly fair, his eyes blue, and he had an abundance of curly, yellowish hair. At school he was nicknamed the Saxon, and the *sobriquet* stuck to him in later life.

Such was Pym Forrester physically; as to his character, let the records which I shall chronicle bear testimony.

Of what we did and said during the first hour I retain only the slightest recollection.

Dick talked, I believe, in his usual even tones, and related various stories of adventure tending to show that at sea the marvellous was no rarer than the commonplace, and Pym interposed a few words now and then, but I, for the most part, sat gazing in silence at my newly-recovered friend.

It was only when the latter began to speak of General Evans that I regained sufficient self-possession to take part in the conversation.

"I cannot understand this apparently chance meeting," he said. "Colonel Godfrey—of course you notice I have joined the Legion, but we will talk of that later—told me that I was to present myself to the commander-in-chief at ten o'clock."

"Were you acquainted with the general?" I asked.

"I had met him once; he is an old friend of my father's."

"And did he know about the wreck of the yacht?"

"Yes; one of his ships picked me up."

"Then the puzzle is easily solved. I told him my story last night, and he planned this meeting as a pleasant surprise."

"And so you're going to try your hand at soldiering, Mr. Forrester?" Dick observed.

"Yes; I have accepted a captain's commission in the Legion. Believing that everybody in the yacht was drowned, I did not care about returning to England, and thought the campaign would furnish me with a little healthy excitement."

Just then General Evans himself entered the room, and with a kindly smile exclaimed, "Well, David and Jonathan have been restored to each other, it appears. Now, Mr. Powell, you can understand the drift of my questions last night?"

"Yes, sir, perfectly."

"Your friend has been transformed since you saw him last," he continued, glancing at Pym's epaulettes.

"Yes, sir, and that troubles me. It seems that I have found him only to lose him again."

"Could not my friends join the Legion, sir?" asked Pym eagerly. "Dick Truscott there would not find the uniform a novelty. I have heard him speak of serving under you at Waterloo."

The general turned towards Dick with a look of interest.

"Were you at Waterloo?" he asked.

"Yes, sir; I won my sergeant's stripes there."

"Would you like to join the Legion?"

Poor Dick hesitated, and guessing at the cause of his irresolution, I hastened to reply for him.

"He is in a dilemma, sir," I said. "The truth is, he would like to be with Captain Forrester, but is unwilling to leave me."

"It looks as if I must take all or none," the general remarked laughingly; "but that is not so easy, as I fear all the commissions are filled up. However, inquiries shall be made, and I will tell you the result in a day or two."

Smiling pleasantly, he went out, after bidding Pym devote the rest of the day to us.

"I must introduce you to some of my new comrades," Pym said, as we turned into the street, "but not now. Let us get away from the crowd; I am anxious to have a full account of all that has happened to you since our separation."

Accordingly we strolled to the outskirts of the town, and sat down on a grassy mound where we could be free from interruption.

Suppressing all needless details, I ran rapidly through the list of our adventures, from the dismal night on the rocks down to our stormy entry into Bilbao.

"My faith," Pym exclaimed, "you have made the most of your time. Why, compared with Dick and you, we of the Legion have been asleep."

He was particularly interested concerning the rescue of

the Spanish lady, and several times questioned me as to the prospects of her recovery.

I repeated the doctor's words, but, at the same time, made no secret of my own belief.

"You are an incorrigible pessimist, Arthur," he laughed, "ever looking upon the dark side of things. Why, in your place I should have built up a splendid romance on such a foundation. Here, I'll give it to you in four chapters. The lady recovers. She proves to be a Spanish princess. She marries the doughty warrior who saved her life. He becomes a powerful Spanish nobleman."

"Who possesses various *castles in Spain*," I added slyly.

Pym laughed again, and explained the joke to Dick, who had not understood the hidden meaning of the words.

"Now," I said, "let us leave the realms of fiction, and descend to sober fact. How is it that you have been transformed into an officer of the Legion?"

"It is very simple," he answered, "and came about in the most natural manner. A troop-ship picked me up in the early dawn, half insensible, but still clinging tenaciously to a broken spar. The vessel was bound for San Sebastian, where I landed with the soldiers, and met General Evans. As an old friend of my father's, he offered me a commission, which I accepted; and since then I have been hard at work learning my duties.—That reminds me, Dick, your knowledge of drill will prove very useful. Our men make good rough material, but it requires working up."

"How many men has General Evans under him?" I asked.

"There are three thousand of us here in Bilbao, another couple of thousand in San Sebastian, and fresh detachments are arriving from England at short intervals. Later on the general hopes to take the field with ten thousand men of all arms."

"But what is your position? Do you figure as irregulars?"

"Not at all; we are an organized portion of the Spanish army, but subject to our own military discipline. We have two regiments of lancers—the Reina Isabella and the Queen's Own Irish; several regiments of infantry, a rifle corps, and a small artillery force. My regiment is the Eighth or Scottish Highlanders."

"Plenty of fancy names," observed Dick, with just a faint touch of sarcasm.

"Yes, I must admit that the general is strong in picturesque description. We have two regiments of grenadiers —the Westminster and the Scottish."

"I saw some of the grenadiers last night," said Dick dryly, and with a strong emphasis on the word "grenadiers."

"Ah! there's the prejudice of the old army man peeping out; but"— after a pause—"the men don't look much like grenadiers, and that's true. Still I believe they will not be found backward when it comes to actual fighting. Anyway, they will have every inducement to do their best."

"How so?"

"Because Don Carlos has threatened to put all prisoners

to death, and from various quarters I hear that the promise will be faithfully kept."

"Pedro told us something of that," I said: "and Dick and I know from experience how fiercely these Carlists fight."

"If we were on their side instead of against them," said Pym thoughtfully, "Don Carlos would be crowned at Madrid before Christmas. None of the Spanish soldiers, except their own brethren, the Chapelgorris, are a match for them."

"Who are these Chapelgorris?" I asked.

"Basques, like most of the Carlists, only they take sides against Don Carlos. Terrible stories are told of the savage feud between the two parties."

"It is a wretched war altogether," I remarked, "and for the sake of humanity I trust it will soon be ended. But although wishing every prosperity to the little queen's arms, I cannot help feeling a certain amount of sympathy for Don Carlos."

"Well, perhaps it is hard on him, but it would be harder still for the nation were he to become king."

This sentiment I repeatedly heard expressed by thinking Spaniards, who, while admitting that the late king acted beyond his powers in changing the succession, nevertheless agreed that the exclusion of Don Carlos would be for the good of the country generally.

Pym did not leave us until the evening, when his duties compelled him to return to his regiment, while we went back to our temporary lodgings.

My fears with regard to the señorita proved unfounded, at least for the present. The doctor, who had just left her room, met us in the passage, and in answer to my question remarked that his patient was neither better nor worse.

"The poor child is still unconscious," he said, "and may remain in that state for several days. But," with a sweeping bow, "the señor's generosity has made it possible for her to have every necessary that may tend to help her recovery."

I asked him if he had been able to discover anything which might establish her identity, but he shook his head.

"No," he replied. "The señorita is young—not yet twenty, I should say—and exceedingly beautiful. Her garments show that she comes from a wealthy family, but there are no marks and no papers."

"Should she die, her fate will cause endless suspense to her relatives," I said; but the doctor did not agree with this, saying that the Carlists would soon be driven off, and then searching inquiries could at once be made.

The next morning Pym, to whom we had pointed out our lodgings, arrived just as we finished breakfast, and I gathered from his face that he was the bearer of important news.

We greeted each other warmly, and then, with a pleased smile on his handsome face, he turned to Dick.

"Sergeant Truscott," he said, "you will report yourself without delay to Colonel Godfrey, commanding the Eighth Regiment. The colonel will give you an order to obtain all necessary articles from the stores."

"What about Mr. Powell, sir?" asked Dick dubiously, "because if he is not to be one of us, I would rather stand out."

I was about to interpose when Pym anticipated me, saying, "The general has some proposal to make Mr. Powell. I do not exactly know its nature, but you may depend it is something that he can accept.—Arthur, you are to see the chief at once, while I take Dick to the regiment. I shall be busy for the next few hours, but will call round here during the evening to learn what has been decided on."

General Evans received me with the courtesy habitual to him, and then came at once to the point.

"I am sorry," he began, "that I cannot offer you a commission in the Legion, for at present there are no vacancies. At the same time, I am unwilling to lose your services. You have already proved yourself a brave and trustworthy lad, and your knowledge of Spanish would make you very useful to me. What I propose then is briefly this—that you should join the Legion as a volunteer, until such time as an opening occurs for being definitely enrolled. You would not be attached to any particular regiment, but would perform such duties as might be necessary. In that way you would still keep in touch with your friend, Captain Forrester, and eventually perhaps find a place in his regiment."

Now this proposal of the general's suited me admirably, and I hastened to accept the offer. I was not much in love with the routine of regimental life, and preferred the greater freedom which such a post as that now shadowed forth would give.

Having signed an order for the officer who was to procure me a billet, the general bade me adieu, and intimated that I should present myself immediately after breakfast on the following day.

The next step was to go with Pedro to the Spanish general, Jaureguy, and this I did with extreme unwillingness.

True, we had not known each other long, but during the brief period of our being together I had formed a great liking for the worthy Spaniard.

Pedro also showed a disinclination to return, but recognizing the futility of grumbling, he passively resigned himself to the inevitable.

I found the Spanish general to be a most charming individual, and I learned afterwards that he was greatly beloved by the troops under his command.

According to common report he had been originally a shepherd, and he was familiarly spoken of both by his own men and by those of the Legion as "El Pastor."

He listened with interest to my narrative, and complimented me upon the successful termination of a dangerous errand.

I thanked him warmly for his kind words, and took the opportunity of pointing out that the credit was mainly due to Pedro.

"He is both a brave and capable man, general," I said in conclusion, "and I trust that his services will not be overlooked."

El Pastor spoke a few words of praise to the soldier, whose honest face glowed with pleasure, and then I turned to go.

"I hope we shall meet again," General Jauregui said, as he grasped my hand; "you will always find a welcome here, and I am sure that my officers will be glad to count you upon their list of friends. Come whenever you have a spare hour."

His genuine kindness touched me, and I walked back to my lodgings feeling that in this pleasant-spoken Spanish general I had gained a valuable friend.

In the evening Pym paid his promised visit, and heartily glad I was to catch sight of his handsome, smiling features.

"Well," he exclaimed, "are you going to stay? What did Evans propose? I am as curious as a woman."

I told him of what had passed, and he expressed himself satisfied.

"Evans will find you plenty of work," he said; "but we shall be able to see a good deal of each other. Little will be done in the fighting line yet a while; we are having a course of training, and it is needed. Dick has been grinding away at his fellows all day, and declares that they are the awkwardest squad he has ever put through their facings."

"What about the horse Cordova gave him? The animal is his own property."

"I'll sell it for him, and get a good price; horses are in demand. Do you stay in this house?"

"No, I have a billet near the general's; but I shall come here now and then to see how my invalid gets on."

"Ah, the princess!" he laughed. "How is she?"

"No better. But I must find the lady of the house and tell her that I am going away."

"All right; I'll go into the street and smoke a cigar. But don't be long."

Having finished my business, I joined him outside, and we went to my fresh lodgings, which were situated in a quiet street standing back from the main square. Here Pym, in spite of his broken Spanish, soon ingratiated himself into the hearts of the people—a respectable artisan and his wife.

"You ought to be comfortable enough, Arthur," he said as we went out; "the man is a trifle reserved, but his wife seems a kindly soul."

I laughed at this, knowing full well that the woman's hospitality owed its origin more to Pym's good looks and winning disposition than to any real partiality for "Los Ingleses."

Indeed my comrade's popularity seemed universal, and nowhere was it more apparent than among the officers of his regiment.

They were, of course, perfect strangers to me; but they received me with such unaffected kindness that my shyness soon wore off, and long before it was time to leave I felt quite at ease.

But when I returned to my solitary chamber, the absence of all my friends filled me with an overpowering sense of loneliness, and it was in a very despondent frame of mind that I finally sank to sleep.

CHAPTER VIII.

THE MARCH TO BRIVIESCA.

PYM'S prophecy that General Evans would provide me with plenty of work was amply verified, and during the next few weeks I had rarely an idle day.

My knowledge of the Spanish tongue served me in good stead, and enabled me to perform many little duties both in Bilbao and at San Sebastian, whither, during this period, I went on more than one occasion.

In Bilbao itself the soldiers of the Legion were busy drilling and learning the use of their weapons, besides cutting trenches, throwing up earth-works, building new forts, repairing old ones, and strengthening the defences generally.

From time to time rumours reached us that the little queen's friends were in sore straits.

Not only were the Carlists active and aggressive in the northern provinces, but they were making considerable headway throughout the east under Cabrera, a cruel but distinctly capable leader.

To make matters worse, the whole country was in a state of seething discontent. City after city threw off its allegiance to the government at Madrid, and broke out in open revolt.

The army commanded by General Cordova—ill-clad, unpaid, and half-starved—lay at Vitoria doing nothing, while the Carlists moved from place to place, gaining an almost uninterrupted series of successes.

"Not much glory to be obtained in this kind of campaign," Pym said one evening. "The men are growing very weary of garrison life, and are eager to be doing something. A long course of drill and digging is apt to become monotonous."

"Better that than moving out to be slaughtered," I suggested.

"Oh, I think we can give a good account of ourselves now," he said cheerily; "the last few weeks' work has effected a marvellous improvement. Even Dick admits that we are beginning to emerge from the grub state. By the way, what is the last news of the princess?"

"I have not seen her yet, but she is mending slowly."

"Have they found out who she is?"

"No; she is not in a condition to be questioned. The doctor hinted something about brain trouble when I saw him this afternoon."

We were walking back towards my lodgings when Captain Simpson of the rifles met us.

"I say, Powell," he cried, "is it true that the Legion has received orders to march?"

"I have not heard anything."

"Cottam of the artillery has put it about that we move in a few days to Vitoria."

"I devoutly hope so," said Pym; "anything for a change."

"Well, I reckon you will find the news true," returned the rifleman as he passed on.

By the afternoon of the next day the rumour had spread throughout the army, and though not officially confirmed, it became evident that a change of some kind was in contemplation.

Numerous orders were issued and promptly executed, stores given out, kits overhauled, bullock-carts requisitioned, mules collected, and various other signs indicated an approaching departure.

Pym was particularly excited by the prospect of active service, and looked forward with confidence to the speedy termination of the campaign.

Alas! he little guessed what miseries and hardships were in store for the soldiers of the Legion, even before they had a chance of meeting the enemy.

Happily the future was a sealed book, or there would have been many heavy hearts in Bilbao that day.

Many of the soldiers had been accompanied to Spain by their wives and children, and as the march to Vitoria was expected to be of a very laborious nature, it was deemed best that the women and children should be left behind.

Several hundreds were sent by sea to Santander, where a depôt of the Legion was established; and very much to my chagrin, I received orders to go with one of these detachments.

This was a severe blow to me, as I had reckoned upon enjoying Pym's company during the march, and my friend shared keenly in the disappointment.

However, there was no help for it—the general's commands must be obeyed; so, after a melancholy farewell of Pym and the trusty Dick, I took my place in the vessel which was to bear me to Santander.

Of the miseries of that voyage I shall ever have a lively recollection. The weather was tempestuous, the sea rough, the ship packed with grief-stricken women and crying children.

One woman, whose husband was in Pym's company, came to me with streaming eyes.

"Mr. Powell," she cried between her sobs, "tell me the truth, for God's sake. What are they going to do with us? They told us at Bilbao that we were to be sent from Santander with the baggage, so that we should join our husbands later on. Now some of these women say that it is all a trick—that we are not going to Vitoria at all, but are to be sent back to England. Tell me, sir, what I am to believe. Why did they let us come, if we were not to stay with our husbands? Do they think because we are poor, and only common folks, that we have no feelings?"

"What is it ye're bothering the gintleman about, honey? Shure, hasn't he got troubles enough of his own, and the rain comin' down like a waterspout? Of course we'll go to Vitoria. Haven't they got horses and carriages waitin' at this blessed place to take us all the way, so that we shan't hurt our feet?"

"Shure, an' it'll be a bad day for the spalpeen that won't take me to my Mick," screamed another, "after spakin' me fair an' all."

"Ye're daft, Biddy Moriarty, an' it's meself that tells ye so, believin' in the officer an' his soft blarney. What good'll ye do runnin' about the country after Micky, an' he wid his head off, most likely, wid a cannon ball? It's home to ould Oireland they're takin' ye an' the bairns."

At these words the woman who had first spoken sobbed anew, and placing a hand on my arm, looked me pitifully in the face.

"Oh, what can I believe?" she moaned. "My poor Jim! I wish we had never left England."

The poor creature's sobs cut at my heart, but I had small means of comforting her.

"Do not give way so," I urged gently; "time enough to grieve when the evil is at hand. One thing is quite certain—this ship is going to Santander."

This statement pacified her to some extent, but did not altogether banish the suspicion in her mind that those in authority intended sending the hapless women and children back to England.

Concerning this matter I knew nothing, and therefore could not speak with any assurance.

"But," I remarked, "it would be the truest kindness to find you all a passage home. Think what miseries you will meet with here. Winter is coming on; there will be long marches, nights in the open, very likely scanty rations, to say nothing of the cruel enemy, who will show you little mercy. No, my good woman; take my word for it, England is the best place for you."

She listened to me very patiently, and then, looking up, said in a tone of pathetic simplicity, "Ah, sir, you forget I am a woman, and that Jim is my husband."

What could one answer to a remark such as that?

Poor little woman, white-faced and tearful, yet with heart loyal and true as any that beat in the breast of hero!

Words can paint only an inadequate picture of the scene at Santander when orders were formally issued that the women and children were to be shipped to England.

Some accepted their fate with a resignation which had in it something of dignity; others broke forth into pitiful lamenting; while still others, with angry words, bitter revilings, and loud menaces, refused point-blank either to be coaxed or coerced.

One of these was Biddy Moriarty, the Irishwoman, who alternately bullied and wheedled every officer in the town, and finally constituted herself the head of a considerable body of malcontents.

These were temporarily installed in the Corban Convent while the process of embarkation went on.

After a lot of persuasion, I induced Jim's wife to go on board one of the vessels, where I secured her a comfortable berth.

"Believe that I am advising you for the best," I said.

"Your heart is a trifle bitter now, but you will thank me in the time to come. And if I go to Vitoria, I will say a word to your husband."

"Heaven bless you, sir!" she exclaimed fervently. "Tell Jim that I shall count the hours till he comes back."

I wished her good-bye, and was leaving the vessel's deck when she came after me.

"I am taking a great liberty, sir," she said; "but you have been so kind, that I thought maybe you would grant me another favour."

"Count upon it as done," I answered, "if it is within my power."

"My heart will be very nigh to breaking in the old home," she said, "as I sit wondering if anything has happened to Jim. It's terrible hard, sir, waiting for news of any one you love—and Jim can't write."

"Then you shall have a letter from me. I'll give him your messages, and write you his answers the first time I meet with him. Keep a good heart; you can trust to my word."

In her gratitude she kissed my hand, and my feelings as I hurried away were, it must be confessed, anything but warlike.

To chronicle the events of the next few weeks would be wearying to my readers, as most of the time was spent journeying to and fro between the towns of Santander, Bilbao, and San Sebastian.

During the second week in November I was at Bilbao, and while waiting for a letter for the commandant at

Santander, took the opportunity of paying a visit to the princess, as Pym called the girl whom we had rescued from the bandits.

The woman of the house exhibited the greatest reserve, and gave me little information beyond a vague intimation that the señorita was better.

Happily, a few doors away I met the genial doctor, who turned back and walked with me for a short distance.

Yes, the señorita was decidedly better, he said in answer to my question—not well, of course, but fairly on the road to recovery. She was conscious of her surroundings, and had, at intervals, asked several questions, though at the same time she resolutely refused to give any account of herself.

"I told her one day," he continued, "that she had been brought into Bilbao by a brave Englishman who had risked his life to save her, and she asked your name, señor. 'Don Arturo Powell,' she repeated after me; 'I shall not forget it. Tell me what he is like, doctor. Give me a faithful portrait, so that if chance should throw this generous Englishman across my path I may recognize him.'"

"I hope you drew a flattering likeness," said I laughingly.

"No, señor; I did as the señorita bade, and described you accurately, that she might know you at a glance."

"Then I wish you would do me a similar favour, and sketch the señorita in like manner."

"Ah, that is beyond my power; I know only that she is one of the loveliest of my countrywomen."

"And will she not tell her name, even to you?"

"No, señor, neither name nor rank. I have learned nothing, except"—and he hesitated strangely—"except that the señorita is a devout Catholic."

"What a lame ending! I imagined that you were about to impart some wonderful secret."

The doctor looked into my face, opened his lips as if to speak, apparently thought better of it, and stopped abruptly.

"Farewell, señor," he said, "until our next meeting."

"The date of which is exceedingly indefinite. In a few days I shall be on the way to Vitoria."

"Then may God and the Virgin hold you in their keeping."

"Amen!" I replied; "and many thanks for your kindly wish."

I walked on a few paces and turned round; the doctor was still standing gazing after me, with an odd look on his face.

His curious behaviour struck me forcibly, and the memory of it long lasted in my mind.

"Perhaps he is wondering what part of the country will provide me with a grave," I said to myself; "but his manner seemed queer from the beginning. Why on earth should he inform me that the princess was a Catholic? And what was it that he half made up his mind to tell me?"

However, there was little opportunity for speculation; my time was up, the vessel waited for me, and in a few hours I was once more at Santander.

Shortly afterwards Colonel Arbuthnot, the commandant at Santander, knowing my wish to go to the front, permitted me to join a detachment which was under orders to march.

It was now the third week in November, and winter was setting in with a promise of unusual severity.

The morning was dull, cold, and cheerless, and I wrapped an ample Spanish cloak closely around me as I rode from the town.

The beginning of the march, at all events, was far from inspiriting. Many of the soldiers had only just recovered from painful illnesses; while, to add to the distress, crowds of women walked along by our sides begging for assistance in getting to Vitoria.

This, of course, we were unable to render, as only a favoured few had been given leave to go with the detachment.

On the evening of the first day we camped by the side of the river Meira, and after attending to my horse, I lay down on the ground and slept.

The next morning we were early astir, and having crossed the river in barges, resumed the journey.

"Not very exhilarating work this, Powell!" exclaimed a cheery voice at my elbow, as plunged in melancholy I rode slowly along.

The speaker was Captain Peyton, quite a young man, with whom I had become acquainted in Santander.

"You are right, Peyton," I made answer, striving to imitate his good spirits—"rather different from the general ideas of sunny Spain."

"And there is worse to come," he added, looking up at the black clouds which hung overhead; "we shall get a drenching before long, or I am much mistaken. However, we shall soon forget this when we are in comfortable quarters."

Happily the rain held off; but early on the following morning it poured in torrents, and we marched all day over the winding mountain road amidst a perfect deluge.

The procession presented the most wretched spectacle. The men—at least, those who could keep up at all—toiled ankle-deep in mud, and had not a dry thread in their garments.

Some, hopelessly beaten, were placed on the baggage-wagons, and lay steeped in wet and exposed at every moment to the pitiless storm.

Of shelter there was none to be found anywhere. The road lay across a succession of bare, bleak, and desolate mountains, over whose craggy rocks the foaming cataracts dashed themselves in a wild fury.

"I say, Powell," Captain Peyton remarked in the afternoon, as we walked on together—I had lent my horse to a sick man—"how our people at home would open their eyes if they could see us. I can just fancy my sisters sitting beside a roaring fire, listening to the storm and saying, 'Fred is lucky to escape this dreary winter.'"

He laughed heartily, seeming to find a comical pleasure in his family's mistaken notions.

I did not respond to his merriment: unwittingly he had touched upon a very tender chord.

Of a real home I had never any knowledge. From my earliest childhood I had lived amongst strangers, who, kindly as they proved, could not quite supply the place of my dead parents.

I had been spared the bitterness of poverty, for my father had left me a moderate income, amply sufficient to satisfy my simple desires; but many a time my heart had yearned for the solace of a parent's affection.

Concerning these things Peyton was, of course, in ignorance, and he rattled on gaily about his sisters and mother and the "governor."

"By the way, some of the fellows at Santander were talking about your adventures before you joined the Legion," he said. "I should like to hear the yarn, if you have no objection, and it will help to while away the time."

"Well, it certainly has that merit; but, personally, I should prefer drier quarters in which to tell the story."

"I wish Johnson were here," my comrade remarked irrelevantly. "Do you know Johnson? He's on the staff. I met him in London before he came out. His uniform is gorgeous—gold lace, waving plumes, and all that kind of thing; it would look pretty in this deluge. You know the sort of man. Looks as if he were carefully preserved under a case, and brought out only on special occasions. I've seen him, when it rained, order a cab to go three doors away. But I'm stopping the story."

"Don't apologize; the tale can wait."

"No, I'm really anxious to hear it."

"A chum worth having, that," he interrupted, when I

told how Dick acted on the night of the wreck; and he drew his breath hard at the description of Don Philip's ruined home.

Every incident interested him, and as he kept up a running fire of comments, it was some time before I could bring the narrative to a conclusion.

"A pity you did not see the girl," he said musingly; "perhaps you will never have a chance now."

"Probably not. No one knows when we shall return from Vitoria."

"If we ever reach it. Listen to the wind; the storm is getting fiercer instead of lessening.—Come, Martin"—to one of his soldiers who was limping painfully—"step out; the sooner we make an end, the better for us all."

"I'm dead-beat, sir, and that's a fact," the man answered; "I'm feared I shall have to fall out."

"Nonsense! never say die. Here, take a bite of this chocolate, and pass the rest along. Wonderfully sustaining, Powell, is chocolate; ever try it?"

"No; I prefer it hot, with sugar and cream.—Here, my man, let me take a spell with that knapsack; you'll march lighter."

"Thank you, sir; I'll have it again soon as you're tired," and relieved of his burden he walked on a trifle more briskly.

"Where do we halt?" I asked after a while; "this is a long march."

"Don't know, I'm sure; some place with an unpronounceable name. A horrid spot, I'll warrant, containing three hovels and a cow-shed."

The last part of the sentence was uttered in jest, but the speaker proved to be a true if unwitting prophet.

It was dark when we reached the apology for a village where the night was to be spent, and not a soul in the place seemed stirring.

Peyton left me in order to perform his duties, and I led my horse into a low, rambling building, from which the roof was partly torn.

The place had at one time been used as a shelter for bullocks, and finding one corner comparatively dry, I tied up my tired animal, and after giving him a feed, took up my own quarters in the manger close by his head.

Before long every inch of the wretched building not directly exposed to the pelting storm was occupied by soldiers, who, drenched with rain and numbed by cold, passed the night as best they could.

For some time I crouched, wet, miserable, and quite unable to sleep.

The wind howled dismally, the tempest, as if in anger, redoubled its force, and through the rents in the crazy roof poured volumes of water.

The soldiers, poor fellows, were worn out, and I think that the majority, in spite of every physical discomfort, slept.

Very early in the morning, indeed before the troops were stirring, I heard my name called, and recognized Captain Peyton's voice.

"Are you there?" he cried, and when I had answered, bade me come out.

I asked him to wait while I attended to my horse, and then, wading through the lake which formed the floor of our sleeping-room, joined him outside.

"I lost you last night in the darkness and confusion,' he said. "Had you anything to drink?"

"Plenty of rain-water. What an awful night it has been!"

"The worst is over; but come, I have a treat in store. If you do not swear eternal gratitude to me afterwards, you are a heathen."

He led me into one of the hovels, and when I saw the room in which he had slept, I did not regret having chosen the bullock-shed.

The floor had once been paved, but the only stones which now remained were in the centre, and served as a fireplace. Beyond a handful of smouldering wood, upon which was placed an iron pot, I could see nothing in the room but a rough settle; the natives apparently did not place much faith in the honesty of the Legion.

"Come and blow," said Peyton; "this fire will take some time to burn up."

The speaker was right. Long before the wood blazed, my throat and lungs were filled with a nasty, dry, irritating smoke, my eyes smarted painfully, and I felt like giving up the task in despair.

"A splendid idea this for a treat, Peyton," I spluttered, between two fits of coughing, "and worth any amount of gratitude. It has the advantage of being cheap, too."

"Wait a bit, old fellow," he said, and forthwith dipped

his fingers into the pot. "Ah, that will do famously Now, you sceptic, behold and marvel."

From a far corner he produced an earthenware basin coarse and thick, into which he put some powdered chocolate and mixed it with the water.

In happier times, perhaps, the beverage would not have been pronounced a culinary success. The water did not boil; it was smoky and impregnated with sooty flakes; sugar and milk were absent quantities; and the smoky flavour was modified, but not improved, by a strong taste of tobacco.

Still it possessed one merit which outweighed all defects—it was hot. I had not discovered until then how cold was the lining of my throat and stomach.

"An admirable decoction!" I gasped, when the last drop of the curious compound had disappeared; "I shall call it 'Peyton's mixture,' and hold it in remembrance for ever."

"You must have been cold, and no mistake," he said, gazing thoughtfully into my face.

"That is where the English language is so lamentably weak. Fancy using a word so absurdly feeble to describe my state!"

By this time the storm had considerably abated, and before the march began it stopped altogether, much to our satisfaction.

Naturally the ground was in a fearfully boggy condition, and hampered our progress; but about ten o'clock the sun came out, and though the clouds quickly gathered again, the temporary warmth was of great benefit in partly drying our draggled garments.

After that night I regularly shared Captain Peyton's quarters, and his cheery conversation and buoyant spirits made me half forget the miseries of the journey.

Still it was with a feeling of relief I learned one morning that the close of the day would find us in Briviesca, and with my comrade I beguiled several hours in anticipating the delights which there awaited us.

CHAPTER IX.

THE ATTACK ON THE CONVOY.

NIGHT had fallen when cold, tired, and hungry, we marched, or to be more accurate, straggled into Briviesca.

Even the most robust of the men were utterly broken down, while many had been forced along only—these were the "good" old flogging days—by the application of the lash.

The detachment was drawn up in the plaza, while the colonel in command took his measures for quartering the men. The place was in darkness, and as far as I could tell, not a native made his appearance.

"This doesn't promise very well," I remarked to Peyton; "I am afraid that our rosy visions are about to vanish into thin air."

"Well, we have enjoyed the anticipation at least, even if there should be no reality." Then turning to one of the men, he said, "Bravo, Carey! that's splendid; you would make your fortune in a cook's shop.—Powell, listen to that little man's description of a Yorkshire pudding. Upon my word, the picture is so graphic that I can smell the gravy."

By some strange and yet not wholly inexplicable freak, the conversation of the soldiers nearest to us had turned upon the subject of bygone feasts, and they were engaged in an animated but friendly controversy concerning the merits of various viands.

It was a trifle incongruous but wholly pathetic to hear them standing there in the darkness and cold expatiating upon the glorious spreads they had once enjoyed.

Each man had some experience to relate, and before the order came to march, almost everything eatable in the animal and vegetable kingdoms had been brought before our notice, cooked in a variety of ways, and consumed with infinite gusto.

"I wonder how much longer these Dons are going to be," said one man, giving a fresh turn to the chat; "they move about as quick as the Tower of London."

"Don't be in such a hurry, mate—give 'em time; they're airing the sheets—that's what they're doing. They don't want to put us in damp beds."

"That's a very good notion, Tommy, and does credit to your intelleck," growled a comrade approvingly.

"Perhaps," Tommy went on, with mock gravity, "they haven't got enough warming-pans. Not that I mind; I ain't particler a bit. A hot-water bottle will do for me; I'm used to roughing it," at which there was a general laugh.

"A capital fellow, that," whispered Peyton to me, "and full of quaint humour. He's the sort of man worth having in your company."

"I should say so. I noticed him this morning carrying a comrade's knapsack and musket, though he doesn't seem extra strong himself."

"No, his spirits keep him up. But he never lets a chance of doing any one a good turn slip by; he is the most unselfish of men. Listen to him now: he is telling them about a Christmas party."

"Well, there we was," Tommy was saying, "the fire a-roaring in the grate, an' the holly an' mistletoe over the mantelpiece, an' everything jolly. 'Lizzie,' says I, 'give father a nudge; I'm goin' to drink a 'ealth.'"

Whose health it was that Tommy proposed to drink I never learned, for through the darkness rang out the order, "Attention! shoulder arms, by the left, quick march!" and we moved off the ground.

Poor Tommy! he did not have the luck to be at another Christmas festival.

The troops were put up for the night in a ruined convent, without bedding or fire, and having nothing but their greatcoats with which to cover themselves.

"Peyton," I said, as we walked about in the gloom, trying to find the lodgings assigned to us, "if this state of things goes on, the Carlists may save their bullets, as far as the Legion is concerned."

"We can't expect luxuries in war time," he answered lightly; but I knew that in spite of this careless air his heart was sore with the knowledge of his men's sufferings.

And if the rank and file fared miserably, we ourselves were not much better off.

The room in which we passed the night was as bare as the convent. The floor was icy cold, the four walls, unrelieved by a single picture, looked bleak and cheerless, while of a fire-place the inmates seemed to have no idea.

Our host—a surly, ill-conditioned fellow—set an evil-smelling lamp on the rickety table, and went away without uttering a word, good or bad.

"There is a bedstead," I exclaimed dolorously, pointing to one corner of the room; "but I doubt its capability of bearing our combined weight."

"Let us try the experiment," my comrade answered; "things are sometimes better than they seem. Is your cloak wet? No! that's capital. I have a rug. We shall do nicely, though I could put up with Tommy's hot-water bottle."

In spite, however, of Peyton's cheery optimism, the excessive cold kept me awake half the night, and the morning found me half-frozen.

Peyton, whose regimental duties compelled him to go out early, had risen without disturbing me, displaying a kindly thoughtfulness for which I felt profoundly grateful.

The room was in darkness, so I threw open the lattice window, and looked forth upon the plaza.

The sight which greeted my eyes was far from enticing, and certainly suggested little of "sunny Spain." The ground was covered deep with snow, and the roofs of the opposite houses were clothed in a similar dress. A few inhabitants of the dreary town moved about, enveloped in ample cloaks, which were drawn over their heads in such a manner as to leave nothing but the eyes visible.

I drew back with a shudder, and shutting the window, groped my way down the wretched staircase to the kitchen.

Here three or four men were huddled round a wood fire, but no one made the slightest movement, and I was pushing my way by force to the flames when Peyton called me.

"Come along this way," he cried; "breakfast is waiting," and he carried me off up the snow-covered plaza. "Evans has marched, and no one seems to be here but the sick. Did you ever see such a forlorn, miserable-looking spot? The houses are dirty, the people are dirty and half-asleep."

"I am thankful we have not to stay here. When do we march?"

"Uncertain; we are waiting for orders. I hope the delay will be short; several of my men are down already. Last night's cold did the mischief," and he sighed heavily.

After breakfast we visited the building known as the Spanish hospital, which was simply an unfurnished house—cold, cheerless, and wind-swept.

Two or three of Peyton's men, amongst whom I recognized Tommy, lay on straw, shivering in their greatcoats.

Poor fellows! their feet were frost-bitten, and they seemed smitten with some mysterious form of low fever that completely sapped their vigour.

Peyton strove hard to address them in his usual cheery style, but the attempt broke down, and his voice sounded husky as he spoke, calling each man by name.

They brightened up wonderfully at this, and more than one fervent, "God bless you, sir," greeted his promise to procure some cooling drinks with which to moisten their parched throats.

Other men also lay there in different stages of the malady, brought on by cold, wet, and insufficient nourishment.

As we passed through the room, I heard one patient talking to himself, and thought that the voice was not altogether unfamiliar.

The soldier lay in a corner on a bundle of dirty straw, and wrapped like all the rest in his greatcoat, which was drawn tightly round him.

Bending over, I looked at his features, and started back in amazement.

"Staples!" I exclaimed; "are you Jim Staples of the Eighth?"

The man's fingers, so wasted that the bones seemed bursting through the skin, closed over my hand and held it tightly.

"Have you come back, Mary?" he whispered. "I thought you would. I have been very ill—caught cold on the mountains; but the pain's gone now. It was in my feet, you know; that's where it hurt most. Captain Forrester was very good to me, but I couldn't keep up. Is that a lark, Mary? Yes, there it is, just rising from the meadow. Shall we go down to the river? I'll show you the place where I caught the big trout."

"Peyton," I said softly, so as not to be overheard, "bring one of the surgeons; I fear the man's dying."

He nodded and left me, while I continued to sit listening to the soldier's incoherent ramblings.

Sometimes he talked of the Legion's terrible march over the desolate mountains, but mostly his mind dwelt upon the happy days of his youth.

Just before Peyton returned with the surgeon, he pressed my hand lightly, saying, "Let us go back, Mary; it will be a nasty night. See how black the clouds hang yonder; it will rain soon."

Then releasing my hand, he threw off his covering, and sat up. His large, sunken eyes, bright with an unnatural brilliancy, moved restlessly round the room, and with a heart-rending cry of "Mary, Mary!" he fell back.

"May God have mercy on his soul," said Peyton reverently, to which the surgeon and I responded with a solemn "amen."

My comrade led me into the open. "Cheer up," he said, "or we shall be having you sick next. Try to think that yonder poor fellow is well out of his troubles."

"And what of his wife?" I replied. "Peyton, I put the poor little woman on board ship at Santander. 'Keep a good heart,' I said to her, and promised to send news of her husband at the first opportunity. Can you wonder that I feel miserable?"

"Not at all, but brooding on it will do no good. Besides, there's plenty of work to be done. Come and help me galvanize some of these petrified shopkeepers into life. I wonder if they ever show any smartness."

We spent the forenoon in collecting a few delicacies for

the captain's sick men, and though the result was far from commensurate with the trouble involved, I shall not soon forget the poor fellows' looks of gratitude.

After the day's work we went back to our room, where Peyton had introduced one improvement in the shape of a *braziero*, by the side of which we sat.

True, the coals were mainly ashes, and the actual heat afforded almost infinitesimal, but still, as Peyton declared, it was a fire, and we drew much comfort from that fact.

The lattice window was, of course, fastened, and I plugged the space at the bottom of the door with a strip of matting obtained from the surly Spaniard, and this proved of signal benefit.

"If we pass another night in this hole, we will have a proper fire," I said moodily, sticking my feet upon the *braziero*.

"And be suffocated by the smoke! I prefer freezing."

"Very good; have your own way," and I stared savagely at the ill-smelling lamp, the light from which could barely be seen through a haze of sooty smoke.

Presently Peyton broke the silence, saying, "That man Tommy will be dead in the morning, and he was one of the smartest soldiers in my company. Did you notice his face when we came away this afternoon? And I can do nothing for him."

"Nonsense," I replied, essaying the part of comforter; "in a few days we shall all be at Vitoria, where he will have every attention."

Peyton shook his head, and though he offered no

further remark, I knew that my words yielded him no encouragement.

Having absolutely nothing to do, we went early to bed; but the cold became so intense that sleep was out of the question, and we gladly welcomed the advent of another day.

Leaving Peyton at the convent where the troops were quartered, I went on to the hospital, and there learned the fulfilment of my comrade's prophecy.

Tommy—I never knew his other name—had died in the night, and his fellow-sufferers told me that the last words his lips framed were a blessing on the captain.

I did what little I could for the poor fellows, and it was wonderful to note the effect produced by a cheery smile, and the utterance of a few kindly, pleasant words.

"God bless you, sir! It's easy to tell you've a good heart anyway," said one long-visaged man, who lay there weak as a kitten from cold and exposure.

"There's the captain," cried another; "I thought he would come. Good-morning, sir! Why, it makes me think of summer, just seeing your face. I only hope that some of us will live long enough to do you and Mr. Powell a good turn."

"Pooh, pooh, Jenkins," said Peyton; "you are overrating the thing. We have done precious little for you, I'm sure," but his grey eyes nevertheless kindled with a light of honest gladness at the man's speech.

"Poor Tommy's gone, sir," Jenkins continued solemnly; "he was talking about you when he died."

"Poor Tommy," echoed Peyton softly; "he was a smart soldier."

"Ay, that he was," came from several; "and a better mate you couldn't wish for."

"May we all deserve as good an epitaph when it comes to our turn," I said, moving away.

We had been four days in Briviesca, and about noon, on the fifth, Peyton received orders to take twenty men and march eastward, in order to learn tidings of a convoy of provisions which had been expected an hour before.

Utterly wearied with doing nothing, I joyfully accepted the offer to join him; and the men, too, exhibited a keen pleasure at the prospect of getting away, if only for a brief space, from such a scene of wretchedness.

We had seen nothing of the Carlists, and, indeed, no one suspected them of being in the neighbourhood; but Peyton, who was of a rather prudent temperament, took every needful precaution.

"'Never give a chance' is my motto," he said, as we marched along over the snow-covered ground; "and it has served me well enough so far."

"It is certainly a good rule when we have opponents like the Carlists to contend with," I answered. "They seem always on the look-out for an opportunity of striking a blow."

"Well, we must not let them surprise us. But, as a matter of fact, I think it very unlikely that they will venture so near our lines."

We marched some distance without finding any traces

of the convoy, when suddenly a mounted soldier was seen galloping madly across the field on our right.

"It is Quartermaster Reid's horse," cried one of the men, "but not the quartermaster."

The rider caught sight of us, and urged the animal on afresh.

Running down the road, I came to a gap in the hedge, and stood there, waving my hat as a signal.

In a few minutes the horseman was with us, and we saw that his left arm hung helplessly at his side.

Both horse and rider were bathed in perspiration, and the man had scarce strength to speak.

"The Carlists!" he gasped brokenly; "they have attacked the convoy. All our men are dead or captured, and Sergeant Dickson's wife is in their hands."

"Did they send you back to tell the news?" Peyton asked contemptuously.

The man's eyes wandered to his broken arm, and with the cuff of his right sleeve he wiped a clot of blood from his face.

"I did my best, sir," he said simply. "The fight was finished when I scrambled on the quartermaster's horse and rode off."

Peyton's face flushed crimson, and he offered his hand to the wounded fugitive.

"Forgive me," he said; "I spoke hastily and without thought. You are a brave fellow, and have borne yourself nobly, I warrant. What was the Carlist strength?"

"Fifty horsemen, sir, putting it roughly; and we were sixteen all told."

"Can we come up with them?"

"Likely as not, sir; they hadn't caught the mules a few minutes ago."

Peyton turned to the men.

"My lads," he said curtly, "I'm going to get the prisoners back. Who is coming with me?"

"All of us, sir," they cried, and their faces lit up with a glow of determination.

Peyton gave the brave fellows a word of praise, and then asked the wounded soldier which route he had better take.

"Begging your pardon, sir," the man responded firmly, "but I'm coming with you;" nor could we shake his resolution.

"The arm will do till we get back," he said; "and as for this cut over the head, it don't matter."

Possessing a little knowledge of surgery, I volunteered to bind up the injured limb; and when this was done, we followed our guide at the double across the field.

We speedily arrived at the scene of the encounter, where nine bodies lay hacked and mutilated in a terrible manner.

The sight filled our men with a kind of frenzy, and Peyton had much ado to keep them from rushing pell-mell on the track of the Carlists.

"Steady, lads," he cried; "too much haste will lead to our undoing. The enemy cannot be far off, and they will call a halt presently to sample the wine."

"Let me take half a dozen men to reconnoitre," I suggested.

The proposal pleased him, but he bade me have a care and not be over-venturesome.

Accordingly, having selected six of the band, I started off with them, keeping well under cover of the hedge.

The trampled snow, and a bloodstain here and there, pointed out the route which the horsemen had taken, and we followed swiftly but with caution.

Our sole hope of rescuing the prisoners rested on the chance that the Carlists, feeling safe from pursuit, would stop somewhere, in order, as Peyton expressed it, to sample the wine.

Even in that case we should be forced to fight against heavy odds; but no one seemed to give a thought to the desperate nature of the undertaking.

One resolution animated the breasts of all—to free our comrades, and most especially the unhappy woman, from the Carlists' grip.

Several stories were in circulation concerning the fate of those luckless enough to fall into the hands of our merciless foes. It was commonly reported that men had been done to death in a most cruel and barbarous manner, and the rumour obtained universal credence.

We pressed on, therefore, in hot haste, and were shortly rewarded by a sight of the enemy in the one street of a wretched-looking hamlet.

The horsemen had dismounted, and while some stood about drinking on the roadside, others sought a little extra comfort within the hovels.

I kept my men well out of view, and sent a message to Peyton, whose band we had outstripped.

The Carlists evidently did not fear surprise; their confidence, indeed, was so great that they had not even taken the precaution of posting sentinels.

"They don't mean staying long," remarked Sergeant Parker, who was at my side; "in a few minutes they will be off. Can you see any of our people, sir?"

"Yes, they are in a group at the other end. You stay here and report to Captain Peyton; I will take the others round by the field, and make a dash for the prisoners directly the captain comes up."

Without allowing time for any objection, I led the other four by a little detour which brought us to the farther end of the hamlet, where we crouched in a ditch so close to the enemy that the men's muskets were almost within touch of some of the horses.

The period of waiting was but short. Almost immediately, in fact, we heard the sounds of firing, a thundering "Hurrah!" the rush of feet, and a medley of cries and groans.

At the same moment we sprang up, leaped the ditch, and rushed at the bewildered foe. Some of the latter ran to the horses, others drew their swords and laid about them vigorously; but taken unawares, they fought in detached groups, without method or order.

Aided by my four comrades, I made straight for the prisoners, and cut their bonds before their guards had time to shoot them, which they would have done unhesitatingly.

"Get swords," I cried, "and lay on;" but the order was not needed.

Furious at the indignities they had suffered, and mindful

of their slaughtered comrades, they threw themselves into the thick of the fight. Then assisting the woman to mount one of the Carlists' horses, I bade her ride like the wind to Briviesca, and report to the colonel what was happening.

Soon, however, it became apparent that we should not require help. The Carlists, who lost several men at the first fire, were driven slowly back; and now those who could seized their horses and rode off.

The mules had already galloped away, fortunately in the direction of Briviesca, and a few of the horses ran after them. About a dozen of the latter remained in our keeping, and these we utilized for the conveying of our wounded.

Sending two mounted men in pursuit of the mules, Peyton drew the rest up in a square, and gave the word to march.

Twice during the journey the Carlists, who had rallied from their disorder, attempted a charge; but, baffled by the steadiness of the soldiers, they retired with two or three empty saddles on each occasion.

At the scene of the original encounter we stopped to take up the mutilated bodies of the fallen escort, and shortly afterwards were met by a strong reinforcement which the colonel himself had brought to our aid.

"Have you seen the mules, sir?" Peyton asked anxiously.

"Yes, they are safe. You have behaved very gallantly, Captain Peyton, and the men with you. I will take care that your action is brought to the general's knowledge."

Peyton bowed his acknowledgments, and then we all moved briskly forward, eager to partake of the provisions which had cost us so dear.

CHAPTER X.

A MISERABLE INACTION.

ON the fourth morning after the affair with the Carlists narrated in the previous chapter, we received orders to march to Vitoria.

The day was bitterly cold—the snow froze as it fell; but in spite of the inclement weather, we left our dreary quarters joyfully, and set out in good spirits.

"Now," said Peyton cheerfully, "we shall have a taste of decent comfort. I wish those poor fellows in hospital were able to come with us."

My own satisfaction was materially increased by the thought of rejoining Pym and the sergeant, and I made light of the discomforts which beset us on the road.

Little real danger was to be apprehended, as we were too strong to be attacked by any of the roving bands which occasionally harried the district, and as a matter of fact we reached Vitoria without encountering an enemy.

We had been travelling three days, and evening was beginning to gather in when we entered the town.

Leaving Peyton, I rode off to find General Evans, in order that I might report my arrival.

The streets were thinly peopled, and the few men of the Legion whom I saw appeared gloomy and careworn.

While crossing the principal plaza I heard my name called, and turning, beheld Pym Forrester.

I dismounted immediately, and the dear fellow shook me warmly by the hand.

"Just arrived?" he said inquiringly. "I began to feel anxious at your long absence. Come with me; you can't see the general this evening—he is busy with some Spanish officers. I have a comfortable billet which you shall share."

He spoke excitedly, and I noticed that his cheeks were flushed and his eyes feverish.

"You have been ill, Pym," I said; "you must take more care of yourself."

"It is nothing," he made answer lightly; "a mere bagatelle. I have escaped marvellously."

"Escaped?"

"Ah! you do not know. I will explain later."

"Is Dick well?"

"He was this morning, and asking after you. He is a splendid fellow, and has done a lot of good. But I fear the strain will wear him out."

Again my face exhibited astonishment, and I said, "You are talking in riddles, old fellow; where is the strain? Here you are in pleasant quarters, with nothing to do beyond ordinary routine work—no marches, no fighting; I should say you are in clover."

In all the years of our comradeship I had never known

Pym lose his temper, but now he broke out in a speech so scathing and bitter that I could only listen and wonder.

"But to-morrow you shall see for yourself," he concluded abruptly; "here we are at the house."

"Can you make the people understand?"

"Fairly well. My Spanish is far from perfect, but frequent practice is improving it."

The landlord willingly assented to Pym's proposal, and took charge of my horse, while he promised that his wife should prepare us a meal.

Pym's room was a decided improvement on my Briviesca lodgings, and the charcoal fire in the *braziero* emitted quite a cheery warmth.

"This is better than Briviesca," I declared; "the memory of that abode of desolation will haunt me for all time."

Pym gave me no answer, but sat staring abstractedly before him until the woman of the house brought in the supper, which included some steaming coffee.

I thought of "Peyton's mixture," and in spite of my friend's gloom, laughed light-heartedly.

"Come, Pym," I cried, "let us make a beginning," and I forthwith proceeded to pour out the fragrant liquid.

Little conversation passed during the progress of the meal, but at its conclusion Pym lit a cigar, and proposed that I should give him an account of my doings.

The description of the women's distress at Santander affected him deeply, but he agreed with me that they were better off in their own country.

"Poor creatures!" he said; "the separation was cruel enough, but they would have met a far worse fate here."

I told him of my promise to Mrs. Staples, and the subsequent death of her husband at Briviesca.

"Staples!" he said; "ah, I know the man. We left him in hospital; he was sinking fast then. Barker of my company was his chum, and will be able to tell you where the poor fellow lived."

"And now, what has been going on here?" I asked, after relating the incident of the attack on the Carlists.

Pym's blue eyes flashed angrily, and he walked about the room as if seeking an outlet for his irritation.

"Your question takes very little answering, Arthur," he replied; "we have been drilling and dying. As far as the Legion is concerned, Vitoria is a veritable city of death. The apathy and indifference—nay, I should say the hostility—of the Spaniards is incredible. On the night of our arrival they cheered us, and put up a few tawdry inscriptions 'to the brave English,' beyond which they have done nothing. The officers of the Legion have billets in the town; as for the men, they are suffering a repetition of the Briviesca horrors. Their quarters are the ruined convents—bare, bleak, and wind-driven. There were a few beds at first, I believe, but they are now in the dogs' holes called hospitals. The rations are detestable, and, even such as they are, insufficient. My heart aches to think that, while we sit here in comparative luxury, those poor fellows are lying yonder on their wretched straw bundles or the flag-stones, cold, wet, and hungry. I told you Dick was alive this morning, but to-night he may be in the hospital —dead. The men are simply dying like sheep."

"But surely something can be done to remedy the evil," I urged.

"I cannot tell," he answered wearily. "Those in authority assert that the Spaniards either cannot or will not make things better. They have no money, the treasury is empty, and so the men die. It is a horrible business."

"But the general can insist upon an improvement?"

"I believe he has done and is doing his best; but short of taking the men home, he is powerless. Besides, the Spaniards are profuse in promises, and so I suppose he goes on hoping."

"What are the men dying of?"

"I don't know; some affirm one thing, some another. Surgeon Blake declares it to be typhus fever, brought on by exposure and insufficient nourishment. Many of the regimental officers and hospital doctors have sickened and died."

"I suppose my genial friend Jaureguy is here?"

"Yes, and in desperate ill-humour. We were treated a few days ago to a specimen of Spanish discipline, in connection with his Chapelgorris. I did not see it, but had the story from a Spanish officer who was present on duty. It seems that, some time ago, the Chapelgorris drove the Carlists out of a village called La Bastide, and then plundered the church. No notice would have been taken of the act, but that the authorities at Madrid complained to General Espartero of the sacrilege; and in order to please them, he resolved upon punishing the offenders. The Chapelgorris were marched out to an eminence on the Miranda road, where they found a large force of cavalry, infantry, and horse-artillery drawn up. They were ordered to pile arms, and being ignorant of what was intended, they obeyed. Then Espartero commanded that lots should be drawn, and by this means ten men were selected for death."

"And were they really shot?"

"Yes, in the presence of the troops. Their sad fate cast quite a gloom over the army. But it is well in keeping with the general wretchedness."

"I must go and see El Pastor; he was very hospitable in Bilbao."

"He is the one Spanish officer in a high position whom I cordially admire. Have you ever met General Espartero?"

"Not to my knowledge."

"You would easily recognize him. He is almost the exact counterpart of General Evans, only that his features are sterner. But you are tired, and I am keeping you up."

I really did feel fatigued, and was glad to lie down on the little bed made up for me in a small cupboard-like room, which was separated from Pym's chamber only by a hanging curtain.

The morning was half spent when my comrade roused me from a heavy sleep.

"You have rested well," he said, and his voice seemed to have recovered some of its normal cheerfulness. "I have been visiting the men, and found Dick, as usual, hard at work. You can guess how glad he was at hearing you were in Vitoria. I told him that you would call round during the day."

"Then he has escaped this mysterious malady?"

"So far," Pym answered, and his face clouded again.

After breakfast my comrade accompanied me to General Evans, who was pleased to express his gratification at the services which I had lately rendered in the north.

Then Pym and I went on to the convent of San Juan, where the Highlanders were quartered.

The day was piercingly cold, and so deep did the snow lie that it was utterly impossible for the men to practise their ordinary drill.

The conversation with Pym had to a degree prepared me for a scene of misery; but his description, vivid as it was, fell far short of the reality.

There are some sights which can never be adequately described, and the interior of the convent on this particular morning was one of them.

The bare walls of the grim old building were desolate enough, but it was the hopelessness expressed in the faces of the soldiers that struck a chill to my heart. As Pym had said, it was a repetition on an extended scale of the Briviesca horrors.

Most of the men were lying huddled together, for the sake of extra warmth, on their bundles of dirty straw, and wrapped in their greatcoats.

Their faces were white and pinched, their sunken eyes

bright with incipient fever, their skins dry and parched, their limbs emaciated.

A few who still preserved a little strength dragged themselves along with listless steps, but the features even of these were marked by a dismal apathy.

The spectacle filled me with sorrow and indignation, and I began to wonder if the people responsible for such a state of things were worth fighting for.

But the coming of Dick, who had just caught sight of us, prevented me from indulging further in these melancholy reflections.

He saluted his captain, and then turned to me.

"Glad to see you again, sir," he said, with genuine heartiness; "I had almost given you up."

I looked at him with a feeling of deep pity in my heart. Nothing could have brought home to me with greater distinctness the hardships which the Legion had undergone than his altered appearance.

The man whom I had last seen strong, sturdy, stalwart—the "Cast-iron man"—was now little else than a physical wreck. He carried himself upright as of yore, but his features were gaunt, his hair thickly streaked with grey, while his uniform hung quite loosely about him.

"You have had a hard time," I said, striving to speak calmly.

"Well, things are not particularly rosy," he admitted; "but we can't expect the luxuries of feather-bed soldiers. Still, I wish that the Dons were a bit handier at cooking.

Come and see my breakfast; it's waiting till I can make up my mind to tackle it."

I followed him across the huge flag-stoned apartment, and this is what he showed me—a cube of black bread, so soft and doughy that the dark colour alone prevented its being mistaken for putty, a strip of tough leather courteously spoken of as beef, and a measure of villanous liquor called *aguardienta.*

I drank a mouthful of this last, and thought I must have swallowed poison, so nauseating was the taste.

"Do the men really live on this?" I asked.

"Yes, when it can be got," he answered significantly. "Sometimes the rations are missing—get lost on the way here, I reckon—then we have to starve for a change. But my time is up; I have a squad to drill in the corridor."

"Surely not any of the men in this room!" I exclaimed aghast.

"Oh yes, we are the fighting crowd; the sick are in the hospitals; we keep only those fit for duty here."

"I am going on to the hospitals to find a man named Barker."

"Belonged to Captain Forrester's company. A smart lad enough, but weakly; couldn't stand the wear and tear. You had better hurry, sir; I daresay he's dead by now. They don't last long as a rule after being removed to hospital. The surgeons do their best, but they are tremendously overworked."

Pym, who had been amongst the soldiers, now rejoined

us; and having taken our leave of Dick, we passed through the hall, and so into the dreary street.

I told my comrade of Dick's advice, and begged that he would lead me straight to the hospital.

This proved to be simply an old house, differing from the convent only in size. Like the building which we had just quitted, it was neither wind nor rain proof, while its floors and walls were bare.

Of hospital necessaries, it possessed a few beds and blankets far from clean; but those who used them were to be accounted fortunate, as the majority of the sufferers lay on straw, with their military cloaks alone for covering.

Pym introduced me to Surgeon Parkes, who appeared scarcely less ill than his patients.

"I am working almost single-handed," he said in explanation of his harassed looks; "one of my colleagues died last night, and another is down with this horrible fever.—Barker? Yes, he still lives; but his case is hopeless. I had him shifted an hour ago to this bed. The fever has left him, but he has no strength; he will die of sheer weakness."

We walked softly to the bed where the poor fellow lay, wasted to a skeleton. I had often heard the expression. "skin and bones," and now beheld a practical example.

So thin was the dying man that the bones threatened to burst through their slight covering. A gleam of pleasure struggled into the sunken eyes at Pym's approach, and with difficulty he extended a hand, which my comrade gently pressed.

"Going, captain," he whispered faintly; "I wish it had been on the battle-field."

It was now that I more fully comprehended why Pym's men so loved him.

He held the sufferer's hand within his, and such a wealth of tenderness illumined his face that one instinctively thought of a mother sorrowing over and comforting her child.

I stood aside, that his words of consolation might not reach my ears; but I knew by the soldier's face that he spoke of hope and peace.

Then raising his voice, he mentioned the name of Staples, and asked about his home.

Barker guessed why the question was put, and sighed heavily.

"Poor old Jim," he murmured; "may God help the little woman. She lives at Budleigh, in Hampshire. That is one comfort I have—there will be no one to mourn for me."

I turned to the surgeon, who was leaving the adjoining bed, and asked sadly, "Can anything be done for him?"

He shook his head.

"All the doctors in the universe could not get him out of death's grip now," he said; "he will die at dawn."

We walked back to our lodgings silent and heavy-hearted, nor did Pym speak, save in monosyllables, till the close of the day.

In the evening I went over to El Pastor's quarters, and having sent in my name, was immediately admitted.

The general, who was attended by several of his officers, received me with extreme cordiality.

"You are right welcome," he said, shaking my hand; "and here is another old friend of yours, who will be glad to see you."

While the general was speaking, an officer stepped forth from the little group, and I recognized Don Philip.

"I heard of you from El Pastor," he said, "and was rejoiced to learn that you were working in the good cause."

"In the same good cause in which our men are dying by hundreds," I responded gloomily.

"I have done what I could on behalf of my gallant allies," said the general; "but, unhappily, I possess little real power, as Raphael here knows to his cost."

He motioned with his hand towards a tall, handsome youth, bright-eyed, and of dark complexion.

"Let me introduce you to Raphael," El Pastor continued; "he is a curiosity—a dead man amongst the living."

"Your remark interests me," I said; "how do you explain the riddle?"

"Of course you have heard of my ten brave Chapelgorris whom Espartero butchered to please the gossips at Madrid? Raphael was one of them.—Tell the Englishman about it, my boy."

The youthful Chapelgorri laughed lightly, and said, "The story is short, señor, and easily told. I was the tenth man on whom the death-warrant fell, and took my place in the line. The firing-party marched out. I commended my soul to God, took a last look at my comrades, and waited. The suspense was so disagreeable that I felt quite relieved when the order to fire was given."

"Pray go on," I said, as he paused in the recital.

"The rest of the narrative is far from romantic," he replied with a smile. "A ball grazed my neck and just drew blood, but that was all. Fortunately I had sufficient presence of mind to fall on my face and simulate death, until the troops were withdrawn. I fear that I gave the burial-party something of a shock, but they were good fellows, and carried me off to El Pastor's quarters."

"Where he shall stay, even if it costs the life of every man under my command," observed the general sternly.

"Your experience must be almost unique," I said, "and I fancy there are few of us who would care to go through it."

Raphael laughed, displaying his white teeth, and I gazed at him curiously, thinking how close he had been to the valley of the shadow of death.

Soon afterwards, remembering that Pym would now have finished his duties, I took my leave, and Don Philip walked with me, wishful to obtain an accurate account of my adventures.

He was very much interested in the story of the girl's rescue, and questioned me closely concerning it.

"Do you know this Rubio?" I asked. "Pedro had heard of him."

"Yes, he is a scoundrel who fights for his own hand. He has changed sides several times, and is now ostensibly a Carlist. His band is the most powerful in Biscay, and the Carlists humour him to keep his friendship. But who the girl may be is hard to tell. I cannot recall the name of any prominent adherent of the queen in the neighbourhood of Bilbao."

"The war makes but little progress," I said after a while, in order to relieve the silence which had fallen upon us.

"No; action is impracticable until the weather breaks up; then, I trust, we shall make a move. Now I must go back, but we shall meet again."

"I hope so, indeed; it is ill parting for ever with a friend."

After leaving the Spaniard, I hastened home to Pym, who had just returned from the convent.

He was weary and depressed, but he brightened up at my coming, and seemed profoundly engrossed in my story of the young Chapelgorri.

After that we sat moodily enough till bedtime, striving, but unsuccessfully, to shake off the memory of the scenes which we had that day witnessed.

During the next few weeks the misery of our lives was wellnigh intolerable.

The winter proved exceptionally severe. The cold was so intense that we shivered even in our room, while at times the rain poured down in a sweeping deluge.

As for the men, Pym's pithy statement continued to hold true—they drilled and died, or, to vary the monotony, deserted.

Beyond drilling, scarcely anything of a military nature was done or even attempted. Often, it is true, the luckless soldiers of the Legion, shaking with cold and weak with hunger, were marched out in the grey of the morning across the snow-clad plains, but they were invariably marched back again without having fired a shot.

The first fortnight of the new year passed in this dismal manner, and then it was rumoured that Cordova had determined upon striking a decisive blow.

For some time past a portion of the Legion had occupied the villages in the direction of Salvatierra, which was strongly held by the Carlists, who were also in possession of a little village called Mandigar.

It was on the night of the fifteenth of January 1836 that orders were sent from General Cordova to march forward the next morning and engage the enemy's attention, while he and General Espartero brought up their troops with a view to delivering a combined attack.

The prospect of actual fighting raised the men's spirits, and after a meagre breakfast, the Legion moved upon Mandigar and drove the Carlists out.

With this success we were obliged to be satisfied, as General Evans had received instructions to act strictly on the defensive until Cordova had completed his arrangements.

Emboldened by our inactivity, the Carlists returned again and again to the attack, and thus a kind of guerilla fight was maintained, which gave the Westminster Grenadiers an opportunity of exhibiting their prowess.

Few of the men slept that night, but spent their time speculating upon the result of the action which every one believed must inevitably take place.

This expectation was strengthened when, early on the following morning, heavy and continued firing was heard in the direction where we imagined Cordova to be.

General Evans accordingly ordered an advance to the heights of Marietta, there to await the instructions of the commander-in-chief.

All day long we stood in the frozen snow, watching eagerly for the Spanish general's messenger, and wondering at his non-appearance.

Young as I was, physical suffering was familiar enough to me, but the agony of that terrible night surpassed all that I had yet endured.

At the falling of darkness I lay down on that bleak hillside with my military cloak as the sole protection from the frozen ground. I had fasted since the early morning, and in addition to the other miseries, was tortured by the pangs of hunger. My head burned, and was so heavy that I could scarcely raise it; my limbs had lost all power of movement—they were like ice.

As the night wore on, so powerfully did the cold grip that I feared it would kill me, yet it was beyond my power to move about.

Pym's company, unhappily, lay at El Burgos, and thus I was deprived of my friend's assistance.

But the dawn came at length, and to my inexpressible surprise I still lived, although unable to rise when the bugles sounded.

In this strait I was discovered by my old acquaintance Peyton, who promptly had me removed to an ambulance.

"You will have a chance of getting into Vitoria," he said; "but keep out of the hospital if you wish to live.—Tovey"—turning to one of the men—"take Mr. Powell straight to his lodgings. Now I must be off."

I just managed to thank him for his kindness, and then fell into a state of insensibility, which lasted, as I learned afterwards, for several days.

My eyes opened on the familiar cupboard which served me as bedroom, and I heard some one moving in the adjoining chamber.

"Is that you, Pym?" I called, and the question was answered by my trusty comrade in person.

"How did the battle go?" I asked eagerly, as he came to my side. "I see you are all right."

He smiled a trifle sarcastically. "There was no fighting, except with the elements. While we lay out on the hills, freezing and starving, Cordova was calmly retreating to Vitoria."

"What! unknown to the Legion?"

"Yes; if the Carlists had taken advantage of the opportunity, we might have been cut to pieces. Our men are very angry about it; indeed, they go so far as to openly accuse Cordova of treachery to the Legion. However, we are well out of it; but were I Evans, I should think twice before co-operating with Cordova again. How do you feel now?"

"Warm," I answered; "and warmth just at present is Paradise."

"I can well believe it, although our sufferings were less

than yours. My company passed the night in a dismantled house."

"Is Dick safe?"

"Yes, but disgusted at the turn of events. Now, I'm going to get some hot coffee, and then you must excuse me for a couple of hours. El Pastor and Don Philip have made kindly inquiries after you, and General Evans looked in himself last night."

Having brought some food and drink, he waited until I had finished the meal, and then, bidding me sleep, went out.

Thus left alone, I endeavoured to follow Pym's advice, and soon fell into a peaceful slumber.

CHAPTER XI.

ON THE TRACK OF THE SPY.

MANY days passed before I recovered sufficient strength to leave my chamber, and even then it was only to walk with uncertain steps into Pym's room.

But these hours of enforced imprisonment were not all lonely. Pym sacrificed most of his leisure to bear me company, and honest Dick Truscott paid frequent visits.

Occasionally, too, I received a cheery message from Peyton, who was quartered in one of the outlying villages, and more than once my Spanish friend called with some little delicacy which his position had enabled him to procure.

After the *fiasco* on the heights of Marietta, matters had relapsed into their former condition. General Cordova, either through sheer inability to move or weak irresolution, remained quiet in the city, while the men of the Legion drilled and starved as of yore.

Pym rarely alluded to these things, but Dick, who had less responsibility, spoke his mind freely.

"This is the queerest kind of campaign," he said one night, when we two were alone. "Here we stay week after week, cooped up in this wretched hole, and as far as

I can see, to no purpose. The men have never had decent quarters since they came, nor a proper meal."

"Are the rations just as bad?" I asked.

"Every bit. Some days we wait hours, and when the food comes it isn't fit to eat. I should like to have half an hour with the people responsible. Upon my word, though it ill becomes an old soldier to say so, I can scarcely blame the men for deserting. No fire, no pay, poisonous food, and little of that, but plenty of drilling and flogging—it's enough to sicken the best soldier going."

"Are the desertions frequent?"

"Hardly a night passes without two or three slipping off—it's getting quite a trade; but none have gone from Captain Forrester's company."

"Have you met with the Spanish soldier Pedro since the Legion has been in Vitoria?"

"No, but I have seen the Don several times; he remembered me at once."

Mention of the Don caused us to talk over our earlier adventures, and so the evening slipped away pleasantly enough, until it was time for Dick to go.

A few days subsequent to this conversation, when I was able to resume my usual duties, I discovered that Dick's account of the desertions from the Legion was well within the truth.

Many of the men, tempted by the flattering promises of Don Carlos, and worn out by the terrible privations they had undergone, sought every opportunity of going over to the Carlist lines.

This, in the case of the cavalry and the various regiments occupying the villages, was easily found; but for the troops in Vitoria the task was more difficult, as no one was permitted to stray beyond the walls.

Nevertheless the losses continued, and it became evident that the Carlist agents were in our midst.

Men who responded to the roll-call at night were missing in the morning, and the officers were at a loss to know how they had succeeded in escaping from the town.

"One thing seems clear," Pym observed. "The emissaries of Don Carlos must be people of some influence, otherwise they would be unable to spirit the men away in this mysterious manner."

Now it happened on that same night I was returning from the cantonments at Salvatierra, whither I had carried a letter from General Evans.

Owing to an unavoidable delay, the hour was late; but I had traversed the road on several previous occasions, and experienced no sense of danger.

The sky was darkened by a curtain of black clouds, and the wind howled dismally; but as the rain kept off, I jogged along quite contentedly.

For half the distance I held to the track—spoken of by the misguided natives as a road—and then, turning abruptly to the left, cantered my horse down a gentle slope, the opposite summit of which was covered by a thick wood.

Being familiar with the route, I felt quite safe, and my horse stepped out firmly but lightly over the hard ground.

Entering the wood, I turned into a narrow glade, bordered on either side by a row of tall, leafless trees.

Here the darkness was intensified, and a sudden downpour of rain added to the dreariness of the night.

The skeleton trees offered small protection from the storm, yet I rejoiced at having chosen this forest route, as it would considerably shorten the journey.

I was just conjuring up the picture of Pym waiting for me in his room, when a vivid streak of lightning passed so close that my horse reared in fright and nearly threw me.

"Steady, old fellow," I said, patting his head soothingly; "'twas a narrow shave, but there's no harm done."

At the sound of my voice the sagacious creature, as if satisfied, quieted down; and I was about to proceed, when an exclamation, uttered somewhere on my left, threw me into a state of wonder.

"That settles it," some one said in good English; "he'll never venture out on a night like this."

So keen was my surprise that during the space of several seconds I sat perfectly motionless and dumbfounded.

Then, acting on the first impulse which found expression in my muddled brain, I rode softly away.

Very soon, however, the idea of flight was tempered by the reflection that, by exercising a little caution, I might make some important discovery, and I pulled up sharply.

What was this Englishman doing in the wood? Whatever his object, I concluded that it must be harmful to the Legion—so much indeed seemed certain.

Again, it appeared very unlikely that he was alone. Who, then, were his companions?

I stroked my horse gently, and considered what was best to be done.

By great good fortune I had avoided the danger; to what purpose should I court it afresh? Why not pursue my original intention, and ride on to Vitoria? What good could I, a mere lad, effect, unaided?

But these questions lost significance in face of that other: What could an Englishman want at such a place and time?

Finally, the very inability to solve this riddle decided my course; at all costs I would turn back.

Dismounting lightly, I tied the horse to a tree a little way within the wood, and gripping my pistol, stole quietly towards the place from which the sounds had come.

At every step I became more fully impressed by the dangerous nature of the errand.

As I have previously stated, the night was dark, and no flash of lightning succeeded to the one which had evoked the stranger's exclamation.

It was too risky to trust myself beyond the narrow pathway, as a false step might plunge me unawares into the midst of an armed band; yet to remain in my present position was practically useless.

Pistol in hand, I stood behind a tree trunk listening intently. The swish of the rain, the sweep of the wind, alone could be heard; and I was on the point of braving in despair the unknown terrors of the wood, when an angry oath reached my ears.

Again it was the Englishman's voice which directed me, but now I could also distinguish broken snatches of conversation in Spanish.

Using the most extreme caution, I crept stealthily in the direction of the unseen hiders, pausing at intervals to listen.

Gliding from tree to tree, I came to a spot where the ground dipped, and crouching close to the earth, waited.

The talking had ceased, but a few minutes' watching convinced me that I had successfully tracked the men to their lair. Right down in the very bottom of the hollow gleamed a tiny spark of fire—the glow from a man's pipe or cigarette.

Soon there came a sound as of some one moving, and with difficulty I made out the figure of a man ascending the slope opposite me.

The next instant he disappeared amidst the trees; there was a low, plaintive whistle, and again all was still.

After a short interval, the signal—for such I took it to be—was repeated, but it obtained no response.

I lay quiet, hardly venturing to breathe, while the man returned to his hiding-place.

"The Englishman was right," he said sullenly; "the storm has frightened him."

"He has never failed yet," returned another voice sharply; "why should he now? Is he made of sugar to be melted by a drop of water?"

These two speakers employed the ordinary Spanish tongue, but now a third uttered a remark in a kind of rude *patois* perfectly unintelligible to me.

The second man, however, answered contemptuously, "These English pigs are dull—they have no wits. Make yourself comfortable, Ricardo. We will give him another half-hour's grace, and if he does not come, we will return."

The other made some grumbling reply, and then they all relapsed into silence, or at least I failed to catch any further words.

All this time the rain kept falling with a steady persistence, and being destitute of any real cover, I was soon in a soaked condition.

The party below I judged to be much better off in this respect than myself, since they, most likely, were lying snugly behind the natural barriers which the broken nature of the ground afforded.

However, in spite of the disagreeableness of the situation, I stuck to my post, though beginning strongly to wish that the rain would cease.

The half-hour came and went, and one of the hidden watchers began to move impatiently, when the silence was broken by a long, sustained cry, as of a night-bird.

The sound came from amidst the trees, and was answered from the hollow.

The darkness had increased rather than lessened, but my eyes being now more accustomed to the gloom, I could just make out the figure of a man come from the wood and disappear in the little valley.

Now having heard the snatches of conversation here set down, I anticipated little difficulty in learning the nature of the new-comer's errand; but in this I was grievously disappointed.

Truly there rose on the air a subdued hum of voices, but the words were indistinct. From the tones of the speakers I gathered that some plan had miscarried, and the Englishman in particular was excessively angry.

For fully ten minutes they kept up the talk, and then a voice which I now heard for the first time said in Spanish, "Tell the general that I will answer for to-morrow night—suspicions—caution—the best place."

An answer of some sort was made to this, as the voice continued, "Then it is agreed—mind the patrols."

By this time I felt certain that the last comer belonged to Vitoria, and without hesitation I decided upon the course to be pursued.

If I could capture the stranger, the secret, whatever its nature, would be in my keeping. To follow him through the wood seemed hardly feasible, owing to the darkness; and this plan, moreover, would involve the loss of my horse.

But if my suspicions proved correct, the man must of necessity return straight to the city, where he could be tracked.

Reasoning thus, I resolved to ride hard to Vitoria, and take up a position close to the nearest gate, where I could easily observe any one who entered.

Of course it was possible that he would select some other point of ingress, but that must be risked.

To reach the narrow glade was the first consideration,

and this took time, as by making a false step I should probably bring the whole band upon my heels.

Once there, I ran swiftly forward, loosed the horse, and mounted.

Thus far all was well; but the journey through the glade occupied a longer period than I had reckoned upon, and I feared that the stranger would reach the plain first, which would prove fatal to the success of my plan.

Having emerged from the wood, I urged my gallant horse to his utmost, and galloped at a headlong pace towards the town, at a little distance from which I drew up.

This second vigil, which lasted till daylight, was, I verily believe, more dismal than the first. Not for a single instant did the rain abate its violence, and I had much ado to quiet my horse, terrified by the frequently-recurring thunder-claps and flashes of lightning.

A sense of failure, too, disheartened me, for as the night hours wore on, and the steel-grey dawn broke in the eastern sky, it became plain that the unknown had escaped.

One chance still remained—that of obtaining information at the gate.

Here again I was completely foiled, as the stolid Spanish sentry persisted in his statement that no one had passed since the gates were shut overnight.

Weary, wet, and crest-fallen, I rode dejectedly through the muddy streets to my lodgings, and found Pym on the point of starting for the convent.

He gazed at my sorry plight in amazement. "Where on earth have you spent the night?" he asked.

"In the open, but you shall hear the story later; I am going to bed," and I proceeded without delay to cast off my dripping garments.

Pym's duties kept him busy throughout the day, but directly on his return, he begged that I would tell him what had occurred.

It was plain that he thought the incident of some importance, and when I finished speaking, he said abruptly, "What do you intend doing?"

"Wait till dark, and then try my luck again."

"It would be better to take a dozen men and make a clean sweep."

"I think not. My object is to get hold of the spy, and at the first sign of suspicion he would bolt. Besides, a dozen men would be too few to surround the band in the darkness, and a larger number would most probably betray us."

"It sounds plausible," my comrade replied thoughtfully; "but I wish you were well through it. Will you ride?"

"No; the horse would prove a hindrance. I intend to post myself in the wood on the other side of the hollow, and wait for the mysterious messenger on his way back."

"Are your pistols in order?"

"Yes, but only to be used as a last resource."

"Let us go together. I can easily get leave of absence."

"It's scarcely worth it, old fellow. I can manage; and after all, you know, I may have discovered a mare's nest."

Pym continued to press the point, but finding that my

determination remained unshaken, he very reluctantly permitted me to depart.

"Should the worst happen," he said, pressing my hand in farewell, "remember that the Carlists show no mercy to soldiers of the Legion."

I nodded lightly, and bantering him on his gloomy forecast, set out.

Making my way across the plain, I entered the wood and traversed the familiar glade as far as the spot where my horse had been tethered on the previous night.

Here I turned to the right and advanced with caution, although feeling nearly certain that it was as yet too early for the arrival of the Carlists.

In a little time I came to a narrow footpath, and followed it to the hollow.

Having thus made sure of the position, I retraced my steps and hid behind a clump of trees a few steps from the track.

Happily the weather was fine, but the wind blew keen, and as I had purposely left my cloak in Vitoria, the cold punished me severely.

To that, however, I paid but little heed, being too much occupied in speculating on the probable results of the adventure.

My plan was simplicity itself. Believing that the stranger would pay his promised visit to the hiding-place, I resolved to follow him on his return, and surprise him near the outskirt of the wood.

It was perhaps an hour after midnight that I heard a

low whistle on my right, immediately echoed by one on the left.

I crouched behind the sheltering trees, and very soon a dark-cloaked figure passed in front of me.

"The mysterious stranger!" I thought, but fortunately remained still. Fortunately, I repeat, for to my surprise the first figure was succeeded by others similarly arrayed.

I lay and counted them to the number of six, wondering greatly all the while what this unexpected procession might mean.

The figures passed on out of sight, while I, devoured by curiosity, crept after them, just in time to see the last descend into the valley.

Almost immediately there arose a clamour of tongues, English and Spanish; but the noise lasted a little while only, as some one, manifestly in authority, called for silence.

Then it was that the truth dawned upon my mind. I realized that I had been watching a party of deserters from the Legion, and that their guide was a Carlist spy.

In a few minutes the correctness of this surmise was made abundantly clear; the men, one by one, clambered up the opposite slope and vanished amidst the trees.

I had barely time to secrete myself before the spy returned. He stood an instant so close to me that I could have felled him to the earth, but his friends were as yet too near, and I forbore to strike.

Fumbling in his pocket, he produced what appeared to be a cigar, and placed it in his mouth. Then, as if doubting the wisdom of the action, he put it back, and strode away in the darkness.

Instantly I stepped into the path and followed quietly.

Evidently the route was familiar to him. He walked on at a rapid pace, showing no hesitation, and as far as could be judged by his firm, even tread, having perfect confidence in his safety.

He was a tall man, and the length of his strides made it awkward for me to keep up with him; indeed, it soon became apparent that the distance between us was increasing.

Now I regretted having refused Pym's offer, and anxious to make up for my stupidity, pressed on with undue haste, guided alone by the sound of the footfalls in front.

The difficulty was enhanced by the tortuous nature of the path, which wound and twisted like the track of a serpent.

Hitherto I had regarded the adventure almost as a piece of child's play, but now I began to be vaguely oppressed by a dread that my intended victim would a second time escape me.

And the mischance followed directly on the fear of it. Suddenly the sound of the man's steps ceased, and losing all sense of caution, I hurried recklessly forward.

It is a simple enough matter to be wise after the event, and looking back, I perceive my folly in its true light. But it was different then; my brain had room only for the single notion that the man had branched off into the wood and would get clear away.

It was maddening to lose my prey in this manner, and I actually ran in the darkness to the next bend in the path.

Here an accident of the most trivial character intervened to save my life.

My foot caught in a tangle of knotted tree-roots bared by the rain, and I fell heavily, while at the same time there was a blinding flash, and a bullet whistled over my prostrate body.

Plainly it was the old story of the hunter hunted; I had stalked my prey to some purpose.

But the imminence of danger braced my nerves and perhaps cleared my vision, for I beheld the cloaked figure of a man standing on the edge of the path.

Springing up quickly, I rushed at my opponent before he had time to discharge his second pistol, and the next moment we were locked in a close if not loving embrace.

Neither of us spoke; breath was far too precious to be wasted in idle words, and in silence we set about the deadly struggle.

To and fro we reeled and swayed like drunken men, and before long it was borne in upon me that I had met my match.

The sweat poured freely down my face; the veins on my forehead stood out swollen and corded; my breath came in short gasps.

Once the spy forced me to my knees; but in his anxiety to terminate the contest, he lost his advantage.

Releasing the pressure for a second, he groped with one hand for his knife; but before it could be used, I broke from his grasp and clutched him afresh.

Then, in the midst of our straining and tugging, I heard

fierce cries and the snapping of wood, and realized that the party of Carlists had returned.

My antagonist laughed aloud, and with a cry of exultation bade his comrades hasten.

With an energy born of despair I got my arms free, and putting all my strength into one terrific blow, sent him crashing against a tree.

It was my sole chance, and it answered admirably. The spy lay bruised and dizzy, and as the first of my new foes sprang to the spot, I bounded away into the darkness.

Once hidden amongst the trees I felt safe, knowing that the Carlists would be afraid, under the circumstances, to prosecute the search.

Nevertheless I continued my course in the most melancholy manner imaginable. My scheme had fallen through completely, as I had to acknowledge to myself with shame and humiliation.

Proud in my own conceit, I had gone forth confident of my ability to carry the enterprise to a successful conclusion; I was returning empty-handed, thankful even at having escaped with my life.

A saying which the soldier Pedro had once uttered rose involuntarily to my lips, "Many go out for wool and come home shorn," and in good sooth I was a striking example of its truth.

So grievously indeed did the sense of disgrace weigh upon me that I actually thought of returning to the scene of the conflict, but a fortunate glimmering of common-sense prevented me from putting this contemplated folly into execution.

Nevertheless it was with extreme reluctance that I finally left the wood and started across the plain towards the city.

So thoroughly were my suspicions concerning the Spaniards aroused that I did not care to make inquiries of the guard, but exhibiting my papers, passed into the town without remark.

Knowing how anxiously Pym would await my return, I went straight to our rooms, and found him still dressed.

"No luck!" he said, looking into my face; "never mind; at least you are safe back, and that is the most important point. Did you learn anything?"

"Only that the Legion will be five men short at roll-call in the morning," I responded moodily, and forthwith related the history of the night's adventures.

"It's a pity that you went alone," my comrade remarked. "Would you know the man again?"

"I didn't see his features, but I should recognize his voice. But it is hardly probable that he will give me a third chance."

"Not for a few days; the fright will make him cautious, and I hope that we shall soon be moving. Don't let the mishap trouble you; things will look brighter after a good rest."

But notwithstanding Pym's good-natured advice, I lay awake a long while, brooding over my discomfiture, and forming fresh schemes for the capture of the man who had thus outwitted me.

CHAPTER XII.

THE END OF THE SPY.

PYM looked very grave that same evening when, in answer to my question, he informed me that four privates and a corporal, lately reduced to the ranks, were missing.

"The evil is growing," he said, "and unless steps are speedily taken to check it, will work a lot of mischief. Desertion is like some diseases—contagious."

"It is evident that there is some one in Vitoria playing a bold game," I observed, "and playing it well. The whole thing looks to me very much like an organized conspiracy."

Previous discomfiture had the wholesome effect of making me more modest, so I made no mention of my intentions; but, privately, I determined upon unravelling the mystery.

During the next week, however, scant opportunity offered of furthering my purpose, as I was kept busy riding to and fro between Vitoria and the various outlying villages occupied by troops of the Legion.

The subject, nevertheless, was constantly in my mind;

and some ten days after the adventure in the wood, a trifling incident happened which had far-reaching consequences.

I had been in attendance on General Evans, and was returning home, when a tavern door just in front of me was suddenly opened, and two men came into the street.

One of them I recognized as Sandy M'Alaine, a member of Pym's company; the other was a Spaniard.

"Burn the note," the latter was saying, "or it may bring mischief to both of us."

Now, the sight of one of our men in friendly intercourse with a Spaniard being quite common, I should straightway have passed on, but for a faint ring of familiarity in the stranger's voice.

This set me thinking, and feigning an interest in the doings of a knot of idlers, I waited while they walked together a little distance.

The Spaniard wore an ample cloak, while a large *sombrero,* drawn low down over his forehead, partly helped to conceal his features.

I could make out little beyond the fact that he was tall, but this did not afford much aid in the work of identifying him.

But I had heard the voice before, and recently—so much was certain.

Then, like a flash of inspiration, there came to me the remembrance of my fight with the spy in the woods; and the mystery was laid bare.

So assured was I of being on the right track that I

could scarcely refrain from openly displaying my satisfaction in the discovery.

There, without a doubt, stood the man I wanted; but how could I conclusively prove his guilt?

My first impulse was to call for assistance and arrest him on suspicion, but conscious of my lack of proof, I resolved to act cautiously.

To this end, I loitered about until the two separated, and then followed the soldier, who walked briskly in the direction of the convent.

At the sound of footsteps the man paused, and recognizing me, saluted.

"Good-evening, Sandy," I said. "Have you burned the letter?"

He stood in the middle of the side-walk, with dazed eyes like one in a dream, and his face was the colour of parchment.

I kept my eyes fixed steadily on his till the power of speech came to him.

"Don't give me up, Mr. Powell," he cried earnestly; "I haven't done anything wrong. Do you think that I would bring disgrace on Captain Forrester?"

"If I thought so for an instant we should not be parleying here. And yet it is a serious thing being caught hand in glove with a Carlist spy."

"The man's a stranger to me," he said; "I don't even know his name. Take me to Captain Forrester, sir, and let him read the letter; it hasn't been opened yet."

This seemed a good suggestion, and I told him that he

should go with me to the captain's lodgings, at which he brightened up wonderfully.

At sight of Sandy, Pym looked up in surprise, which increased as I explained the nature of the soldier's errand.

"This wears an ugly look, M'Alaine," my comrade said sternly; "perhaps you will tell us what you know, before we examine this document," which Sandy had laid on the table.

Now, whatever the result of this informal investigation might be, it soon became abundantly plain that the Scotsman was quite innocent.

He told his tale in a simple, straightforward manner, and every word bore the impress of truth.

Set forth baldly and without circumlocution, the story amounted to this. That evening he had been accosted by a strange Spaniard and invited to drink, an offer which Sandy accepted with the utmost willingness. Accordingly the two entered a tavern, and after several glasses of wine, the Spaniard began cautiously to compare the state of the Legion with that of the British troops serving under Don Carlos. Then he mentioned that a certain person—a deserter to the Carlists—had entrusted him with a letter for Sandy M'Alaine, to which he—the speaker—would require an answer on the following night.

"That's the story, gentlemen, without a lie in it from beginning to end. I told the Spaniard I would meet him again, and was going back to the convent when Mr. Powell stopped me. But there's just one thing more I should like to say. The man who wrote that letter is an old friend of mine, and I don't want him to get into trouble through me. Perhaps you could keep his name out of the mess?" and he looked at my comrade appealingly.

"I think we can promise that," said Pym. "Of course, if he is caught he will be punished as a deserter; but that is another matter altogether."

"That's all I ask, sir. As to the deserting, he's made his bed and must lie on it."

The letter, which we now opened, was brief and to the point. The writer expressed his satisfaction at having joined the Carlists, and strongly urged Sandy to do likewise. But the sentence which made the greatest impression on Pym and myself was the following: "You can trust the bearer; he smuggled me out of Vitoria."

Pym looked at me significantly. "The man in the wood," he said, and I nodded in assent.

"This must be probed to the bottom," he continued. —"M'Alaine, go to your quarters, and remember to keep a still tongue in your head. I will pledge my word that no harm shall come to you."

Sandy saluted and went out unconcernedly, having an unbounded faith in his officer.

I took up the letter, saying, "What is the next step, Pym?"

"I must show that note to the colonel. The subject is far too serious for us to settle on our own responsibility. I will see him in the morning, and be guided by his advice."

"The general expects me directly after breakfast; shall I mention our discovery to him?"

"Better wait a bit, I should say, and hear what the colonel proposes to do."

I very much fear that my duties the next day were performed in a rather perfunctory manner, since my thoughts would persist in wandering to the affair of the spy.

Oddly enough, too, it chanced that General Evans kept me exceptionally busy, so that the night was growing late when I finally reached home.

So great was my curiosity that Pym had hardly an opportunity for speech before I began to question him concerning his doings.

"The train is laid," he said, "and to-morrow evening will see it fired. But I don't like the business, Arthur, and that's a fact. A fair open fight I can stand well enough, but this underground burrowing goes against the grain."

"But surely we are acting rightly in protecting ourselves against spies," I suggested.

"Perhaps so—and yet! Ah well, talking will not mend the mischief. M'Alaine has had a second meeting with the Carlist, and has arranged to join him to-morrow evening with a few others, who, he told the Spaniard, are eager to desert."

"Where is the rendezvous?"

"You will be surprised. The meeting is to take place at the house of Don Jose Elgoez!"

"What! the chief contractor for the army?"

"Yes. Don Carlos has been happy in the selection of an

agent. His position affords him unrivalled facilities for work of that kind."

"Just so; he can smuggle the men out as ordinary peasants going on a foraging expedition. But we must act with caution; he is enormously wealthy, and has powerful friends."

"That is precisely the colonel's argument; and in order to make assurance doubly sure, he has placed the management of the enterprise in my hands. I shall make one of M'Alaine's party."

"That will expose the trick at once."

"Why? The Spaniards do not know me, and I shall borrow a sergeant's uniform for the occasion."

"What is my share to be?"

"Your part is done; it would be folly to risk your being recognized by the spy. Besides, the danger is trifling."

"Which to you makes the work doubly unattractive. If there was a moderate chance of your getting a stray bullet, you would welcome the adventure."

"There is certainly some truth in that remark," Pym answered with a laugh; "this seems to me like hunting a chained lion."

"Danger may lurk even in that. Do you take Dick?"

"Assuredly. Next to yourself, I would rather have Dick at my side than any man in the Legion. But really everything is so ridiculously easy that I am half ashamed of my part. At dusk to-morrow we shall go singly to Don Jose's house, and there, I imagine, shall be transformed temporarily into Spanish peasants. The guard at each gate will be warned, and directly we set foot outside the walls, our party, including the spy, will be promptly surrounded and made prisoners."

"Have you considered that they may have a secret way out, beyond call of the guard?"

Pym mused a while. "There is just a chance of it," he replied thoughtfully; "but I scarcely think it likely. However, it may be as well if you keep watch at a safe distance upon the contractor's house."

This I readily agreed to do; and then, as the hour was growing late, I went into my little room.

Throughout the next day I was filled with impatience, and welcomed the coming of the evening shadows with a lively satisfaction, though, like Pym, I felt that the adventure was shorn of half its interest by the absence of danger.

At the appointed time I stationed myself near Don Jose's house, and before long perceived Sandy M'Alaine and Pym—the latter dressed in sergeant's uniform—steal cautiously up.

One by one, and at irregular intervals, the others followed, until all the party had gathered inside the contractor's dwelling.

As to what was taking place there, I could only conjecture; but directly upon the arrival of the last man the doors were shut and the place was wrapped in darkness.

Evening passed into night, and still the silence remained unbroken. Little by little the noises of the streets died away; the last straggling soldiers had returned to quarters;

the populace had retired within doors; the taverns were emptied of their brawling customers; the lights in the neighbouring houses disappeared; Vitoria slept.

The hush and darkness of the night made me nervous and excited. All manner of vain imaginings crowded into my brain—thoughts grotesque, absurd, illogical, yet having power sufficient to weigh down my spirits.

Midnight was just sounding when a trifling incident somewhat relieved the tension on my nerves. A tall man, almost concealed by an ample cloak, walked down the street, and after standing at the end for perhaps five minutes, returned in the direction of Don Jose's house.

I let him pass my hiding-place, and then followed with cat-like tread.

Even now no lights were exhibited within the building, but soon there arose a faint hum of voices and the sound of clanging doors, while a little later I beheld the gleam of lanterns.

Completely hidden in the darkness, I waited breathlessly, staggered by the simplicity and boldness of the spy's scheme, although I had more than half expected this very arrangement.

Yet in spite of, nay, perhaps because of its marvellous audacity the plan had already been successfully worked, and I felt compelled to pay a silent tribute of admiration to the author of this daring enterprise.

Without any attempt at secrecy, the party emerged from the courtyard, and now I saw that the sham deserters were dressed as Spanish peasants, and acting as muleteers.

I could not count the men with any degree of accuracy, but guessed the number to be from twelve to fifteen, divided apparently into two distinct groups, the soldiers of the Legion having doubtless been separated from the genuine peasants.

At the head of the throng walked a tall man, who seemed to be the person in authority.

It was quite easy to track them, as the leader courted rather than shunned publicity. An accredited agent of the Christino army, none would be likely to imagine him guilty of treachery, and chance passers would naturally conclude the party to be composed of simple peasants engaged in their ordinary avocation.

And in acting on this surmise the spy proved his sagacity.

Without undue haste, and in the most natural manner, the men traversed the deserted streets, making for the San Juan gate.

Here they halted, while their leader produced his papers, which the officer on duty gravely examined and gave back.

Then, at the opening of the gate, the men fell into their places, whipped up the mules, and moved forward.

For the first time I was enabled to distinguish Pym and the sergeant, and noticed without much surprise that they had drawn very close to their unconscious victim.

The critical moment was fast approaching, but I regarded the result as a foregone conclusion, and this confidence was very shortly completely justified.

At a given signal those in the secret closed round the

conductor, so that he was shut in, without a chance of escaping.

The spy accepted his defeat with philosophic calmness.

"'He who would catch fish must not mind getting wet,'" he remarked coolly, and then relapsed into stolid silence.

Giving the prisoner into Dick's charge, Pym drew up his men, now reinforced by a portion of the guard, and gave the word to march.

"To strike the iron while it's hot is excellent advice, Arthur," he said; "we will finish our work by placing the chief rogue safely under lock and key."

"Do you think that Don Jose has any inkling of what is going on?"

"Not the least. He is a wily scoundrel, and I expect will give plenty of trouble later."

"Others must look to that; we have only to get hold of him."

So well had Pym's secret been kept that only those who had actually assisted in the capture knew what was being done, and we marched straight to Don Jose's house without interruption.

Here Pym, bidding his men preserve strict silence, distributed them so as to guard every means of exit, and passing into the courtyard, knocked at the door.

Then ensued a whispered colloquy, carried on in too low a key for me to catch the words; but at the end of it Pym called me, and I went up quickly.

The door had been opened by Don Jose himself, who,

bearing a lighted lamp in his hand, led us into a kind of office.

He was still dressed, and though some notion of the truth might have entered his mind, it was plain that he did not realize the danger of his position.

But his haughty demeanour vanished and his cheeks paled with terror when Pym, speaking with a slow deliberateness, said, "Don Jose Elgoez, I regret that duty compels me to arrest you on a charge of treason. Your house is surrounded by my men, so that escape is impossible."

The hapless Spaniard sat and gazed at us as if we had been visitors from another world. No word did he speak; but his limbs trembled, and the corners of his mouth twitched in an agony of fright.

"Do you hear me, Don Jose?" Pym said; "you are my prisoner. Your accomplice is already in my hands."

Then the Spaniard, making a great effort, banished his fears and confronted us boldly.

"Dog of an Englishman!" he cried, "when General Cordova hears of this insult, you will have cause to rue your action."

"As to that, let others judge," replied Pym coolly; "I am but an instrument.—Arthur, you will stay here in charge until a proper guard is sent. Let no one enter or leave, and see that everything remains as it is now.—Come, Don Jose, I must beg that you will accompany me," and the Spaniard, finding himself powerless, left the room with my comrade.

By this time day had begun to break, and it was with a feeling of satisfaction that, shortly after Pym's departure, I saw the approach of a body of men who had been sent to relieve us.

It was too late to think of bed, but the excitement of the recent doings prevented me from feeling fatigue, and after breakfast I was ready for the day's work.

As was natural, the tidings of the contractor's arrest created an intense sensation, and the most extraordinary rumours began to circulate.

Everywhere men congregated in groups to talk about the incident, and the Spaniards, both soldiers and civilians, appeared thunderstruck.

One opinion, however, I heard uttered repeatedly, and with the most assured confidence.

"These English dare not harm Don Jose," the Spaniards said to each other; "they will have General Cordova to deal with."

At General Evans' house I met Pym. He had already made his report, and was surrounded by a crowd of officers, all eager to learn the story.

"Ah! Powell," exclaimed one of them, "the general has been inquiring for you. Forrester here insists that it is to you all the credit belongs."

"You shall have the true tale another time," I answered; and having sent in my name, I was immediately ushered into an inner room.

The general, who was looking unusually grave, came to the point at once.

"This is an awkward business, Powell," he began; "what do you know about it?"

I told him exactly what had happened, and then he said tersely, "Put it down in black and white; make two copies—one English, the other Spanish," and with this order I complied.

"It is a queer case," he mused thoughtfully, while I was writing; "the man has high connections, and has always been thought loyal. However, a court-martial will get at the truth. Meanwhile, hold yourself in readiness to appear as a witness."

Most of the officers were gone when I left the general, but Pym was still waiting, and we set off together.

"We seem to have made a startling capture," my comrade remarked; "have you heard the latest rumour?"

"The town is filled with idle tales."

"But Mounsey, who relieved you, vouches for the accuracy of this one. After you left, the troops took possession of all the traitor's effects, and found amongst his stock a large quantity of drugs, besides bones and chalk ground to powder."

I recoiled a step involuntarily, horror-struck at the implied accusation.

"It seems incredible," Pym went on; "but the men firmly believe that he has made a practice of mixing these things with their food. However, the rascal will meet his deserts; we have abundant proof of his treachery."

"Yet his fellow-countrymen are certain that he will be set at liberty; they think that his high standing will save him."

"They put their trust in a broken reed. If the man be found guilty, all the influence in Spain will not get him off."

"You forget that General Evans, after all, is only a subordinate."

"In this instance he will be the master. You may take my word for it that all the gold and all the power in Spain will be unable to screen this unhappy wretch."

As Pym had predicted, the result of the court-martial was a verdict of guilty—the only one, indeed, which could have been returned, so overwhelming was the evidence of organized treachery; and Don Jose was condemned to die with his accomplice.

Yet not until the last hour did the hapless man despair of obtaining a reprieve. It was rumoured that he offered to give the whole of his fabulous wealth in exchange for his life; it was known that the most powerful chiefs were making strenuous efforts in his behalf.

Whether Cordova, if left to himself, would have yielded to these arguments and entreaties, I cannot tell, but all knew that bribes and threats alike were lost on the English leader, and at length it was resolved that the prisoners should pay the penalty of their crimes.

On the morning of the twenty-eighth of March 1836 various companies of the Legion marched into the great square, and after a tedious delay, formed round the platform with fixed bayonets.

The balconies of the neighbouring houses were crowded with Spanish soldiers—chiefly Chapelgorris—who evinced in the most unmistakable manner their satisfaction at this even-handed justice.

The men of the Legion stood at attention, and in admirable order, while in the distance was heard the muffled drums beating the Dead March.

Presently the dismal procession appeared in sight, and a deep hush fell upon the assembled multitude as the prisoners, attended by about a score of priests chanting the prayers for the dead, slowly approached the place of execution.

Don Jose first ascended the fatal platform, and having received the sacrament from his confessor, seated himself on a kind of chair in front of a stout pole which pierced the flooring. Then his hands were pinioned, an iron collar was placed round his throat, the executioner turned the screw, and all was over.

Immediately afterwards, his luckless assistant met a similar fate, and then the troops filed off to their respective quarters.

"I fancy that the Carlist agents will be chary of interfering with our men for a while," said Pym that evening; "Don Jose's execution will teach them a much-needed lesson."

"If we stay idling here, the men will require very little inducement to desert," I answered; "they will go of their own accord. It has always been a mystery to me why we were brought here."

"Perhaps to swell the numbers of Cordova's army," Pym suggested. "But the winter is breaking up now, and we shall get to work. I heard this morning that there is every likelihood of our being sent north again; the Carlists are closely investing San Sebastian."

"Any change will be welcome," I responded gloomily; "I am heartily tired of Vitoria."

"Our experience has been far from exhilarating, I admit; but a soldier must learn to take the rough with the smooth, and at least we have lived through the worst of it. But you are fatigued, and thrown out of gear by the events of the day; I should advise a long night's rest."

"Perhaps it will do me good," I said; "and things generally look rosier in the daylight."

CHAPTER XIII.

IN DESPERATE STRAITS.

PYM'S remedy for mental depression did not meet with entire success, and thus it chanced that I eagerly seized the opportunity for action which my old Spanish ally Don Philip just then offered me.

The miseries which the Legion had suffered in Vitoria, the veiled hostility of the citizens, the apathy and indifference exhibited by many of the Spaniards high in command, a hopeless sense of doing absolutely nothing in furtherance of the queen's cause—all these combined to excite in me a strong desire to get away. Therefore I lent a willing ear to Don Philip's proposal that I should join an expedition the leadership of which had been given to him.

The offer was made about three weeks after the execution of the two traitors, and I went at once to get the general's permission.

"The service is a hazardous one," he said, "and in my opinion almost certain to fail. Still, if you want to see the Spaniards fight, I will grant you leave of absence. I must tell you, however, that in a few days the Legion will be on the way to Santander."

"We shall be back before then, sir," I replied, "either defeated or victorious."

"Very well; maintain the honour of the old country, but don't let your courage lead you into recklessness. I wish you a safe return."

"Thank you, sir," I said, and withdrew, much gratified by the nature of the general's remarks.

I had agreed to meet Don Philip at the end of the hour, but first of all I hastened to find Pym.

The interview was necessarily brief, but this, I think, rather pleased us than otherwise, since we had little time in which to dwell upon the perils of the enterprise.

"Did the Don give you any details?" my comrade asked.

"None; but I gathered from Evans that there is a fight in prospect."

"As you are going, I wish that I could make one of the party; but that, of course, is out of the question."

"Remember me to Dick," I said, "and—and in case anything should go wrong, to those at home."

I pressed his hand, asked him to take charge of my horse, and then, my time being nearly up, hurried away to the place of meeting.

Don Philip received me with enthusiasm. "Ah, my friend," he cried, "your general has given his consent; I expected it. Come! the men are waiting; we go to strike a great blow."

Being quite ignorant of the Don's intentions, I could not well indulge in criticism, though it appeared to me that a force of five hundred men was scarcely capable of performing any noteworthy enterprise.

Still, the very fact that Don Philip was in command afforded a guarantee that something would at least be attempted, and if at all practicable, carried to a successful issue.

I have before remarked upon the superb powers of endurance possessed by the Spanish soldiers, and these proved no exception to the rule. Hour after hour they tramped on through the night, with long, swinging, tireless steps, over rough roads, along narrow paths, through rugged ravines, and yet few showed symptoms of fatigue.

We had started in the dusk of evening, and morning light found us still marching over a wild, rocky, and to me totally unknown country.

"If these sturdy fellows fight as well as they march," I said to Don Philip, "they should do great things."

My comrade looked pleased at the compliment. "They are good soldiers," he replied; "you will not be ashamed of their company."

Yet in spite of their ability to endure fatigue it seemed to me that there was a want of elasticity in their movements, while I missed the look of aggressive resolution which is so marked a feature in our own countrymen.

It was broad day when we halted at the head of a narrow pass, and here I was agreeably surprised by the thoroughness of my old ally's military knowledge.

His position was carefully chosen, and he proceeded to make it secure against any sudden attack.

"The Carlists are educating us," he said, "and in the end the pupils will prove more than a match for their teachers. Half of our defeats have been due to panic, caused by the marvellous vigilance of our adversaries. We have rarely fought except at a disadvantage."

"They will have hard work to surprise us here," I observed.

"We are going to turn the tables this time. But I will tell you what is intended to be done while we breakfast."

Most of the men were now eating the meagre rations which they had brought with them, while a few, stretched on the rocks, were already asleep.

"We have broken bread together before," Don Philip said courteously, as I sat down beside him; "I trust that we shall do so again."

Then while we ate and drank, sparingly enough, it must be confessed, he unfolded the object of the expedition.

"It would take too long to explain the reasons for the step," he began; "but General Cordova is anxious to capture the Carlist stronghold of Ovaro, a half march from here. El Pastor offered to take it with his Chapelgorris, but the general deputed the task to me."

"Ah!" I responded, "there is a little jealousy between the Chapelgorris and the regular troops, is there not?"

"You are right," he answered smilingly, "and therefore we shall do our very best to succeed."

"Are you acquainted with this stronghold?"

"Unfortunately, no. Still I have a capable guide—your old servant Pedro, now Sergeant Gamboa."

"You could not have a better."

"I am glad you think so; he is a shrewd fellow, and devoted to the cause. Well, we shall reach Ovaro at midnight, and while a part of the troops delivers a feigned attack on one side, you and I, with a few picked men, will follow Gamboa by an unused path to the top of the cliffs. To-morrow Ovaro will fly the royal flag."

"Amen to that," I replied, and secretly resolved that the English lad should not be the last inside the Carlist fortress.

Throughout the middle of the day I slept soundly, and on waking strolled round looking for Pedro.

I found him stretched on a rock gazing thoughtfully into space. At sight of me he sprang up, and evinced the utmost pleasure when I congratulated him upon his promotion.

"Ah, señor," he said, "I heard of you in Vitoria, but it seemed that chance was against our meeting." Then, lowering his voice to a whisper, he added, "Why are you here?"

"To get a share of the credit for the Legion," I answered laughingly. "Surely you don't expect to fail?"

He shook his head doubtingly. "If Don Philip's troops were Chapelgorris," he said; "but these southerners, *carajo!* they may run at the first shot."

"Well, at the worst we can count on three who will stand fast."

"Yes," he said; "and of these one is an Englishman, and the other two Biscayans. But we shall see."

This speech, coming from a man like Pedro, was far from

reassuring, and tended rather to depress my spirits, though I feigned to laugh at his lack of faith.

Directly night fell, Don Philip, who had explained the situation to his officers, ordered the troops to fall in, and addressed them in a few simple but spirit-stirring words.

Then, led by Pedro, we began slowly to file from the pass, almost in perfect silence.

The rain kept off, but happily for us thick, black clouds hung overhead, effectually screening us from the gaze of chance passers-by. The officers issued their orders in whispers, and the only noise was the faint thud made by the men's sandalled feet.

At length we came to a temporary halt, almost within striking-distance of the fort. All was still, not a light glimmered; it seemed as if the contemplated surprise would be complete.

Don Philip quietly gave the last instructions to his second in command, who was to make the sham attack; and then, turning to Pedro, told him to lead the way.

Slowly, under cover of the friendly darkness, we advanced across an undulating plain to the foot of the cliffs, which at another time we should scarcely have dreamed of scaling, even had they been undefended.

Up we went, toiling painfully, it is true, but still we ascended, and the silence in the fort remained unbroken.

Thus far the enterprise had proved signally successful, and we began to congratulate ourselves that for once our active foes were caught tripping.

I pressed close on the heels of Don Philip, and a dozen

sturdy fellows panted after me, leaving their comrades in the rear.

Suddenly a loud yell and the noise of firing told that the feigned attack had commenced, and Don Philip urged his men to hasten.

Fired by the prospect of victory, the Christinos redoubled their energies, and though I strained every nerve to keep pace, two of them passed me.

Then it was that, without a word of warning, the hill-side blazed with flame, and a storm of bullets swept through our little band.

So unexpected was this reception, that for a few seconds those of us who had escaped stood unable to move.

Don Philip, as was fitting, recovered first from the temporary stupor.

Caution and secrecy could no longer avail aught; the time had come for a daring and reckless bravery.

I could distinguish little of his features, but his eyes flashed through the darkness, and I caught the sheen of his naked sword.

"Forward, my lads, forward!" he cried passionately. "*Viva Isabella Segunda!*"

We took up the cheer, and from the heights above us it was responded to by a mocking laugh and a shout of "*Viva Carlos Quinto!*"

Then I heard Pedro calling, "This way, señor. To the walls, men—over the walls," and the Christinos carried me forward in a burst of momentary fury.

The frenzy of the rush cheated me into the belief that

we should sweep all before us, and I cheered exultingly; but, alas! the force of the wave soon spent itself.

A second volley and a third, each better directed than the initial one, thinned our numbers, and the survivors paused irresolute.

I think that perhaps the darkness paralyzed their energies. Death came to them in a flash from out of the gloom—death, swift, sudden, and unperceived.

Whatever the result might have been, the downfall of Don Philip rendered defeat certain.

Still untouched, I was toiling after Pedro, when a cry of "The colonel's killed!" caused me to turn round.

I had just made out a group of figures, some few paces in the rear, when the Carlists fired for the fourth time, and with a sharp cry of pain Pedro sank on the ground.

By this time the situation had become desperate. As far as could be judged, I was the sole unwounded man left on the hillside. A few of those fatally hit lay groaning in agony, but the others had vanished.

The triumphant cheers of the Carlists rang out above me, and then all was silent.

I ran swiftly to Pedro, and found that he was badly hit.

"Can you walk?" I asked anxiously. "Don Philip is down, and the rest have fled."

The tidings galvanized him into fresh activity. "The cowards!" he exclaimed contemptuously. "Ah, if only they had been the brave Chapelgorris! But, señor, you must go; the Carlists will be here in a few minutes, to finish with knife and bullet the work of death. Señor, I beg that you will go," and in his excitement he half rose from the ground.

"And leave you to be butchered? Hardly likely, my friend; that is not our English custom."

"But, señor, I pray of you, think. Why should you die? The Carlists will be here directly; they will cut you in pieces for sport. Fly, señor, if only for the sake of your English friends."

I seized him by the waist and lifted him to his feet. "Rest on me," I said—"so. Now we will try together."

The poor fellow had been struck in the side, and movement caused him intense pain; but so great was his anxiety on my account that he stifled every sob which rose in his throat.

Half-way down the hill he came to a halt, and raised his hand in warning.

"It is useless," he whispered faintly; "the Carlists are at work. They have begun on the other side; at the bottom of the hill we shall walk into their arms."

Pedro spoke the truth. I could hear in the distance cries of pain mingled with outbursts of mocking laughter, shouts, oaths, *vivas*, and the sounds of men bounding from one spot to another, like hounds on the track of game.

My comrade renewed his appeals that I should seek my own safety; but I refused to abandon him, and breathed a silent prayer for strength to meet my death with fortitude.

Had I been alone I might have escaped, at least for a time, by venturing down the steep cliffs on my right; but hampered by a wounded man—

Yet that was the only chance, and perhaps it were better to die so than to be butchered by the ferocious Carlist soldiery.

I told my idea to Pedro, and he urged me to make the attempt.

Already the Carlists were at the bottom of the pass, and now their comrades from the heights were coming down, stabbing the wounded, and uttering many a brutal jest in their savage glee.

Leaving Pedro for a moment, I went to the edge of the cliffs and peered into the black abyss. The darkness which had hitherto stood us in good stead was now both a help and a hindrance. It hid us from the Carlists, and at the same time prevented us from seeing anything ourselves.

Taking out my sword, I lay flat on the ground and dangled the weapon over the cliff. A paroxysm of joy seized me as the point struck on a ledge of rock, and I could hardly check myself from hurrahing aloud.

"Pedro!" I whispered—he had dragged himself across—"there is ground, solid ground; we are saved."

Getting a firm grip of a piece of rock, I let myself down very cautiously, till my feet found a resting-place, and, scarcely a minute before the Carlists reached the spot, succeeded in placing Pedro by my side.

Hardly daring to breathe, we crouched low in the darkness, while the soldiers, little dreaming that two of the beaten foe were so completely at their mercy, passed by.

For fully an hour we lay without word or movement,

and then everything was hushed once more in the silence of night.

As I had calculated, the move saved our lives for the time being, and the Carlists returned to their stronghold. Except ourselves, the dead alone remained on the hill-side.

Yet the evil was only put off for a little while. Even if we were not discovered by the enemy when daylight came, hunger would compel us to move.

Pedro, whose wound made him half delirious, moaned piteously for water, and I could not let him suffer without attempting to relieve his agony.

"Lie quite still," I said; "I will come back in a few minutes."

Remembering that a stream ran at the foot of the pass, I scrambled up the rock and made my way with caution in its direction.

Once I stumbled over the dead body of a fallen Christino, and a thrill of horror ran through me as my hands came into contact with the soft, wet flesh, for the soldier had been stripped naked by the victorious enemy.

But discomfort and misery, recent fatigue and present peril, were alike forgotten when I came to the side of the sparkling stream, and throwing myself down, drank deeply of the precious liquid.

Then filling my flask and Pedro's water-bottle, I began the return journey, finally rejoining my comrade without mishap.

I do really believe that the Spaniard wept tears of

gratitude when I placed the flask to his lips and bade him drink.

"Señor!" he whispered, "may the good God repay you; I never can."

"Tut!" I answered, "I owe you one or two lives still, and before long shall most likely be further in your debt. Try to sleep; in the morning we must plan some means of escape."

Brave words these last; but the coming of dawn showed clearly how difficult was the task before us. The shelf on which we lay stretched a few yards to our right and left, and then descended abruptly on both sides in straight walls so smooth and of such polished surface that nowhere could even the wild goat have found safe foothold.

A glance to the front of us showed that descent there was equally impracticable, and our only outlet was the path from which we had fled.

"Pedro," I said, "we must camp here till dusk, and then, Carlists or no Carlists, make the best of our way out."

"But this spot is too open, señor; we can be seen from the hill. Yonder, where the bluff overhangs, will be the better place."

Pedro was too weak to walk alone, but with my support he was able to gain that part of the platform where the rocks projected above us.

Here, as his quick sight had discerned, our position was much more secure, since we found ourselves in a natural recess which completely hid us from the view of outsiders.

This change of quarters, indeed, proved our salvation,

and in the following manner. Towards the close of the forenoon we heard the tramp of men in the pass, then the sound of voices, and some one leaped lightly on to the ledge of rock.

Pedro, sick as he was, grasped his sword resolutely, while I, with both pistols at full cock, peeped forth from our hiding-place.

The ghastly spectacle which greeted my sight unnerved me, and I shivered as with an ague. Three Carlist soldiers stood on the edge of the cliff, two of them bearing in their arms a man's dead body.

All three were laughing and chatting gaily, and as I looked they swung their burden far out into the abyss.

Then one made a remark at which his companions laughed uproariously, and the three turned away.

Only when the last of them disappeared did I breathe freely, and my lips trembled as I related to Pedro what had occurred.

He, poor fellow, was beside himself with anger, and lamented bitterly that he could do nothing to avenge his fallen comrade.

"Patience!" I said; "the opportunity will soon come,' but he shook his head mournfully.

However, as the day wore on, and we neither saw nor heard anything further of the enemy, his spirits rose, and he began to canvass the possibility of getting away.

"If the Carlists have not closed the mouth of the pass, there may be a chance," he said; "but I feel so weak."

"Strength will come when you hear the ping of the

bullets," I answered laughingly. "Danger makes a capital tonic."

But when the deepening shadows of evening warranted us in starting, I realized how terribly his weakness would handicap us. It consumed ten minutes of valuable time to get him into the pass at all, and at every step forward he leaned more and more heavily upon me.

The outlook was dreary enough, but I did my best to keep up his spirits, though possessing little confidence myself in a successful termination to the adventure.

We halted at the stream, and when our thirst was quenched, I bathed my comrade's wounded side, and bandaged it with wet rags.

"Ah, señor," he exclaimed gratefully, "now I am better; now I can walk."

This new accession of strength did not last long, and very soon I was forced to support him as before. In that short time, however, we had got out of the pass, and were proceeding across the plain.

The memory of that night of horror dwells with me yet. Even now I sometimes start from my sleep, shuddering in the belief that I am dragging Pedro this way and that, dreading at each moment to hear the crack of a Carlist rifle.

We had gone only a few yards across the plain when my last hope failed. Even in the daylight I should have found it perplexing to steer a proper course for Vitoria, yet it speedily became manifest that I must not expect any assistance from Pedro.

My unfortunate comrade, harassed by the pain of his

wound and fainting from hunger, seemed to lose his mental balance. He walked by my side, but the action was mechanical—there was no purpose in his steps; and had I left him a single instant, he would simply have lain down.

Time and again I begged that he would gather himself together and direct me; but he was hopelessly lost. We formed a striking example of the blind leading the blind.

Hour after hour we stumbled on in the dark, going I knew not where—perhaps round and round in a circle; and I grew sick and dizzy.

Had we come to a road, I should in my misery have followed its course, even had it led straight to a Carlist outpost; but, whether for good or ill, we never left the endless succession of hill and valley.

My comrade hung so upon me that my body ached with the weight of him, and I prayed fervently for the coming of dawn, even though it should expose us to the view of our enemies. Better, I felt, a speedy death than a continuance of this misery, now wellnigh intolerable.

With the opening of day Pedro's strange lethargy began to disappear; he gazed at the barren country with a look of interest.

Then he wrung his hands, crying, "Señor, forgive me; I have led you astray; we are nowhere near Vitoria."

"It is my fault," I answered; "I should have taken proper notice of the route. But where are we? Do you recognize this place?"

He shook his head disconsolately, but made no other reply.

Bad as the situation had been, it was now worse.

At any moment we might be spied by the Carlists, and Pedro could scarcely trail one foot after the other.

With food and a rest we might do much, but how could we obtain them?

"We must look for a wayside house and take the risks," I said. "We can but die there as here."

Again Pedro urged that my life was being sacrificed to no good purpose; but finding that his remarks annoyed me, he desisted, and silently fell in with my suggestion.

Truly we were in a pitiable plight. Everywhere death lay in wait for us, and we were powerless to avert our fate.

I knew perfectly well the terrible risks we ran in seeking shelter; but what else could be done, with both of us almost starving, and Pedro utterly incapable of making much further progress?

At length that which we sought appeared before our eyes. On the slope of a hill we perceived a long, straggling building, comprising, as we knew, houses, stables, piggeries, and offices, all under one roof.

"Courage, Pedro!" I cried; "yonder we shall find food and rest."

"A long rest, señor, from which there will be no awakening."

"Then we will die like men, my friend; you for Spain, I for the honour of merry England."

A weary trudge brought us to the door, which was ajar, and I looked inside.

"Fortune favours us," I said; "our only enemies will be a woman and a boy," and so saying, I boldly entered.

CHAPTER XIV.

BREAD CAST UPON THE WATERS.

THE inmates of the kitchen comprised, as I have said, an old woman, and a boy of perhaps fourteen years, so that we plumed ourselves upon our good fortune.

Whether fear or pity actuated the woman, I could not determine, but whichever the motive, it caused her to treat us with unusual kindness.

Perceiving that Pedro had been injured, she undid the rude bandages, bathed the wound, anointed it with oil, applied fresh wrappings, and all with such deftness and dexterity that I marvelled at her skill.

Then, setting meat and bread on the table, she motioned us to eat, while directly afterwards she produced wine and two cups.

This she did without uttering a word, either voluntarily or in answer to questions, and her example was faithfully copied by the boy, who stood staring at us, open-mouthed.

It must, moreover, be confessed that, on the appearance of food, neither Pedro nor I lost much in speech, nor did we wait for a verbal invitation to begin.

So absorbed indeed were we in our pleasant occupation

that it was only when the eatables had disappeared we noticed that the boy was missing.

I ran to the door and looked out, but could see nothing of him.

Then I addressed the old woman, sternly demanding to know what had become of her companion.

"*Quien sabe?*" she replied coolly. "Perhaps he has gone to water the oxen, or to bring the soldiers; how can I tell?"

"Pedro, the little rascal will betray us," I said; "let us go."

He rose and tottered towards the door, but once outside, stopped.

"Señor, it is hopeless; my time has come," he said. "But with you it is different; you are unhurt, and have time to get away."

While he spoke I was casting round for a suitable spot on which to make our last stand, since it was naturally impossible to adopt his suggestion.

"There is some brushwood yonder," I said, pointing to a spot higher up the hill; "it will afford a little cover. Can you make shift to reach it?"

"I will try," he answered faintly; "but I wish you would leave me. I feel that your blood will be on my head."

We had just reached the brushwood when the tramp of numerous feet told that the Carlists had arrived, and looking out, I saw that the house was surrounded.

In a few moments the leaders came out from the building, and with a shout rushed towards our hiding-place.

"They will offer us quarter, señor," my comrade said, "but you must not accept it; better to die now than be tortured to-morrow."

I nodded in answer, keeping my eyes fixed on the advancing Carlists, and was impressed even in that time of peril by their sturdy appearance.

I had little faith in Pedro's prophecy, believing that our enemies would kill us at the first onset; but while they were still some distance away, the leader gave the order to halt.

Tying a piece of white rag on the end of his sword, and waving it aloft, he called upon us to surrender, promising in that case to spare our lives.

"He lies," whispered Pedro fiercely, "he lies; do not trust him."

Finding that we kept silent, the Carlist officer issued some command to his men, who spreading out came with a run to hem us in.

The spot was ill adapted for a successful defence, as it could easily be turned on three sides, while in front the cover consisted simply of a few bushes.

The weakest position, however, acquires a certain strength when held by desperate men, and certainly none could ever be more utterly reckless than we were on that memorable morning.

Such horrid stories of Carlist butchery circulated throughout the Legion that I actually courted death in preference to being captured; and having emptied my pistols, I sprang sword in hand amongst the crowd with a loud "hurrah."

Now this cry of defiance led strangely enough to quite unexpected results. The Carlists, angered by their losses, pressed savagely around me; a dozen swords were uplifted, when some one called out, "Inglese, Inglese! keep him for the torture."

"Gaspard speaks sense," shouted another; "knock the foreigner down!" and while one vigorous stroke sent my sword spinning into the air, a second stretched me on the earth.

"Lie still, Señor Inglese," said a brawny ruffian, dexterously binding my wrists with cord; "you shall dance enough to-morrow," and the pleasantry, which I but dimly comprehended, was greeted with a volley of brutal laughter.

But the cries of merriment were suddenly drowned by a yell of rage close behind us, and I heard the name "Pedro Gamboa, the Biscayan," uttered in every conceivable form of passion.

Raising my head, I beheld Pedro in the centre of the Carlists, who danced round him in a kind of frenzy, barely able to restrain themselves from plunging their swords into his heart.

"Oh, oh, comrades, we will have rich sport in the morning!" roared one; "bring them along, Pedro and the Englishman; they shall dance together."

One of the men stuck his sword into me as a signal to rise, and being placed in the middle of the column, I was dragged off with my captors.

Once on the march I caught a glimpse of Pedro, and saw that the Carlists were carrying him, as it was manifestly impossible that he could, in his weak condition, keep pace with their long, swinging strides.

Others besides Pedro were being carried too, and three of them would never fight for Don Carlos again.

Happily for my wounded comrade, the march took up little time, and we soon arrived at a dreary-looking, half-deserted village.

A few peasants came into the street and laughed derisively at us, but the soldiers thrust them back, bidding them wait till the morning.

A little distance beyond the village stood a building somewhat larger in dimensions than the others, and here the Carlists halted.

"Señor Englishman," said the chief, with a mocking bow, "this is your lodging for a few hours; you will share it with the traitor Pedro."

I passed into the room, and the men who bore my comrade flung him down without ceremony.

"The accommodation is rather poor, señor," the officer continued, "but you must make the best of it; the inconvenience will be only for a short while."

"Trapped, señor, and kept for the torture," Pedro said, as the door was locked and bolted. "For myself I care little, but thinking of you makes me a woman."

"Courage!" I exclaimed; "at least these savages shall not have the satisfaction of seeing us flinch. But why are they so angry with you?"

"They look on me as a renegade, and believe that I betrayed my comrades. I served with some of these men in the Army of the Faith when King Ferdinand lived. My leader was Rubio."

"Rubio!" I echoed, thinking of our adventure at Bilbao.

"Yes, he is a scoundrel, but scoundrels are of use in these days. What are you trying to do?"

"Gnaw through this cord. You don't suppose that I am going to give up hope while there is a chance of escape!"

Pedro laughed, not unkindly, but rather pityingly. "They will jeer at you, señor, and say that you are a coward."

"I intend getting out if it is feasible, for all that. Will you help me?"

Pedro looked at me stolidly. "Señor," he replied, "in our tongue we have a saying, 'When a friend asks, there is no to-morrow,' yet I warn you that we shall fail. Listen!"

The fastenings of the door were being undone, and half a dozen of the Carlists came in.

They looked at us and laughed tauntingly; but Pedro lay as if asleep, while I regarded them with a contemptuous stare.

Keeping well away from our corner, they squatted on the floor in a half ring, and lighting their cigarettes, began to play some game with a pack of dirty cards; while I, resolute as ever to seize the first opportunity of flight, watched them with ill-concealed interest.

Unhappily the excitement of the game did not lessen their vigilance, and when, during the afternoon, food and drink were brought in for us, they bound my legs securely before untying the cord which fastened my arms.

"Now, Englishman," said one, "your arms are free for the next ten minutes; then they will be tied again."

"Eat, señor," Pedro advised; "it will keep up your strength," and somewhat reluctantly I acted on his counsel.

Towards dusk our jailers lit two lamps, and by the fitful illumination continued their never-ending play.

A long time I kept awake, eagerly observing every single movement; but at length, worn out by fatigue, I fell into a sound slumber.

When I awoke the sun was streaming in through the barred window, and the room was filled with men, who laughed and jested boisterously.

"Come, Señor Inglese; come, Pedro, old friend," shouted one of them; "it is time. We are keeping the spectators waiting."

The men cut the thongs which bound our limbs, and ordered us to rise.

Pedro preserved his demeanour of apathetic indifference, nor could his tormentors wring a sign of suffering from him by taunt or blow.

As we marched through the street of the village he leaned across and whispered, "Forgive me, señor," and I smiled at him cheerfully.

In truth, my attention was mainly occupied by the endeavour to comport myself as an English lad should do in the presence of death.

I did not wish to exhibit a foolish and vain-glorious

bravado, which was altogether foreign to my feelings; but at the same time, I honestly wanted so to bear myself that I might bring no discredit on my country.

Therefore, I walked with head erect and firm step through the thronging crowds that had come in from the outlying districts to see the sport.

I thought of Pym and Dick, my trusty English comrades, and of my friends in that dear mother-land which I should never more revisit.

Our captors halted in an open glade, and fastened us to two stakes, which side by side had been securely driven into the earth.

"Courage, señor!" said Pedro; "it will soon be over."

"What are they going to do?" I asked.

He glanced significantly at two men who, each bearing an armful of partly green wood, now approached, and for an instant my spirits quailed.

Could it be true that the ruffians really intended to burn us?

But the wild clamour of the mob stopped abruptly, and looking up I saw a girl picturesquely dressed come spurring into the glade.

As she reined in her horse, the Carlist leader stepped in front, and making a low obeisance, spoke a few hurried words.

That the speech referred to us I felt assured, and the more so when the girl replied.

Her eyes flashed with contemptuous scorn, and she spoke in anger.

"I tell you, they shall not be tortured," she cried; "I, Juanita Eizmendi, forbid it."

The officer, still carrying on the conversation in a subdued key, spoke again, and his companion rode a few paces towards us.

"An Englishman!" she exclaimed; "why, he is a mere lad."

Then in passable English she said, "What is your name, señor?"

Secretly wondering at the question, I told her who I was, and how I came to be in such an unpleasant position.

She gazed searchingly into my face, and then leaving me in a state of the utmost astonishment, rode back to the officer.

"The señorita is the daughter of a famous Carlist chief who was killed by the Chapelgorris," said Pedro; "I have heard the name of Eizmendi often."

"She seems to be using her influence in our favour," I remarked; "but why, is more than I can tell."

The girl, still on horseback, was surrounded by the Carlist officers, who were arguing vehemently, while the crowd waited impatiently for the sport to begin.

Finally the leader, advancing a few paces, addressed the people, who replied with a howl of rage and menacing gestures.

At the same instant the girl, putting herself at the head of a body of soldiers, rode to the stakes, and gave orders that we should be unbound.

The Carlists, who looked half inclined to mutiny, cut

the cords and immediately formed round us, as much for our protection from the disappointed peasantry as to prevent our escaping.

Half dazed by this unexpected change of fortune, I walked mechanically by Pedro's side, only vaguely realizing that, on account of some unexplained reason, our lives were for the moment spared.

It was well that we were guarded by a strong escort, as otherwise the country people would have torn us piecemeal; and as it was, they made two or three ugly rushes.

It was only when we were once more inside the building that I felt at all safe, and even then I half expected that the angry mob would drag us out by main force.

Instead of thrusting us into our former apartment, our captors marched us up the stone staircase, and on the first landing one of the men threw open a door which led into a small room.

"You will stay there until his majesty's pleasure is known," he said sullenly, and with an evil leer on his face, left us.

The room was destitute of furniture, so we sat down on the bare floor and looked inquiringly at each other.

I asked Pedro what this strange occurrence might signify, but he was at a loss to supply any explanation except one, which I thought out of the question.

"Most likely it is the game which the cat plays with the mouse," he said; "and the end will be the same. As we Spaniards say, 'The mouse does not leave the cat's house with a belly full.'"

"A pithy remark," I answered; "but it does not weaken my confidence in the señorita's goodwill. If she can do anything for us, she will."

"But why?"

"Because she is a girl, and pities us."

"If she is the daughter of Don Manuel Eizmendi, she will show little mercy to the enemies of Don Carlos."

"At all events we still live, and that is something for which to be grateful."

But it appeared that we were to experience further marks of favour. Presently the door was opened, and a soldier carrying food and drink came into the room.

Placing the tray on the floor, he said, "Thank the señorita for this, as well as for your lives."

"We do most heartily," I replied; "and I shall be glad if you will tell her so."

The man mumbled some answer and departed, leaving us more astonished than before.

"'A wise man changes his mind, a fool never,'" quoth Pedro. "I will show wisdom by agreeing with you."

"And gratitude by eating the provisions," I added with a laugh.

"This is a better dish than they gave us yesterday," Pedro observed, as we made an end of the meal, and we fell to speculating again on the reason for the change.

At nightfall the soldier brought in a substantial supper and a couple of thick blankets, the latter of which, more especially, proved a very welcome gift.

Long before this I had, of course, endeavoured to find

a way out of our prison, and had come to the conclusion that the sole means of escape was through the barred window, while to sever the bars a stout file was needed.

Over and over again Pedro and I, in turn and together, tugged and strained at them, but they were too firmly secured, and resisted our utmost strength.

"We might as well spare ourselves the trouble," Pedro said at length; "unless we can get a file, there is no chance of our succeeding."

Several days now passed uneventfully, but one morning we were thrown into a state of excitement by a visit from our fair preserver.

At sight of her, Pedro and I sprang to our feet and bowed courteously.

"The señorita does us much honour," I was beginning, but she checked me.

"This is the wrong time for compliments, Don Arturo; I am the bearer of evil tidings," she said gravely. "Thus far I have been able to protect you from the fury of the people, but I can do so no longer. Even now they are clamouring for your death."

"At least we owe you our warmest thanks for the kindness you have shown to us—strangers and enemies."

"Not exactly strangers," she replied, with an odd smile, "and not always enemies. You do not know me, yet I owe my life to your heroism. I am only returning kindness for kindness. Have you forgotten the unhappy girl at Bilbao?"

"Is it possible that you are the same?" I exclaimed in

astonishment. "But I am at a loss to understand. If you side with Don Carlos, it seems that we delivered you from your friends."

"That is partly the truth," she responded; "and yet you did me a signal service. I fled, not from the soldiers of his majesty, but from evil men who profess allegiance to his cause as a cover for their own ill deeds. However, let us speak of that which more nearly concerns you. The officers have decided upon your execution to-morrow morning, in spite of all my efforts to save you."

"The señor is a brave lad; he does not fear death," Pedro said.

"He is too young to die, and he shall not.—Don Arturo, let me confess the truth. For a time a sense of loyalty to my king held me back, but I hesitate no longer; you shall be free. I have planned everything. Listen. Here is a file, and I give you my pistols; they are loaded. To-night, when it grows dark, you must get through the window; a rope shall be fastened outside by which you can descend in safety. The eyes of my friends will be closed. Keep clear of the village, and follow the road eastward. At the end of a mile you will find an opening through the hills which will lead you to Elgoibar, whence you can travel easily to Cestona. After that you must use your own judgment."

"One moment," I said eagerly, for the girl turned to go. "What will happen when it becomes known that we have fled? We will not buy our safety at your expense."

She raised her head proudly, and her eyes flashed with a haughty disdain.

"The question is well in keeping with your generous character," she replied; "but you can go in confidence. It is true that my power is insufficient to protect you openly, but there are few in our ranks who would dare to raise their hands against the daughter of Manuel Eizmendi. Farewell, señor; we may never meet again—indeed I hope not, since your sword will be drawn against my king and my country."

"Farewell," I said; "perhaps, when this unhappy war is over—" But she would listen to me no more, and with a sorrowful gesture quitted the room.

I waited with impatience until the jailer locked the door, and then, while Pedro talked loudly to drown the noise, started to work at the lowest bar.

Intoxicated by the prospect of coming freedom, I worked away with a will, and soon discovered that the task would not present much difficulty.

At the jailer's usual time of entering we sat down in assumed indifference, and the fellow placed our supper on the floor.

"Eat well, señors," he exclaimed, with a malicious grin; "the next meal may take long in serving."

"Are we to be starved then?" I asked.

"You will find out in the morning," he replied, and with a laugh fastened the door.

Left to ourselves, we ate the food which had been brought, and lay down to wait for the coming of darkness.

As far as we were concerned, everything was in readiness; the bars were sawn so nearly through that a vigorous pull would wrench them asunder, and the way would be clear.

"Suppose the señorita has failed in getting the rope fixed," I suggested.

"Then we must go without," answered my comrade doggedly. "Rope or no rope, I have spent my last night in a Carlist prison."

I walked to the door and listened. All was silent in the corridor, and the house seemed wrapped in sleep.

I felt that the time had come; delay now could only prove dangerous, and in a whisper I bade Pedro break the bars.

"Do you feel the rope?" I asked, as he squeezed his head through the opening.

"Yes, it is here, tied to a hook in the wall. Shall I go first?"

"Yes, and wait for me at the bottom."

Leaning out of the window, I groped for the rope, and with an inward prayer for safety, slid to the ground almost into Pedro's arms.

"Those who fixed the rope will remove it," he whispered; "let us get away, and may God bless Juanita Eizmendi."

"Amen to that," I said fervently, and fingering one of her pistols—I had given Pedro the other—stepped out in the darkness.

A fire blazed on the hill which had so nearly witnessed our execution, but upon that we turned our backs, and walked briskly along the road to the path of which the señorita had spoken.

Occasionally Pedro was brought to a halt by the pain in his side, but for the most part he pushed along bravely, buoyed up by the knowledge that every step led us farther from danger.

"Once at Cestona, we are safe," he said. "From that place I can lead you into San Sebastian in spite of the Carlists, or we can go to Bilbao."

"We will make for San Sebastian; I am anxious to meet with my friends of the Legion."

"Very good, señor; then San Sebastian it shall be."

It was still dark when we passed Elgoibar, but Pedro was now on familiar ground, and led the way as confidently as if the sun shone; while from the señorita's words we felt sure that little danger would be met with from the Carlists in this direction.

This proved to be the case, as we arrived at Cestona without mishap, and found that village occupied by a detachment of Christinos, whose officer received us with great kindness.

"If you don't mind, señor, we will stay here a few hours while I get my wound attended to," Pedro said, and with this of course I willingly complied.

CHAPTER XV.

UNDER FIRE.

IT had been our intention to leave Cestona in the evening, but the surgeon who examined Pedro insisted that the wounded man should remain in the village for several days at least, and I decided to stay with him.

My comrade chafed sorely at this compulsory inaction, although the officer in command of the Christino detachment assured us that nothing of importance was going on elsewhere.

The Carlists, he said, had surrounded San Sebastian with triple lines of entrenchments so strongly fortified as to be considered impregnable, and intended, on the arrival of their heavy artillery, to bombard the town.

For the present, however, all was quiet, and indeed the weather forbade the carrying on of any warlike operations.

Scarcely a day or night passed without a heavy downpour of rain, which rendered even the level roads practically impassable for vehicles, while it had also the minor effect of keeping me shut up in the dirty little village inn.

At length, about ten days after our arrival, the surgeon pronounced Pedro capable of travelling, and the Spanish officer very kindly gave us what information he could concerning the Carlist positions.

"From here to Onio," he said, "you are not likely to meet with danger; but keep well away from the main road, which is in the enemy's possession. The difficulties will begin after you pass Onio, for the Carlists have numerous outposts, and their fortifications stretch to within half a mile of San Sebastian itself."

"Then the best plan will be to strike straight for the coast, hide ourselves during the night, and slip into the town at dawn," said Pedro.

"Yes, but go to work carefully. You will be placed between two fires, and our friends are likely to do you as much harm as the enemy."

This idea, though far from pleasing, was undoubtedly true; and I suggested that it might be safer to make for Bilbao, and take our chance of finding some craft going to San Sebastian.

This plan, however, was open to several serious objections, so I did not press it, especially as Pedro expressed his confidence in being able to get past the Carlist lines.

Finally we set out amidst the good wishes of the Spaniards, who supplied us with both food and weapons.

"If the war lasts, Pedro, I shall learn as much about the country as you know yourself," I remarked, and my comrade laughed pleasantly.

Happily little rain had fallen since the preceding day, and we jogged along comfortably enough over the hills, through brake and fern, with the spreading oaks and the chestnuts waving their newly-leaved branches above our heads.

Here and there, too, we caught glimpses of neat cottages peeping through the trees, surrounded by gardens and orchards, and occasionally by small patches of sprouting corn.

Down the slopes ran numerous streams, somewhat swollen by the recent rains, yet cheering to the sight nevertheless.

So calm was the scene, so thoroughly peaceful and home-like, that for the time I could almost have brought myself to believe that the cruel war existed only in my imagination.

Alas! in what sombre colours was the truth to be displayed even before the rising of another sun!

But of the future, happily, we were ignorant, and we walked along with scarcely a thought of sorrow.

Pedro, however, was too wary a campaigner to allow himself to be deceived by external appearances. He picked his way carefully, and ever as we advanced his keen glance shot from right to left in search of possible foes.

After passing Onio he turned westward for a little distance, and then once more bore due north.

Towards evening the clouds began to gather again in heavy masses, and just as we entered a thick wood the storm burst.

"This will suit us well," my comrade said. "We can rest here a while under the shelter of the trees without fear of discovery; the Carlists will stay close by their watch-fires to-night."

"But we must not be too far from San Sebastian when the dawn breaks."

"If all goes well, we shall be at the convent of San Bartolome between three and four o'clock in the morning. Meanwhile, we may as well make ourselves comfortable. Here is a place that will do famously; we shall hardly get wet even."

He led the way to a miniature dell surrounded by branching chestnuts, and sitting down on a heap of bracken, we prepared to pass the time with as much patience as we could muster.

For nearly two hours the storm raged with unusual violence, and then suddenly stopped, causing me to fear that after all the night would be too fine to suit our purpose.

In this supposition I was fortunately mistaken. Although the rain had ceased and the wind moderated its fury, black clouds still obscured the sky, and we could not discern a single star.

"Now, señor," said Pedro, as we prepared to move out, "come quietly. Everything is in our favour; and if we are taken, the fault will be our own."

"I will be careful," I answered; "I don't mean to fall a second time into the hands of the Carlists."

"We must keep clear of that. As my countrymen say, 'He who stumbles twice over one stone deserves to break his shins.'"

On the outskirts of the wood my comrade paused and bade me look to the east, where the flames from numerous watch-fires shone with a ruddy glow.

Then, turning his back upon them, he struck out at a swift pace, meaning to make a wide sweep, which would bring us back to the ground between the first Carlist outpost and the town.

Over the open spaces Pedro walked quickly, and I followed without question, well content to trust my safety in his keeping.

Occasionally he stopped and listened, but no sound broke the silence of the night.

At first we went westward, but gradually began to bend back, and my comrade redoubled his caution.

Had I been alone, the expedition must have ended in disaster; but Pedro's familiarity with the district enabled him to avoid the most serious dangers, and eventually to bring us within a few yards of the Hernani road, at a point several paces to the south of the San Bartolome convent.

It was now about three o'clock in the morning, and unless the garrison fired upon us by mistake, we were out of danger.

I stood leaning against a tree trunk and wondering whether the Legion had arrived in San Sebastian, when Pedro suddenly sank on the wet, clayey soil.

"Down, señor," he whispered; "listen! do you hear that noise?"

I placed my ear to the ground, but could detect no sound, and said so.

My comrade, more keen of hearing, declared that he could distinguish the tramp of a large body of men marching from the town towards the convent, and soon it became plain to me also.

This was an unexpected incident, and increased the difficulty of the situation.

Two questions immediately presented themselves for answer: What was the explanation of this movement? and how would it affect us?

The same thought came to us both. The Legion had arrived in San Sebastian, and General Evans was about to assault the Carlist positions.

"We must make ourselves known as quickly as possible, before the troops move forward," I said.

"Wait," replied Pedro; "there is a party coming this way."

By this time the main body had come to a halt near the convent, and now we could perceive a few men advancing along the road.

They drew up right opposite us, and one of them, evidently an officer in high command, spoke softly to the others, most probably issuing his final instructions.

As they turned to go back he raised his voice a trifle, and then I knew him to be the brigadier-general commanding the brigade of which Pym's regiment formed a part.

"General Chichester," I cried, but not too loudly, "don't fire; we are friends who have escaped from the Carlists," and bidding Pedro come after me, I left my hiding-place and walked over to the knot of officers.

"Who are you?" asked the general sternly, taken aback at my appearance.

"Arthur Powell, sir; a volunteer in the Legion, which I left at Vitoria."

"Powell!" he said kindly; "why, my lad, this is against all the rules; you are mustered out of the service, marked 'dead' some weeks ago. However, you have turned up at a good time. Who is the other man?"

"Pedro Gamboa, sergeant in the Spanish army, and a sterling soldier."

"Has he guided you past the Carlist pickets?"

"Yes, general."

"He is trustworthy, you say?"

"You have but to try him."

"Then he is the right man in the right place.—Sergeant Gamboa, will you place yourself under my orders?"

"Yes, your excellency; but I must report myself to General Jauregui as soon as I can."

"Come with me, then; I will put things right with El Pastor.—Powell, you will find Captain Forrester with his company.—Gentlemen, it is time to be moving."

At the convent I saw the men of the Legion drawn up, and pressing closely after General Chichester, made my way to the left, where his brigade was stationed.

My heart bounded as I caught sight of Pym at the head of his company, yet there was little in our meeting which to an outsider would have betokened the intensity of our feelings.

"Thank God, Arthur!" he said with suppressed emotion, as I grasped his hand; "Don Philip told us to give up hope."

"I thought he was killed."

"No, but badly wounded.—Steady there, men; close up, cover your files, and be silent; there must be no talking. —Ah! there goes Reid's brigade to the right."

"Are the Irish in the centre?"

"Yes. I fancy General Shaw will have the bulk of the fighting to do."

"Where is the rest of your regiment?"

"At Santander, and all the Fourth; but Evans decided to attack without them.—Now, my lads, as quietly as you can; and mind, no firing."

It was certainly marvellous with what little noise the men succeeded in marching off the ground.

The nearest Carlist outpost was scarcely more than two hundred yards away, yet the enemy apparently remained in complete ignorance of our movements.

Guided by Pedro, we advanced swiftly but silently to our point of attack, when suddenly a musket shot was heard from the centre. Swift as lightning-flash this was answered by a volley from the nearest Carlist picket, and then, in quick succession, volley after volley came from the different pickets all along the enemy's lines.

There was no further need of caution. "Forward!" shouted our chief, and "Forward!" was the cry of every officer.

Such a medley of sounds arose as to be almost indescribable. The whiz of the bullets, the groans of wounded men, the shouts of those not hit, the encouraging cheers of the officers, the *vivas* of the Carlists, all mingled together in a strange confusion.

"Come on, men," I heard General Chichester say; "don't stop to fire—use your bayonets. Over this wall—drive them out."

We had arrived at a stone wall several feet in height, behind which a party of Carlists lay in concealment, and they saluted us with a rattling volley.

Several men dropped; but the rest of us clambered over somehow, and the enemy did not wait for the touch of steel. Not that they feared us, but their plan was to seek the shelter of every bit of cover, from behind which they could do terrible execution with little harm to themselves.

Away they went, active and nimble as mountain-cats, scudding across the field in the grey of the morning, eager to get behind the next wall, while we, forbidden to fire, lumbered after them. I say lumbered, because fleet of foot as some of our men were, the Carlists outpaced them with the greatest ease.

Half-way across the field stood a house from which, as we neared it, was poured forth a telling fire.

"Captain Forrester, take your company and clear that building," said the general; "then follow us."

"Come on, lads," cried Pym, waving his sword; "never mind who falls; we mustn't lose the brigade."

Then it was as we darted off to the right that I saw Dick, who came up to my side.

"Back again, sir," he said cheerily; "I told the captain you were bound to turn up.—Push on, lads; are we going to let the captain take the place by himself?" for Pym was several lengths in advance.

"Mind the ditch, men," called back Pym; "there's a ditch round the house—this way," and with a flying leap he cleared the trench, followed by Dick and myself, together with twenty others.

The building was loopholed for musketry, and the Carlists seemed determined to hold it.

Perhaps, however, the sight of their comrades in retreat disheartened them, as after delivering one volley they withdrew from the windows; and while we burst in the doors on one side, they rushed out at the other.

Meanwhile the remainder of the brigade had met with a stubborn opposition. We could perceive that they were still attempting to clear the wall, and there seemed to be no stop to the rattle of musketry.

The men whom we had dislodged from the house, scattering far and wide, were speedily out of sight, to reform doubtless behind the next wall, while we ran after Pym to where Chichester's weak brigade was opposing the enemy.

At this spot the Carlists were strongly entrenched. The ground immediately beyond the field rose abruptly, and at the bottom they had cut a deep and wide ditch; while the slope itself was defended by walls, earthworks, and barricades of barrels filled with soil.

As I have stated, General Chichester's brigade was weakened by the absence of the Fourth Regiment and the major portion of the Eighth, while the few hundred Spanish regulars under his command did not appear particularly anxious to meet the withering fire of their compatriots.

The battle by this time had become general, and from all quarters rose the sounds of the conflict.

The Irishmen, led by General Shaw, were going forward with splendid resolution, reserving their fire, clearing wall after wall at the bayonet's point, until they approached the wind-mill battery, loopholed for five hundred Carlists, who stood each man at his post.

Their shrill "hurrah" as they dashed at the post came floating over to us, and at the same time we prepared for a final attempt to break through our portion of the lines.

On the wall, and then over, the officers leading; in the ditch, some dead or wounded, others scrambling up the wet sides; on the hill slope, pushing, slipping, struggling, some falling with a half-uttered cheer yet on the lips, while their comrades, pausing only to speak the dead man's name, pressed on with renewed ardour.

The Carlists fought with dogged stubbornness, holding each barricade till it was no longer tenable, and then, under cover of a well-directed volley, retreating with marvellous celerity to the next.

Step by step, however, we advanced, winning our way, until the last obstacle was cleared and the enemy in full flight towards their second lines.

General Chichester drew us up, and spoke a few words of praise, but the halt was only a temporary one. An officer whom I recognized as being on the staff of General Evans came galloping with fresh orders to be at once executed.

Thus far the attack had been perfectly successful, but

now a more serious trial awaited us. The first line had been carried at a heavy cost; the second was likely to be defended with still greater tenacity.

Hitherto we had been favoured by the partial darkness; now, in the morning light, the enemy could observe every movement, and prepare accordingly for our reception.

Moreover, it was quite plain that this second line of defence was far stronger than the first. Fortification after fortification rose, one behind the other, on a series of heights, some of which were defended by heavy cannon, while, commanding all, towered the strongly-built and entrenched redoubt of Lugariz.

Towards this post our course lay through enclosed fields, over walls, across ditches, past loopholed houses, while every single bit of cover sheltered a lynx-eyed Carlist.

"We shall have warm work, Arthur," said Pym, wiping his face; "but a victory to-day will do away with the idea held by some of our friends at home, that the Legion can't fight."

"This will be the last day's fighting for a good many of us, Forrester," said Major Mitchell, a gallant young officer attached to the Eighth Regiment, and the remark came back to me with a peculiar significance when, a couple of hours later, I saw the body of the speaker, who had been mortally wounded while heading a desperate charge.

At the time, however, we had scant leisure for thinking. By a simultaneous movement the three brigades marched forward to the attack, and very shortly we were again in the thick of the flying bullets.

On our immediate left were the three regiments which composed the Irish Brigade, and I saw that the Seventh had already suffered severely.

But now, as we advanced, the Carlist artillery thundered out, and ball after ball ploughed a passage through our ranks.

Still we went on, closing up silently when each fresh gap was formed; but the men began to show signs of impatience, and only the habits fostered by firm discipline prevented them from rushing to the attack in a tumultuous throng.

At length we reached the first position, and having cleared it after a protracted struggle, found ourselves under temporary cover.

But the real work was only just beginning. The heights above us were strongly held by the enemy, who, directly we moved into the open, shattered the head of the brigade by a murderous fire.

Again and again we charged up the incline only to be thrown back in disorder.

The nature of the ground prevented our maintaining any regular formation. Walls and ditches, deeply-cut trenches, ingeniously-fixed barricades confronted us almost everywhere, so that our men were compelled to break up into small groups, each endeavouring to force an opening.

It seemed as if the whole hillside had been sown with muskets, in such thick showers did the bullets fall, while officers and men alike dropped fast.

In one of these mad rushes I lost sight of Pym, and was

borne onward by a crowd of men belonging to the First Regiment, who appeared bent upon forcing a way at all costs.

Higher and higher we climbed, shouting in triumph at our success, when suddenly a hundred muskets rang out a few yards above us, and the gallant little party dropped almost to a man.

The few who were left standing turned and ran, and I with them.

Pym, who was now in command of the shattered two companies, and, indeed, almost the sole officer of the Eighth unhurt, was sorrowfully reforming his men.

I gave a glance along the ranks, and my heart throbbed with pain; Dick was missing.

Pym saw and understood the cause of my despair. "I hoped he was with you," he said.

I shook my head sadly, and was running back, when a man called out, "Sergeant Truscott is on the far side of yonder ditch, sir. He's badly hit—dead, most likely, by this time; the Carlists are taking pot-shots at all the wounded."

I looked at Pym, who led his men forward to the very edge of the cover, and directed them to keep up a heavy fire.

"It's no good, captain," cried one; "the sergeant's dead, and you'll be killed before you go a dozen yards."

Pym did not answer, but, turning to me, said, "Ready, Arthur?"

I nodded, and away we went shoulder to shoulder in

the wild race, heedless of the bullets which whizzed past us or tore up the ground at our feet.

I ran like one in a dream, conscious only that Dick lay dead or badly wounded, and that I must bring him in at all hazard.

Once my foot slipped, and I fell headlong; but before Pym could pause, I was on my feet and rushing forward as before.

Many a time my comrade and I had raced against each other in sport, but never at this pace. Pym's face was deadly white, and his eyes seemed starting from their sockets, while I, no doubt, presented a similar appearance.

Still we were unharmed, and now only the ditch separated us from our trusty friend. I was on the point of leaping in; but Pym, who could not speak, motioned to go round by the lower side, thinking in that way to give the Carlists less chance of hitting us.

Dick's eyes were wide open, and he looked up with an affectionate smile. "God bless you, brave lads!" he murmured; "but you shouldn't have risked your lives for me."

We bent over to raise him, and I shall never forget the moment when we stood upright, with him in our arms. As if by common consent the firing stopped, and it seemed to me, judging by the volume of sound, that all the Legion had gathered together in order to cheer us.

The soul-stirring British "hurrah" fired my blood, and I knew that my cheeks were crimson with pleasure, for I was by no means insensible to praise.

The truce was short; the Carlists began firing anew, and the return journey was attended by much greater danger, as we were forced to proceed slowly.

It was done at length; and a great shout went up from the men of the brigade when, panting and exhausted, but unwounded, we staggered into cover, and laid Dick gently on the ground.

Some one asked if the sergeant still lived, and hearing that he did, gave him some brandy; while others crowded around us, eager to assure themselves that we were unhurt.

"Bravely done!" exclaimed the brigadier, who now came up; and then a familiar voice said, "A gallant deed, and a kindly one.—Soldiers, the Legion is honoured by possessing such officers."

The speaker was General Evans, and as he caught sight of me, his face betrayed the astonishment which he felt.

"Powell!" he exclaimed, stretching out his hand, "I thought you were killed!"

"Not yet, sir," I answered; and then the brigadier spoke a few words in a low tone to his chief.

The general addressed himself again to me, but I could not understand his words nor distinguish his features; the ground rocked to and fro, my head grew dizzy, and had not Pym caught me in his arms, I should have fallen heavily.

"He must have been hit," one of the officers said, and then I fainted.

CHAPTER XVI.

I RECEIVE PROMOTION.

THE first words which greeted me upon recovering consciousness were, "Are you better, señor?" spoken in Spanish; and starting up, I beheld Pedro, whose head had been cut by a splinter of shell.

"Where are the others?" I asked. "Where is the sergeant?"

"The English soldier has been taken away in the ambulance; the Legion has carried the second line of entrenchments, and is getting ready to assault the Lugariz fort."

"Then I must go; my place is at the front."

"It is impossible, señor; the general directed that you should be taken to the hospital."

"I'm all right, Pedro," I answered lightly; "the Carlists didn't touch me. I must have fainted, but that was all."

Then I went on, slowly at first, picking my way between the dead bodies that strewed the hill which had been so obstinately defended by the Carlists.

In the distance rose the sounds of cheering, the rattle of musketry, the booming of cannon, and I knew that my comrades were engaged in a desperate task.

Pedro, loyal-hearted as ever, kept by my side, having plainly resolved that death alone should part us.

As we approached nearer to the scene of conflict, we found that the battle now raged entirely round the fort of Lugariz, to hold which the Carlists were straining every nerve.

It stood on the top of a steep hill, the sides of which, formed of red clay and wet with heavy rains, offered an almost insuperable obstacle to a successful charge.

Up to this time it was clear that our men had made little progress; but suddenly a mighty shout heralded some fresh movement, and mounting a barricade, I saw two war-ships steaming closely into the shore.

Almost immediately a joyful cry ran through the Legion: "The regiments from Santander!" and rushing down to the foot of the Lugariz hill, I made my way to where Pym stood with the remnant of his company.

He shook his head at me reproachfully, and was about to speak, but a cheer from his men prevented him.

"Here comes old Godfrey with our boys," cried one. "Now the Carlists 'll catch it. Give 'em a rousing cheer, lads," and the wearied soldiery responded with a will.

"Glad to see you, Godfrey," said General Chichester to the colonel; "you have come at a good time. Take your regiment up the hill, and turn the enemy out of the fort."

"Very good," replied the colonel coolly.—"Steady, men! Attention! With cartridge, prime and load; but not a shot without orders," and having given the word, he led his men into the open at the double.

Up they went in gallant style, while the bullets tore through their ranks, and the cannon balls crashed amongst the trees or ploughed the ground at their feet.

Higher and higher they mounted, while we who looked on cheered again and again as obstacle after obstacle was surmounted.

And now Captain Henderson of the *Phœnix*, which had anchored close to the shore, opened a tremendous fire upon the fort, and the example was followed by his gallant colleague in the *Salamander*. Nor were the guns belonging to the Legion idle. Bomb succeeded bomb, rocket after rocket rushed hissing through the air, while the cannon balls battered against the walls of the redoubt.

The noise was terrific, the destruction great, but the Carlists proved themselves foemen of mettle. Undaunted by the havoc, they stuck gallantly to their posts, returning, as far as they were able, shot for shot from their big guns, and keeping up a heavy fire upon the advancing regiments.

Just then Pym received orders to take the two remaining companies of the Eighth forward; and away we dashed, eager to have a share in the victory.

But the battle was nearly over. The fort was taken; the Carlists were in full retreat. They had done all that brave men could do, and, though beaten, were most assuredly not disgraced.

When we reached the fort we saw them running swiftly down the slope towards a farmhouse, with the men of the Legion hot on their track.

"Take your company forward, Forrester," cried the colonel; "that house must be cleared," and Pym gave the word of command to his men.

It was the enemy's last effort, and a gallant one, though futile.

But the soldiers of the Legion, having tasted of victory, could not be withstood.

Leaping the walls and ditches, scrambling through the hedges, heedless of the fallen, the survivors swept on and burst without a check into the building.

Having outstripped Pym's company, I was in time to enter amongst the first. Several of the Carlists were yet in the house, and a number of the brave but cruel Chapelgorris rushed towards them with savage cries.

I knew that to balk them of their prey would most likely be the signal for my own death; yet it was out of the question to stand there and idly look on at such a scene of bloodshed.

Without further hesitation I sprang between the two parties, crying in Spanish, "For shame, Spaniards! would you bring disgrace on the cause by such cruelty?" Then in English I continued, "Men of the Legion, are you British soldiers or savages? Will you let these men be butchered, or will you help me to save them?"

"Let 'em be," called back one surlily; "they stabbed our mates fast enough when they got the chance."

This was true and could not be gainsaid, but fortunately a few of the more humane ranged themselves by my side.

Turning to the Carlists, I bade them lay down their

arms. "You are my prisoners," I said; "I am an English officer—your lives are safe."

The moment had been full of peril, but now the danger was past; several officers of the Legion entered the room, and the Chapelgorris were compelled, reluctantly, to forego their vengeance.

Pym had drawn up his company in the orchard, and suggested that the prisoners, having been disarmed, should be marched back in the midst of his men—a plan which I gladly adopted.

The battle had meanwhile ended, and while the army was being re-formed on the heights, for the purpose of ascertaining the number of the killed and wounded, I hurried into San Sebastian.

Dick had been carried into the San Elmo hospital, and the orderly at once conducted me to the bed where he lay.

At first he seemed to be sleeping, but as I bent over him, his eyes opened and he smiled.

"Not hurt!" he said; "thank God for that! I was afraid you had thrown your life away for mine. And the captain, where is he?"

"On the field with his regiment; he has not a scratch."

There was no mistaking the genuine pleasure which the sick man's face showed at these tidings.

"Now my mind's easy, and I shall get better," he said. "How did the fight finish?"

"We have captured all the positions, but at a heavy loss."

"Ah! these Carlists are tough customers; they'll give

us plenty of trouble before we've done with them," and I quite agreed with his remark.

I told him of the part the Eighth Regiment had taken in the battle—a piece of information which gratified him extremely.

Presently, with a glance round the apartment, he said, "This is a sight better than Vitoria; the natives have been bringing in things all day, and our fellows are treated just like the Spaniards; they don't seem to make any difference."

Dick's praise was well deserved. The apartment was large and lofty; the beds, with everything belonging to them, were scrupulously clean; and the surgeons were clever, kind-hearted men, under whose treatment the patients would have every chance of recovery.

Dick's wound was in the leg, but the doctor who had made a casual examination did not anticipate any serious trouble. Considerably cheered by this intelligence, I left the hospital and returned to the battle-field, intending to pass the night with Pym.

Pym's first inquiries naturally bore upon the condition of our wounded comrade, and I delivered the surgeon's report.

"That's a weight off my mind," he said; "I should be sorry if any grievous hurt happened to poor old Dick. You see, I feel a certain responsibility, because if I had not joined the Legion he would have been in England now."

"That is probable, but not, I think, absolutely certain; he has always been partial to an adventurous life. Have the returns been made out yet?"

"Not officially, but our loses are heavy. It is reckoned that a hundred officers and about nine hundred men are either killed or wounded. Have you seen the general?"

"Not since the morning. I thought to-morrow would be soon enough to show myself, as I have nothing particular to tell him."

"Remember I have heard little of the story beyond the fact that the expedition failed."

"Totally!" And I related what happened up to the moment when the assailants fled.

"Don Philip was brought into Vitoria half dead," he interposed. "I didn't see him myself, but those who did said his grief was pitiful to witness."

"I am not surprised, he counted so surely upon capturing the castle."

"How came you to be beaten?"

"Well, in the first place, the southern Spaniards are no match for the Carlists; and, secondly, the latter were prepared for our coming. The surprise was on the wrong side."

"Then they gave you a hot reception?"

"So hot that I doubt if the Legion would have faced it."

"But I can't understand why you were left behind. You were not wounded?"

"No, but my old ally Pedro was."

Pym nodded. "That lets in the light," he said thoughtfully; "you risked your life to save his. I might have guessed it was something like that. Go on, Arthur; tell me all about it."

His brow clouded when I described the scene in the glade, and he uttered an exclamation of anger. "What savages they are!" he said.

"But the Chapelgorris equal them in ferocity."

"True enough. How strange that there is always so much more cruelty in a civil war than in one between two different nations! But we will leave the moralizing till another season. I am burning with impatience."

"Which is less painful than burning in reality—an experience which we only just missed. But you shall hear."

At the mention of the señorita, he interrupted me, crying, "The princess! Arthur, the princess! My romance is working out apace. Here ends the second chapter."

"You have guessed rightly, Pym. My deliverer was the princess herself. But that affair of her rescue was strangely muddled. She is, it seems, a thorough Carlist, so that our desperate ride was undertaken in order to save her from her friends."

"A good many people would be glad to have that done for them," he interposed with a sly twinkle.

"Perhaps so, but it is comical to look back on. Her real assailant was a noted mountain robber named Rubio, who has apparently joined hands with the Carlists."

"Then your princess is a great heiress, as I prophesied. The scoundrel intended either making her his wife or holding her to ransom. Bravo, Arthur! the story grows in interest."

"The reality was exciting enough," I observed, and proceeded to relate the manner of our escape.

"I wonder what has become of Pedro," I said, when Pym had finished talking about my adventures.

"Gone off to his own people, most likely; you will find him to-morrow."

"If he is alive."

"Yes, that is an important consideration, but there isn't any reason why you should doubt it; the odds are in his favour."

We slept that night on the field of battle, and the next morning, after formally reporting myself to General Evans, I sought the Spanish lines.

El Pastor's first words were a proof of Pedro's safety.

"I have to thank you, señor," said the Spanish general, "for your gallant devotion to one of my countrymen. Sergeant Gamboa came in last night, and has told us of your noble conduct."

"I only did my duty, general, such as any man would have done. I could not desert the comrade who had once saved my life."

"It was a generous deed, señor; and her majesty's ministers shall be informed of it."

I thanked the speaker, and inquired if Pedro would remain in San Sebastian.

"Yes," El Pastor replied; "yesterday's work has created many vacancies, and I have room for a man like Gamboa."

We chatted together some time longer, and then, having spoken with several of his staff who were known to me, I returned to the position occupied by the Eighth Regiment.

The look of sorrow on the officers' faces made it plain that some misfortune had occurred, and in answer to my implied question Pym told me that Major Mitchell had died in the hospital.

"There was not a more daring officer in the Legion," said my comrade mournfully, "nor one more beloved."

I remembered how he fell at the head of his regiment, in perhaps the very fiercest charge of the whole battle, and how, stricken to death though he was, he still waved his sword and faintly cheered his soldiers on.

Yesterday, young, brave, handsome, loved by his men, respected by all; and now—

Ah, well, he had died a soldier's death, and it was fitting that he should receive a soldier's burial.

The scene on that lovely summer day when his body was committed to the grave lingers still in my memory.

It seemed as if all San Sebastian had gathered to pay homage to the fallen officer. The balconies along the line of route were filled with Spanish ladies, who looked on, many of them with moistened eyes, all with unaffected grief.

In the great square General Evans stood amidst a host of officers belonging to every regiment in the Legion, who waited sorrowfully for the coming of the solemn pageant.

El Pastor, too, together with the chiefs of his division, had assembled to pay their token of respect to the dead hero; while in striking contrast with the waving plumes, the gold lace and bright-coloured uniforms, were to be seen the civilian costumes of San Sebastian's leading inhabitants.

Suddenly the solemn stillness was broken by the impressive notes of the Dead March, and the Eighth Regiment—the soldiers with their arms reversed—marched into the square. Here the procession was joined by the officers, and with slow, measured steps, it began to wind up the steep hill, where, in a little nook hidden amongst the craggy boulders, the major's last resting-place had been prepared.

The spectacle was one many times to be repeated before the survivors of the Legion left that ill-starred country; but none, I think, made such a vivid impression upon me.

It was with a feeling of depression that, on the conclusion of the ceremony, when the last volley had been fired, and the soldiers marched back to the strains of some gaily-played music, I went to visit Dick.

"You have been burying a gallant fellow," said he, "and one that everybody loved. Some officers are brave enough, but Major Mitchell was more than that—he was kind."

"Yes, the men will feel his loss," I assented.

"Well, it will mean a step up for the captain, I suppose; he deserves promotion, if any one does."

I had been too busy thinking about the dead man to reflect that his death would leave a vacancy for another, and I shuddered a little at Dick's remark.

"It doesn't sound nice," he admitted; "but, after all, the living count more than the dead, and I shall be proud to salute Mr. Forrester as major."

At this point the surgeon's visit interrupted our conversation, and I took my leave, promising to call again when opportunity offered.

I did not, of course, broach the subject to Pym; but a day or two later his appointment as major was officially announced, and his well-merited promotion caused the liveliest satisfaction amongst the men of the Eighth Regiment.

That same evening an orderly brought a message directing me to proceed at once to the general's quarters.

The chief was conversing with several of his principal officers, but he stopped on my entrance, and smiled kindly.

"Well, Powell," he said; "so you have come out of the fight all right. How is the sergeant?"

"Mending nicely, sir; Doctor Martin hopes to have him fit for duty before long."

"That was a very gallant action of yours and Forrester's, but not so brave as that of sticking to the Spaniard."

This speech took me by surprise, as I had said nothing concerning Pedro except to Pym, and I stammered out a halting reply.

The general enjoyed my confusion, and laughed good-naturedly.

"Powell is clearly one of those who 'do good by stealth, and blush to find it fame,'" observed one of his officers.

"Rather an uncommon trait in these days," replied the general. Then, addressing me, he went on: "General Jaureguy has told us the story, and it does you the utmost credit. To do as you did down there at Ovaro shows a far truer bravery than exposing yourself to the enemy's bullets in the heat of battle."

"I did what I thought to be my duty, sir."

"And we are proud of you. I speak not for myself alone, but for all the gentlemen with me."

Several of the officers were Spaniards on the general's staff, and one of them, a tall, stately man, coming forward, shook my hand.

"Señor," he said, "allow me to thank you on behalf of my countrymen for your generous and humane conduct; we shall not readily forget it."

Again I tried to speak, but could not; this unexpected praise overpowered me.

But a further surprise was in store, and I could scarcely believe my ears when the general said, "This is a fitting time to redeem the promise which I made you last year. General Chichester has offered to take you as an extra aide-de-camp; you will, therefore, join his staff with the rank of captain."

"You will have every opportunity of being in the front," said the brigadier-general laughingly.

I cannot pretend to describe exactly what took place after that, but the interview must have come to an end somehow, as I presently found myself outside and hurrying to tell Pym the great news.

The dear fellow congratulated me with a hearty enthusiasm, and I must confess that very little sleep visited me on that memorable night.

I soon discovered that, as General Chichester had hinted, my new post would be far from a sinecure; and though nothing of consequence occurred during the next three weeks, he found me plenty of work, which kept my time fully occupied.

The morning of the twenty-eighth of May had been selected on which to make a further forward movement, having for its object the capture of Pasages, a seaport lying east of San Sebastian, and now in the hands of the Carlists.

For several hours I was busy carrying orders to the various posts, but when the dawn broke the preparations were complete.

Down by the edge of the Urimea, which we had to cross, Colonel Colquhoun's thirty cannon were drawn up, but hidden from the Carlists by the high embankments. Behind the walls and houses the various regiments stood in close column until the word was given, when General Chichester's brigade marched into the open.

Immediately the Carlists came down from the opposite heights in order to oppose the passage of the river. But now the artillery boomed out; thirty pieces of cannon sent shot and shell crashing into the enemy's columns; the earth quivered; everything was enveloped in thick clouds of black smoke, and under its cover we advanced at the double into the swiftly-flowing stream.

Pym had brought my horse from Vitoria, and the gallant little animal, plunging and snorting, carried me safely over.

The Carlists, terribly shaken by the artillery fire, did not attempt to hold their positions, which our men took without firing a shot.

The Chapelgorris, led by El Pastor, dashed after the flying enemy, but General Chichester ordered his brigade to stand firm.

At the same time Lord John Hay brought his ships in gallant style up the narrow inlet leading to Pasages, and the town was ours.

Meanwhile, with the most marvellous celerity, a pontoon bridge was thrown across the river behind us, establishing a direct and permanent thoroughfare between San Sebastian and our new positions, and across it at once poured a string of artillery and ammunition-wagons. The whole affair lasted such a short time that we were amazed at our success.

"This is a good morning's work, gentlemen," said the brigadier, as we sat our horses and watched the Chapelgorris returning reluctantly from the pursuit; "now that Pasages is lost to them, the enemy will find it awkward to procure the necessary supplies."

"If Cordova were at hand with his troops, we could keep those fellows on the run," remarked one of the officers.

Our chief laughed. "We need not put any dependence in Cordova's promises," he said; "what we can't do ourselves will go undone. But we must make sure of our ground.—Powell, ask Colonel Clarke to fortify that hill to his left—the one that overlooks the river."

I saluted and galloped off with the order, and very soon the troops were hard at work strengthening the positions which the Carlists had abandoned.

On my way back I passed Pym, who was happily uninjured; and this, indeed, was the case with almost the whole of his men.

"A pleasant change from the last fight," he said, as I drew up for a moment's chat. "Do we stay here or go on?"

"We are not to move, I believe, unless General Cordova sends reinforcements; our numbers are too scanty to keep the Carlists from slipping in behind us."

"Don't put yourself too much in the way of any chance bullets," he said, as I rode off, and I laughed back lightly in answer.

At present there was little prospect of danger, and I slept that night in the queer little town of Pasages as calmly as if I had still been behind the ramparts of San Sebastian.

CHAPTER XVII.

A LETTER FROM HOME.

LIKE our own countrymen, the Carlists possess in a great degree the merit of not knowing when they are beaten; and the wisdom of our leaders in immediately fortifying the captured positions was soon made patent.

The Carlist general, Eguia, recognizing the loss his party had sustained by the capture of Pasages, made several determined attempts to regain the town, but the most desperate was that begun on the morning of the sixth of June.

The various regiments of the Legion, together with El Pastor's division, turned out as usual at daybreak, in order to be ready for any assault, but had only to repel a feeble and half-hearted attack upon one of the pickets.

The noise of the firing died away, the birds trilled forth their morning music, the sun rose in glorious splendour, everything was quiet and peaceful; but for the previous alarm, one would hardly have imagined that two armies lay so near together.

The men piled their arms and lay down, some to sleep, some to smoke; while a few, perchance, talked in whispers of their far-off homes and the loved ones there.

It was at this time that General Chichester sent me with a message to El Pastor, telling me to rejoin him at Alza, where the First Regiment was stationed.

I rode off gaily, delivered my message, and after pausing a moment to exchange a word with the faithful Pedro, started on the return journey.

The village of Alza, whither General Chichester had gone, is situated westward of the Urimea river, and stands on a hill.

It was a place of the greatest importance, as it commanded the town of Pasages, and, as I have mentioned, it was held at this time by the First Regiment, which formed a part of Chichester's brigade.

I cantered along, picking my way, for the ground was wooded and hilly, while the cut ditches and embankments rendered it impossible to keep a straight course.

I had arrived at a point between four and five hundred yards from the village, and expected to hear the challenge of the sentry, when suddenly there came a puff of smoke, a sharp cry, and on turning the corner my horse carried me straight into a band of Carlists, who had just crept out from the belt of trees beyond.

The body of the fallen sentinel lay prone on the earth, and I saw at a glance that the man was dead, but even had he lived I could not have helped him.

His comrades on the outpost discharged their pieces and ran back to the picket, while half a dozen Carlists sprang with savage glee towards my horse's head.

The knowledge that a single moment's irresolution meant

death steeled my nerves. My pistol was ready, and as the first of the assailants leaped forward, he dropped with a groan. Then, like a flash of light, my sword swept from one side to the other, while my good horse bounded away.

A volley of bullets swept past me, but in another second I was out of sight, and galloping madly towards the men of the picket, who to the number of perhaps fifty were already prepared to oppose the enemy.

Right willingly would I have drawn rein and taken my place amongst that plucky handful, but my duty lay elsewhere; and shouting to the officer that I would tell the general, I flew by.

I met the brigadier with his aide-de-camp Major Townley, and the leader of the First Regiment, near the old church, and pulled up.

"The Carlists, sir!" I cried breathlessly; "they are advancing on the picket; they will be here in a few minutes."

"Are there many?"

"I saw two pieces of cannon and the Navarrese Regiment; others, I judge, were behind."

His decision was taken without hesitation, and he ordered the colonel of the First Regiment to post his men behind the wall of the churchyard.

"We will meet them there," he said, "and our fire will check their rush.—Powell, ride with all speed to Colonel Godfrey, and tell him to bring up the Eighth at once. Mind, there isn't a minute to be lost. Ah, the picket is being driven in."

I wheeled my horse and galloped off swiftly, feeling sure

that, unless help speedily arrived, the Carlists would make themselves masters of the village.

In this view, as I afterwards learned, my judgment proved correct. The Navarrese—than whom there were no braver soldiers—advanced coolly and with the utmost steadiness in face of a withering fire. Led in the most daring manner by their officers, they threw themselves upon the men of the Legion and hurled them back, the brigadier himself narrowly escaping capture.

Meanwhile, the troops in all directions were turning out. Everywhere I heard the rattle of drums and the bugle-calls, while men hurried to their stations and finished dressing as they ran.

On the Ametza hill the Eighth were drawn up, and I rode straight to the colonel, who was impatiently waiting for instructions.

Instantly upon the receipt of the brigadier's order he gave the word to advance; and thus it was that, without a pause, I found myself returning in the direction of Alza.

The battle now raged along the whole line, but most furiously at the first point of attack. The firing in the neighbourhood of the village went on uninterruptedly, while every now and then, above the rattle of musketry, sounded the thunder-claps of the big guns.

"General Chichester is having a bad time down there," said the colonel, as we hastened on; "the enemy seems to be throwing all his strength against this part of the field."

We had worked our way nearly to Alza; but the ground, as I have mentioned, was extremely wooded, and now from behind a thick hedge issued a close and compact fire, which laid many of our men low. The field directly before us was held by the victorious Navarrese, who, ever to the front, were intent upon sweeping us out of existence.

But although our advance was checked, the Navarrese, in spite of superior numbers, could not make further headway. Again and again they dashed from their cover only to be repulsed, while in a similar manner the Eighth were thrust back time and again from the hedge.

Anxious to rejoin my chief, I rode off to the left, when the sight of what was going on almost beneath my feet caused me to pull up. The two bands which, of all that fought on that dreadful field, were fired by the fiercest passions—the Chapelgorris and the Chapelchurris (the Red Caps of the Christinos and the White Caps of the Carlists)—had met in deadly fray.

My thoughts were carried back to that period in our own history when the houses of Lancaster and York—the Red Rose and the White—struggled for supremacy.

As in those days father fought against son, brother against brother, so now did these men from the same province, the same district, nay, the same village, turn their weapons against each other. The insane fury always excited by civil war swept away every vestige of pity and kindness—in truth, I might say of humanity itself.

Fascinated by the spectacle, I reined in my horse and watched. From my position on the hilltop I could obtain an unimpeded view of the action. Others saw it too, and the firing slackened.

There was little of military order in the combat; it was a wild rush by the two parties from opposite directions, the swiftest being first. Bayonet met bayonet, red caps mingled with white; and then gradually but surely the Chapelchurris drove their antagonists back.

The victors paused for a moment in order to recover breath, and then with a loud *viva* prepared to follow up their success.

To me, a spectator, it seemed impossible that the Chapelgorris could withstand the fresh onset. But to my surprise they did not wait for it. A youthful leader—a mere lad he appeared—snatching a red flag from one of his men and waving his sword, bounded forward.

The effect was simply magical. His swarthy followers did not stop even to shout, but poured after him in a wild, impetuous, living torrent. I looked on with beating heart. The red cap and the red flag were swallowed up in the crowd, only to reappear some distance ahead, and I could not refrain from cheering at the sight.

But now the bugles of the Legion sounded an advance, and two companies of the Scottish Grenadiers, launching themselves against the flank of the battling Chapelchurris, forced them back upon the village.

The spell was broken, and with a word to my horse I galloped off to the brigadier, who immediately dispatched me with fresh orders to the colonel of the Fourth Regiment.

Finding that it was out of their power to retain possession of Alza, the Carlists set fire to the houses and retreated some little distance, while we blundered after them through the dense and blinding smoke.

On we went through woods and orchards to the point where the enemy made their last stand. The regiments first up halted for the others; and amidst a roar of cheers, the ping of bullets, and the hissing of rockets cleaving the air overhead, the Legion swept on.

Twice the rush was stayed, but each time the check proved a temporary one, and soon the Carlist army was in full retreat.

We were now on ground hitherto occupied by the enemy, and the frightened peasants—men, women, and children—were seen running from the houses carrying provisions and such of their household goods as could be most easily removed.

"Powell," said the brigadier, "do you see that white-washed building at the edge of the wood? Ride and tell Colonel Godfrey that is our limit for the present. If we do not advance further, it will serve as an outpost."

I went accordingly, and the colonel gave orders for the recall to be sounded, to bring back those who, incited, I fear, by the prospect of plunder, had gone too far.

I saw Pym, who, now that the fight was over, was exerting himself as usual to temper the passions of his men, and to prevent them from committing any useless damage.

And it was marvellous to see what a hold he had obtained over them. The most obstinate and the most sullen thawed under the influence of his cheery voice and genial smile; the most passionate smothered his anger at the major's bidding.

Not that I would have you imagine he gained their affection by pandering to their faults. The secret of his success lay in his personal bravery and strict sense of justice.

On the battle-field the soldiers knew that their dashing young officer never shirked danger; in quarters, that he never acted unfairly. No man really innocent ever feared to lay his case before the major, or ever made his appeal in vain.

Those men, rough and unlettered for the most part, recognized his sterling honesty, his genuine kindness, the sympathy which he felt for them, and in return they gave him both their trust and admiration.

"He's a real gentleman," said one of them one day as I was passing, "and none of your make-believe sort."

The encomium was just: Pym was a gentleman in the highest sense of this much-abused word.

He gave me a cheery smile as I passed him. There was little leisure for speech, but it did each of us good to know that the other was safe.

For several weeks succeeding the battle of the sixth of June, little was done by the Legion beyond fortifying the positions newly acquired, strengthening the old ones, drilling, and keeping a sharp eye on the enemy's movements.

Notwithstanding our previous successes, the Carlists were far from being disheartened; and on two or three occasions I had to turn out ere dawn broke to learn the cause of the firing going on perhaps half a mile away.

Indeed, so clear was it that they would take advantage of any relaxation in vigilance, that the troops were regularly called at dawn and stood under arms until broad daylight.

Of course, the more impatient spirits grumbled at this continued inaction, but the wiser ones knew it to be inevitable. The Carlists who opposed us had over twenty thousand men whom they could hurl upon our positions at almost any given time; while General Evans, after providing for the defence of his lines, could lead perhaps five thousand into the field.

All this time Cordova, the Spanish general, lay basking in the sun, possessing, as far as could be judged, neither the energy nor ability to prevent the Carlists from doing just as they pleased.

And if the Legion had to be satisfied with extending its positions a little, yet that was better than being pushed back into San Sebastian.

But this period of idleness, I must admit, had its pleasures, which we keenly enjoyed.

Many an hour did Pym and I pass together, talking of old times and drinking in the beauty of the scenery which lay around us. Sunny Spain in truth it was now, and I did not cavil at the title.

Patches of ripening wheat; fields of beans; orchards with thousands of bright-green apples; woods gloriously leaved, the dancing sunlight displaying to perfection the exquisitely varied greens; winding streams, silver-bright, losing themselves in the distance; the brushwood-covered mountains towering skyward—all made up a luxurious picture which at this lapse of time my mind's eye delights to dwell upon.

On our left glinted the green waters of the Bay of Biscay, with the British war-ships close inshore, while farther out the merchant vessels, looking like huge sea-birds with flapping wings, scudded merrily before the breeze.

At such times as these Pym's eyes grew moist, and I knew that his heart was speeding seaward over the waste of waters to that happy Devonshire home where his loved ones dwelt.

Sometimes we were joined by Peyton, the inventor of the famous "mixture," and the sight of his laughing face banished all melancholy. His lively spirits acted as a tonic, and he was always ready with some merry jest or humorous story.

One night he came in high glee to tell us of a rather ludicrous mishap which had occurred to some of the men in his company.

"They were getting their evening rations," he said, "when I heard a tremendous noise in one quarter, and hurried over to find out what was going on. There were four of my fellows surrounding a Spaniard, and bullying him awfully. Of course, he didn't understand a word they said, but every now and then he broke in with a most elaborate bow and a pacific 'Si, señors.'

"How the squabble would have ended, I can't say; but one of the four, catching sight of me, cried, 'Here's the captain; let's tell him about it.'

"'What's the matter, Bob?' I asked. 'What harm has the Spaniard done?'

"'It ain't the furriner, sir,' he said; 'it's his dog as has eaten our rabbit.'

"'And the blessed old dummy stands there a-wagging his head, and saying, "See, see," as if he was a-showing of a diorama,' chimed in one of the others, while they all stared savagely at the wretched Spaniard.

"'I can see lots of things,' said Bob mournfully; 'but what I want to see most of all is my share of the rabbit.'

"By degrees I learned that, in some mysterious way, two of my worthies had obtained a rabbit, the third was the fortunate possessor of some ripe beans, and the fourth had contributed an armful of cabbage."

"They were in luck," said Pym; "why, they had materials for a civilized feast."

"But there was one drawback. The rabbit, unfortunately, had only two hind legs, and each man wanted one. The dispute waxed hot, but finally they arrived at a satisfactory conclusion, when Bob, turning round, uttered a cry of dismay—the bone or rather meat of contention had vanished. Engaged in their exciting argument, they had not noticed the hungry Spanish dog prowling around in search of supper. However, when Bob called out, the animal rose up a few yards from them, and showing every sign of satisfaction, trotted leisurely away, with the men in pursuit."

"Then the banquet was reduced to beans and cabbage," I said.

"Yes," replied Peyton, with a twinkle; "but ill-luck still dogged the poor fellows. With a little coaxing, I got them back to the lines, and left them cooking their remnant of supper. When I passed by later, on my way here, they were stretched on the ground groaning most dismally. 'Well, men,' I said, 'what's the matter now? Have you lost another rabbit?'

"Bob turned up the whites of his eyes in the most ghastly manner, and cried, 'We're poisoned, captain, we're all dead men; the dirty scoundrels have put poison in the cabbage.'

"You will never guess the mistake they had made. I looked at the greens which had been left over for another meal, and found them to be very fine leaves of the tobacco-plant."

"Rather an unpleasant method of enjoying the weed, one would think," said Pym; "but I expect they didn't eat enough to do any real harm."

"They looked very bad, and I sent for Davis, who gave them a strong emetic. He thinks they will be better in the morning," and our mercurial friend went on to relate another ludicrous story.

A few days after this I came upon Pym reading a letter, and at sight of me he waved it aloft triumphantly.

"From your father?" I asked.

"From all the family, I think," he replied, with a smile; "every one has put in a little bit. And you are not left out, my boy; from the *pater* down to tiny Sis, each has a word for 'dear Arthur.' But we will read it together; it really belongs as much to you as to me."

And such a letter! A lump rose in my throat as sitting down by Pym's side I glanced at the various hieroglyphics, from the plain handwriting of Sir Nicholas Forrester to the scrawls of little Sis, whose contribution consisted chiefly of printed letters at varying angles, and a string of crosses.

"The papers contain a full account of Truscott's rescue," Sir Nicholas wrote; "and your mother has bought up all the copies procurable. It gave me considerable gratification, not so much on account of its bravery, as of its humanity. It has always been held as an article of faith that an English gentleman must of necessity possess personal courage, but I would have you bear in mind, my dear boy, and Arthur also, that this is not the sole attribute of a gentleman. Kindly sympathy, generosity, a spirit of self-sacrifice—these as well must be added to his list of virtues. Had either of you fallen on that May day, my grief would have been great indeed, yet tempered by pride in your unselfish devotion."

"A father to be proud of, Arthur, eh?" said Pym, with his eyes aglow; "but let us see what the little mother writes—God bless her!"

"My poor boys, my heart is sore for you; I would that you were here to put your arms round my neck! Will you be spared to come back to me? I pray every night that this dreadful war will cease, so that you may return. I am weeping, Pym, my dear"—the paper here had been saturated with tears—"but I am going to be very brave, and send you some practical advice."

"That's the little mother all over," said Pym, glad, I fancy, to seize upon anything that would help to relieve the tension of his feelings; "now we shall have 'A treatise on how not to catch cold, together with an invaluable recipe for curing it, if caught.'"

The little sally came at the right moment, for the lump in my throat was swelling painfully, and the words in the letter seemed running into each other.

But the laugh did us good, and Pym read out his mother's directions with a playful commentary of his own. At the end of the page, however, the pen had been laid down, and the sentence finished by a fall of tears.

"God help her!" said Pym softly. "Arthur, do you understand the meaning of that?" and he pointed to the tell-tale stain.

I nodded without speaking. I guessed, as Pym guessed, how in the very act of writing a horrid doubt had entered the gentle lady's mind.

What if, even while she wrote, one or both of us had fallen victims to a fell disease, or the bullets of the enemy?

I could picture the scene quite well—see the frightened look on her face as the thought caught her, hear the sob that rose to her lips, watch the pen slip from the nerveless fingers.

It was well for us that the remainder of the letter came from younger members of the family, who furnished us with lighter topics. In reading about Evelyn's doings at the county ball, and how Harry won the Exeter steeple-chase on Lightning Flash, the grip at our hearts somewhat relaxed.

Then came Sam's paragraph, mainly descriptive of the new pony, which he had already taught to jump the gate leading out of the home field; and, finally, the sprawling characters of darling little Sis, nearly undecipherable, but none the less welcome on that account.

And through it all there ran a vein of hearty, loving affection—love and admiration for the noble brother fighting on a distant shore, ay, and for me too.

Pym folded up the precious missive, and placed it carefully in his pocket.

"Hardly the kind of letter to read just before going into action, Arthur!" he said, and his remark was just.

I sat there a long time in silence, forgetful of the war and its object—of everything, in fact, but that peaceful English household and their beautiful home.

I saw the rambling but delightful building, the flower-decked garden, the trim lawn, the green fields beyond. I walked in fancy through the picturesque lanes, the hedges clad in their summer robe, and brilliant with wild roses. From a distance came wafted the scent of new-mown hay; I heard the lowing of glossy-coated kine, and the merry laughter of children as they gambolled in the meadows.

"No!" I answered at length, and my voice sounded strange to me; "it is as well that the letter from your dear ones came now, in our hours of idleness."

Pym linked his arm within mine, and we walked to and fro silently, our hearts too full for overmuch speech.

CHAPTER XVIII.

THE REPULSE AT FUENTERRABIA.

THE Legion's spell of inaction was broken on the tenth of July.

For several days previously I had been hard at work, and on that evening I rode down with General Chichester to where his brigade was quartered.

It was a glorious evening, and the soldiers, who had not been made acquainted with the intended operations, were enjoying themselves in various ways; but the first sound of the bugle brought them to their feet.

In a few minutes the scene became animated and exciting. Officers issued orders, sergeants were beating up their men, and there was a continual running to and fro, which clearly showed that something unusual was contemplated.

This conviction deepened into certainty in the minds of all when the Rocket Brigade came down, followed by hundreds of mules laden with ammunition.

Close behind them plodded the mules belonging to the quartermasters of the different regiments, carrying rations of salt beef and biscuit for several days.

"Looks like a three days' march," said one man, as I rode by on my way to Colonel Fortescue, commanding the Rifles; "but where are we to march?"

"Into the sea," laughed a comrade; "that's the only way open. They're serving out the canteens to dip up the water with."

"Perhaps Evans means to take us down to Madrid to see the little queen."

"That's it, Sandy; the canteens are to put our back pay in."

"There's going to be a royal review and fireworks."

"The fireworks will be there, right enough," another joined in, pointing to the Rocket Brigade.

"Tommy, better eat this salt horse now; it'll be carried easier, and very likely you won't want it to-morrow."

Remarks such as these were bandied about in low tones from man to man, while the preparations went steadily on.

At length all was ready, and after waiting an hour or two until dusk had well set in, the final order was issued, and with the Rocket Brigade and mountain guns in the van, the Legion marched away in the direction of Pasages.

Our actual destination, known only to a few, was the town of Fuenterrabia, lying several miles eastward, and quite close to the French frontier.

In order to keep the enemy ignorant of our design, it was necessary to march in the dark, an operation which proved both tedious and difficult.

The road was simply a succession of rocky ascents and

declivities, while in some places the extreme narrowness of the path rendered the journey full of real peril.

Pasages was, however, reached with few mishaps, and here the regiments waited their turns to be ferried across the water, for which purpose Lord John Hay had sent down all the boats available from his squadron.

Thus far the march had proved troublesome enough, but now it seemed as if our trials were only just beginning.

East of Pasages the hills rise steeply from the sea, and it was up their rocky sides that our course lay.

A very little climbing convinced me that it would be safer and more comfortable on foot than on horseback, and I suggested to the brigadier that we should dismount.

"Perhaps it would be wiser," he said, getting down carefully, and his example was speedily followed by all the mounted officers.

Some distance below the summit was a piece of level land, and here each regiment as it came up was ordered to halt.

The soldiers obeyed gladly, and many of them spent the short interval before the dawn in sleep.

The brief rest, I think, did every one good; and when the sun rose out of the east, tinting the summits of the hills with gold and purple, we pushed on with a fresh energy.

At length the top was reached, and we found ourselves on a high ridge which northward sloped to the sea, while on the south it was bounded by a wall of rock almost perpendicular.

"Can you see the ships, Powell?" asked the brigadier,

who was anxiously scanning the surface of the bay with his glass.

"Yes, sir; they are steaming slowly straight ahead of us. There are the four steamers and a number of gunboats. They seem to be regulating their speed by ours."

"What is the meaning of that firing in the front? Ride forward and find out."

I pushed my horse ahead, and discovered that the Chapelgorris, who were in advance, had come into contact with a Carlist outpost.

The enemy, however, after firing a volley, disappeared, and the Chapelgorris continued their march unmolested.

From then until we halted on the ridge overlooking Fuenterrabia the Carlists offered no opposition, and more than one officer of the Legion began to fancy that the expedition would consist simply of a military promenade.

The view from the position which General Chichester's brigade took up was a glorious one, and I looked at it in admiration.

Beneath us lay the town; on our left hand the waters, now calm and peaceful, of the Bay of Biscay; on our right, hill and dale, bright with golden wheat, luxuriant vines, heavily-fruited trees, and with picturesque cottages nestling on the hill-slopes.

At some distance, but not far away, stretched the beautiful land of France, with the Bidassoa sparkling and dancing between the two countries.

But the beauty of the scenery was soon to be spoiled by the horrors of the battle-field.

Up the river from the sea the gunboats made their way, firing at the town; while the larger vessels, anchoring at the mouth, threw shot and shell at the Carlist redoubts.

Then the noise was taken up, as it were, at our feet, and we saw the Sixth Regiment descending the slopes between the town and a primitive-looking bridge which spanned the river.

The brigadier sat his horse impatiently, awaiting the signal to lead on his brigade, but until that moment arrived we had ample opportunity of observing almost every incident of the fight.

The contest at once resolved itself into a struggle for the bridge. Our gallant lads were at the end nearest to the town, but the other side was in possession of the Carlists, and as far as could be judged, they had strongly fortified it.

"Our troops must take that position," said Pym, who was standing close to me, "or they will be between two fires. Ah, I thought so. Shaw is giving the orders."

For a moment we held our breath, and then joined in the loud "hurrah" which rose from the Sixth as with fixed bayonets they rushed at the foe. Men dropped on all sides, but the survivors sped on, encouraged by the cheers which resounded from every regiment.

Already we were shouting ourselves hoarse at their success, when up from the ground sprang a body of Carlists nearly two thousand strong.

No one waited for a signal; each man, levelling his piece, fired into the thick of the throng and reloaded as quickly as possible. Then, elated by the temporary triumph, they swarmed out from their entrenchment, swallowing up the handful of Chapelgorris and the remnant that remained of the Sixth.

I trembled with excitement, and every soldier throughout the brigade waited with intense eagerness for the order to descend the slope. The brigadier attempted in vain to conceal his impatience, and each officer craned his neck to catch the first glimpse of the expected aide-de-camp.

Meanwhile the struggle waxed hotter and more furious. The Chapelgorris and men of the Sixth, as I have stated, were surrounded by the Carlists, but now the regiment of Lancers came down at a gallop; the enemy fell back, some of them into the river, where many of the Legion had previously leaped in order to escape capture.

Still no orders reached us, and the impatience of the men broke out into a loud swelling murmur, and a demand to be led against the foe.

To stand still, idly watching the slaughter of our comrades, was painful—most of us thought it humiliating; and every one heard with relief the sharp words of command, "Attention! with cartridge, prime and load."

Helpless to prevent the atrocity, we perceived the Carlists killing their unhappy prisoners without mercy, and the least warlike amongst us thrilled with a hot desire to join in the strife.

But we were doomed to disappointment. The forward movement had barely begun when Chichester received instructions to hold his brigade in check, and the men halted with a sullen growl of disapproval.

Doubtless those who were directing the battle knew better than we what to do, yet I could scarcely wonder at the angry looks of the troops fated thus to remain passive spectators of the scene.

The brunt of the battle was now being borne by the Third and Tenth Regiments, together with a detachment of the Chapelgorris, who fought wherever the strife was fiercest.

With varying fortunes the contest went on, victory inclining now to one side, now to the other; and through it all the Carlists maintained their reputation for brilliant and daring courage.

No loss daunted them or weakened their resolution. Several times I beheld them charge in face of a heavy fire, and continue their advance till not an officer was left to lead them.

"They have had about enough now, one would think," exclaimed an officer behind me, as once more they were driven slowly back.

"Listen to their *vivas*," said another; "what are they cheering for?"

"Fresh troops," responded the first speaker—"a new regiment coming to help them, most likely. Can you make out anything, Powell?" for I was eagerly peering through my glass.

"A man on a white horse, galloping like mad," I answered. "Here, take the glass."

"A splendid fellow, too—rides like a fox-hunter. But they aren't cheering that one man surely!"

They were though, and cheering as triumphantly as if an army were coming to their aid.

Whoever the new-comer might be, that moment in his life was well worth living for. Nearer and nearer he came—gallant rider on a gallant steed—and the shouts of the Carlists made the welkin ring again.

The wounded stopped groaning to join in the cheers; muskets were elevated in the air, caps stuck on the bayonets' points and waved exultingly.

"Rather stagey," said Conyers, the man behind me, as the officer walked his horse through the opened ranks.

"Not a bit of it; it's genuine enthusiasm."

"Wrong time to find fault with a man when he's going to throw his life away," added Pym.

"True enough, Forrester. It seems a pity, too; he'll never reach the bridge."

"If he gets over, it's all up with our fellows down there; nothing will stop his men as long as he keeps on his feet. Look at him; he means business."

He was facing his followers and evidently making a little speech; then turning suddenly, he stretched out his sword in the direction of the English regiments, and his action was greeted by an enthusiastic cheer.

We on the height waited breathlessly, every eye fixed on the gallant leader, and I on my part, had it not been fatal to our chance of success, could have prayed that his life might be spared.

But the supreme moment had come; the last word was spoken, and waving his sword, he darted forward.

With head erect, he sat his horse as steadily as if leading his troops in a march past, while they, equally daring, followed in close column.

"Now!" cried Pym, and as if in obedience to his signal, the report of a volley rang out; the bridge was shrouded in a curtain of smoke, and we waited in hushed expectation to witness the result.

What had become of that chivalrous leader?

Slowly the fog lifted, and I almost felt like cheering as I saw the white horse and its rider still untouched.

The officer was now leading quite six lengths in advance. I could see the gleam of his sword, as, waving the weapon above his head, he urged the troops on.

Now they neared the head of the bridge, and were met by a second volley more disastrous than the first; but again the leader escaped scathless.

Careless of death, heedless of the flying bullets, he rode on; and the Carlists, nerved by the sight of him, advanced with a stubborn determination.

A quarter of the distance was traversed—a half; he was calling upon them for the final effort.

Terrible as all warfare must necessarily be, the spectacle of that man, calm, steadfast, unflinching amidst a shower of bullets, had in it an element of grandeur.

But the odds which he faced were far too heavy, and suddenly a babel of cries arose. "The horse is down." "And the man." "The Carlists are retreating." "They are carrying him back." "Look! the Chapelgorris are going to charge." "Why, there isn't more than a score." "The leader's only a boy."

Demoralized by the fall of their officers, the Carlists were indeed retreating; and even before the firing had ceased, a small band of Chapelgorris, headed by a youth, dashed across the bridge.

The leader was the same stripling whose daring recklessness I had witnessed at Alza on the sixth of June. Fleet of foot as all the Chapelgorris were, they failed to keep up with him. They were several paces in the rear when he reached the Carlists, but without a second's delay he dashed in, while we looked on and wondered.

"The flag!" excitedly shouted one of the men of Pym's regiment; "the young chap's after the flag, and he's got it too."

I could not distinguish exactly what was taking place, but there seemed to be a brief struggle, and then with his cap gone, bleeding and panting, the youngster emerged from the throng carrying a Carlist flag.

We cheered vehemently as he darted back with his comrades, and almost before the incident could be properly realized, the bridge was empty.

The youthful Chapelgorri was a stranger to us, but I made up my mind to find out through General Jaureguy who he was.

By this time the tide had ebbed, and the Carlists, fording the river, landed on the opposite side at various undefended points.

"Are we never going to be called down?" asked Conyers impatiently; "it looks as if we were to be kept here all day."

No one answered him, for the simple reason that no one knew; but towards evening we perceived that the different regiments were being brought out of action.

Many were the exclamations of anger and regret at the sight, and it was in a sullen humour that the soldiers responded to the summons to mount a range of pickets along the hillside.

The remainder of Chichester's brigade, together with the regiments that had borne the brunt of the battle, lay down amongst the rough furze to wait for the morning.

Whatever the object of our hurried march had been, and regarding that I heard many opinions, there was little doubt that we had met with a real and substantial check.

The Carlists remained in possession of the battle-field, while at the break of day preparations were made for our immediate return to San Sebastian.

Unfortunately General Evans had been seriously unwell for several days past, and at the close of the fighting on the previous evening, was forced to return in one of the steamers which formed part of the expedition.

The enemy, however, content with their victory, did not attempt to interfere with our arrangements, and the cheerless march back began in peace.

That night we slept in Pasages, and on the following morning returned to our old quarters in and around San Sebastian, where the news of a further disaster awaited us.

During our absence at Fuenterrabia, the Carlists had surprised the Ametza hill—one of our positions, which was guarded by the First Regiment—and after a desperate struggle, succeeded in capturing it.

Several days passed without bringing me an opportunity to visit El Pastor; but one morning, having left Dick, who was rapidly recovering strength, I went on to the Spanish quarters.

"Glad to see you, Captain Powell," exclaimed the general, "though I am sorry it is in the old place."

"You would prefer being in Fuenterrabia?"

"Yes, or marching from there against Irun. You did not get hurt last week?"

"You forget that General Chichester's brigade formed the reserves; we had a good view of the fight, but that was all."

"Ah, I lost several men, and gained nothing."

"One of your officers captured a flag. It was a dashing feat."

El Pastor's features softened into a pleased smile.

"That was young Eizmendi; he is scarcely more than a boy, but never backward when there is work to be done."

"Eizmendi!" I echoed in surprise; "the name seems familiar. Why, it is that of the señorita whom we carried into Bilbao—Juanita Eizmendi, she called herself."

General Jauregu y spoke a few words to his orderly, who at once went away.

"I have sent for him," he said to me; "he is a gallant lad. I should like you to know him."

Very soon the young hero of Fuenterrabia came up, and El Pastor introduced us to each other.

I looked at my new acquaintance with interest. He was quite young, of a slight build, but well-knit, muscular, and vigorous. He carried one arm in a sling, and an old scar from a sword wound disfigured his cheek.

The general repeated my remark concerning the incident of the flag, and the young man bowed low with a grave courtesy.

"Captain Powell has a question to ask, Alphonso," El Pastor said; "but, unfortunately, I must leave you to talk to him by yourself. I have promised to meet General Evans."

"I am very much at the señor's service," responded the youthful Chapelgorri; and the general, with a further apology for going, took his departure.

"Pardon me if the subject seems irrelevant," I began; "but it refers to a lady who bears your name—the Señorita Juanita Eizmendi."

My companion controlled his features with an effort, and looked at me without speaking.

"Perhaps it is only a curious coincidence," I suggested; "and yet the likeness between you is most marked."

"You are talking of my sister, señor," he replied.

"But the señorita is on the side of the Carlists!"

Just for one moment I thought that his reserve would give way; his eyes flashed, and he seemed struggling with a rush of words. But his habitual pride restrained him, and he answered coldly,—

"There are few families in these northern provinces which this war has not divided."

"It chanced happily for me that the señorita was a follower of Don Carlos, since to that fact I owe my life," and I told him the story of my escape from the Carlist prison.

He listened eagerly, and when I finished, held out his hand, saying, "Then you are the Englishman who saved my sister from the brigand Rubio! Señor, I owe you a debt of gratitude which nothing can repay."

"You mistake," I answered, smiling; "it has already been repaid, and with interest. The señorita gave two lives for one."

"And the man Pedro! Was he one of your companions?"

"Yes, and the most important. Without his aid we should never have entered Bilbao."

"I must seek him out. Is he here in San Sebastian?"

"Yes, El Pastor can easily find him for you; his name is Gamboa."

"I shall remember it," he said, and then he began to question me concerning his sister's welfare.

By degrees he related his history, which, as he said, was typical of scores of others in the neighbourhood.

His father, Don Manuel Eizmendi, had been violently opposed to the government of the queen, because he foresaw the abolition of the *fueros*—the immemorial privileges of the Biscayans. Swayed by this consideration, he had eagerly invited Don Carlos to accept the lordship of

Biscay, hoping by this means to secure the independence of his province.

On the other hand, Alphonso, who had largely imbibed liberal opinions, and who was looking forward with a genuine enthusiasm to his country taking a more prominent place amongst the nations of Europe, threw in his lot with the constitutional party.

"And the señorita naturally followed her father's teaching," I said.

"My sister is a stronger Carlist than Don Carlos himself," the young man answered. "She looks upon him not only as the rightful king, but as the champion of her church. She is a devoted Catholic, and believes—although I am sure she is in error—that the supporters of Queen Isabella are enemies to religion. It is this mistaken notion which more than all else has roused in her a spirit of fanaticism. But, as I have said, our family is hopelessly divided. I have several relatives who have sacrificed everything for Carlos."

This meeting with Alphonso Eizmendi was the first of many, and we had long talks together, sometimes alone, sometimes with Pym, who was most favourably impressed by the Spaniard's bearing.

"It is a melancholy situation," observed Pym, one evening after Alphonso had left us; "and I do not wonder at his habitual sadness."

"Yet it is inevitable; he must help the cause which he believes to be just."

"Yes, he must be loyal to the truth. He cannot fight

against his convictions; but the task is a peculiarly painful one nevertheless. I doubt if I should have sufficient courage to make the sacrifice."

"Fortunately you are not likely to be tested," I said, with a smile; "and now, to change the subject, have you seen Dick lately?"

"This afternoon. He is getting on nicely, and will soon be out. He told me that General Evans has been twice to see him. By the way, is the general better?"

"Not much. I fancy that he is harassed a great deal by the Spanish authorities. For one thing, the troops are clamouring for their pay, and there isn't a dollar to be got from Madrid."

"That is likely to cause trouble; the men won't be put off with promises for ever."

"There doesn't seem much chance of their getting anything else at present; but perhaps the British commissioner will be able to do something—he has just gone to the capital."

"I hope so, indeed, for the honour of the Legion," my comrade replied; "but I must admit that my faith is small."

It was growing late, and we did not discuss the subject further, but subsequent events brought back the conversation vividly to my mind.

CHAPTER XIX.

MUTINY.

THE small cloud hinted at in the previous chapter rapidly began to spread, although few of us suspected how soon it would burst.

I was seated one morning in the brigadier's room, engaged upon some official correspondence, when Colonel Godfrey entered. His face was flushed, and he looked both distressed and angry. This much I perceived in a momentary glance, and then resumed my work.

An exclamation from my chief caused me to look up again.

"The Eighth!" he said in amazement—"impossible!" and then stopped.

"It may be impossible, but it's the truth for all that," returned the other grimly.

"But they will not persist in such folly. After all, it is a passing madness."

"I should call it an organized conspiracy; the movement has been regularly planned."

"But what is the grievance?"

"There is more than one, but the most pressing refers

to the back pay. The men want their money, and won't be put off with fair words."

"Where are they?"

"In quarters."

"After dinner, march them down to the sands, but without their accoutrements; I will come across. We must stop this before it goes farther," and then the conversation was carried on in a lower key.

I had not heard the actual cause of the commotion, but it was easy to guess at the truth; and indeed before long every one in San Sebastian knew that the Eighth Regiment had openly refused to obey orders.

As usual in such cases, the story was told in a hundred different ways, grotesque or comic, according to the fancy of the individual narrator.

But all the versions rested on the same foundation, and however greatly they differed on some points, that ugly word to a British soldier—mutiny—cropped up in each.

That the Eighth had refused to relieve the First at Alza seemed an undeniable fact, but beyond that all was lost in a cloud of conjectures.

The outbreak, whatever its nature, had occurred at a most unfavourable period, General Evans being seriously ill, and unable to exert either his influence or his authority.

It was between two and three o'clock when I accompanied General Chichester to the spot where the discontented regiment had been drawn up.

I looked at Pym, whose naturally bright face had for once lost its expression of cheerfulness.

Poor fellow! I pitied him from my heart. He had been so proud of his men, so confident in their loyalty, so enthusiastic in their praise, that this sudden revolt came to him with a terrible shock.

The brigadier halted in front of the troops, and raised a hand for silence.

He was a gallant officer, whose bravery and zeal in the service of the Legion had gained him the respect of all, and I judged it likely that he might be able to eradicate the seeds of discontent.

"Men of the Eighth Regiment," he began, "what is the meaning of this? Why have you refused to do your duty?"

He stopped speaking and looked straight at the men, who shifted their gaze uneasily and preserved silence.

"Will none of you tell me?" he asked. "In common fairness to yourselves, to the officers of the regiment, and to me, you owe an explanation of this monstrous and unsoldierly conduct. Are you afraid to answer? I pledge you my word that no one shall suffer for speaking out."

There was a slight cheer at this, and after another minute's hesitation a soldier stepped from the ranks.

"General," he began diffidently, "I'll take you at your word. I'm not much of a speaker, but I'll try to tell you in a few words what the fuss is about. You'll allow that up to now my mates have done their duty. We starved in Vitoria, we froze on the hills, and the Carlists can tell whether we've been backward in the fighting."

"True for you, mate, and no mistake," interrupted some of those near him.

"Well, general," the orator continued, "meaning no disrespect to you or to any of the officers, but speaking as man to man, I reckon that for the future it's to be 'No pay, no soldiering.' We've done our share; now it's for the Dons to do theirs. A man can't go on fighting with an empty stomach. And now, general, I hope that you'll not take offence at a few plain words from a plain man."

The ice being thus broken, several others followed, but they added nothing of importance to what their comrade had already said.

"Now listen to me," exclaimed the general, "and give a straightforward answer to my question. If you get this money, will you do your duty?"

An enthusiastic "yes" broke from the troops, and when the noise died away the brigadier spoke again.

"You shall have your money," he said, "if it can be raised by any possible means."

The regiment greeted this announcement with another outburst of cheering, and then General Chichester, attended by Major Townley and myself, rode back to San Sebastian.

By the evening he had succeeded in obtaining possession of a considerable sum of money, which was placed in charge of Captain Kymer, the paymaster of the regiment, and I began to think that the worst of the storm was over.

But even this action of the brigadier was powerless to allay the growing dissatisfaction. Until all the arrears were paid up, the men respectfully but firmly declined to march, and neither threat nor entreaty availed to shake their determination.

They had learned, and quite naturally, to distrust the Spaniards' promises, which had been repeatedly broken, and nothing short of the actual payment would satisfy them.

Finally they were marched to the convent of San Bartolome and the buildings in the neighbourhood, where I visited Pym an evening or two afterwards.

"I rather expected that you would come to-day," he remarked, as I went into his room. "What a disagreeable business this is!"

"You seem to have been taken by surprise, after all," I said; "and yet the men must have deliberately planned the outbreak."

"There can be no question about that; but they only made up their minds the night before. We had them drawn up in the morning, and when the colonel came he gave the word, 'Shoulder arms!' His face was a study when, out of the whole regiment, only one file obeyed. I stared in dismay at the major in command. But you know Godfrey; it takes a lot to daunt him.

"'Lieutenant Shields,' he said, 'did you hear my word of command?' and young Shields replied, 'Yes, sir.' Then he questioned the major and myself, but of course we were unable to give him any information. 'Very well,' he said, and rode off to the right of the regiment, while we looked on. He stopped in front of the Grenadiers, gazed at them as steadily as if nothing unusual was taking place, and gave the order, 'Right section of the Grenadiers, by themselves, shoulder arms!'"

"A skilful manœuvre that," I said; "a single section

would not care to disobey. Once get the men broken up, and their power for mischief is gone."

"The scheme answered admirably until he reached the third company, but then some of the others began cheering, the Grenadiers took the muskets from their shoulders, and their comrades followed suit. Godfrey was in a towering rage, and I felt too much ashamed to look any one in the face."

"Poor old fellow! I can quite understand. Still, you must admit that the men have a just grievance; they have not been well treated. If they get their pay, everything will go right."

He shook his head despondingly, saying, "There's worse to follow. Half the regiment declare that they only signed for one year, and that their time is up in August. My dear Arthur, the Legion will be overwhelmed with disgrace."

"Not a bit. That little man Tupper who spoke to the brigadier was quite right; the soldiers have fulfilled their part of the contract, and it's time for the Spaniards to do something. As to the period of service, that matter ought easily to be settled. Those who volunteered for the year only must be given their discharge and sent back to England."

"We shall see," he responded gloomily; "but I anticipate trouble," and the events of the next day proved the accuracy of his forecast.

The spirit of insubordination showed itself in regiment after regiment, and the climax was reached when a body of Lancers was marched to San Bartolome to be tried by court-martial for refusing to serve beyond the year.

I was standing in the square with Pym and a few other officers not engaged on the trial, when a loud hurrah from the convent, where the Eighth was quartered, warned us that something extraordinary was going on.

"There's mischief brewing," exclaimed one, and we all ran to the entrance.

The sounds became plainer, and we heard distinctly the fixing of bayonets and the angry cries of the soldiers.

Pym rushed to the foot of the stairs, hoping that the sight of him might calm them, and the rest of us followed, with swords out and pistols ready cocked.

The din was deafening, but Pym made a gallant effort to get a hearing.

"Men of the Eighth," he cried, "what is it that you are about to do? Listen to me. Will you bring disgrace on your old regiment and on your officers? Put down your arms. Don't let people be able to say that a British regiment shot down its own officers."

His words were heard only by those on the lowermost steps, while shouts of "Clear them out!" "Fire on them if they won't go!" came from the throng higher up and in the corridors.

Some of the more impetuous officers brandished their swords, as if it were possible for our little handful successfully to oppose a whole regiment in deadly earnest.

Pym folded his arms and cried sorrowfully, "Scotsmen! will you make me ashamed of you for ever?"

"Push on there," came from above in angry tones; "what are ye dawdling for? Out into the yard, mates! Rescue the Lancers! Justice for the Lancers!" and the cry was everywhere repeated.

Pym made yet another effort. "The Lancers will have justice," he said; "can't you trust your own officers?"

"It's no good, major," responded one of those on the bottom step, a decent, well-spoken man; "we haven't anything against you, sir; but the Lancers are in the same boat with us, and we are determined to stand by them. Why should they be tried? There's nothing to try them for."

"Stop that parleying down there; are we to be kept waiting all day?"

The situation had become desperate. The muzzles of thirty muskets were pointed over the balustrade of the stairs; the fingers of thirty angry men were at the triggers; one little click, and the place would run with blood.

I glanced at Pym; his face was white, but with honest indignation, not fear.

He had done his best and failed, as in the same case the commander-in-chief himself would have failed.

Recognizing the futility of physical resistance, I had, following Pym's example, sheathed my sword, and now stood by his side in the centre of the lobby.

Suddenly the crush from the stairs became so great that those in front were pushed forward, and the next instant, by the sheer impetus of numbers, we were borne bodily through the open doorway.

The court-martial was hastily abandoned; tables and chairs were overthrown; and the mob, shouting for justice, filled the square.

It was a disgraceful scene, and one not easily to be forgotten.

Fortunately, however, no blood had been shed, and Pym with the other officers of the regiment were already regaining control of the men. Godfrey, too, came up, and for a time at least order was restored.

I rode back to town that evening with a deep sense of mortification and a feeling of doubt as to the Legion's ultimate success.

A few days later I learned that the regiment had been sent to Santander, and called at the hospital to tell Dick.

I had not seen him for some little time, and was extremely gratified at the marked improvement in his health.

"I had begun to give you up, sir, and the major too," he said, as I shook hands with him; "but I suppose this wretched business has given you both enough to do."

"You have heard about it then?"

"Why, yes; little else has been talked of lately. Still, I didn't think our regiment would have begun the row."

"They have been sent to Santander."

"To keep them out of mischief. Ah, well, it doesn't matter much whether they're in Santander or some other place. Now that the fire is started, it's bound to go on blazing. There was a man of the Sixth in the bed next to mine, and he told me some queer things. Three-quarters of his regiment will lay down their arms in the beginning of August; that was their bargain with General Shaw, he says, when they signed on. They came out for one year; and when the time is up, they're going home."

"Still, they might urge their claims in a reasonable way, without bringing disgrace on the Legion," and I described the scene at the convent of San Bartolome.

"What a good thing they didn't fire!" he said. "Had a trigger been pulled, even by accident, not one of you would have got away. The biggest cowards in the crowd would have fired off all their ammunition out of sheer terror. An armed mob is an ugly thing to deal with."

"You would have been proud of the major," I said; "he faced them without flinching."

Dick's eyes glistened with pleasure; I knew that he loved Pym like a son.

"It was a dangerous experiment though," he remarked after a while; "it might have cost him his life. Men don't stop to think much when their anger's up, though they would be sorry enough afterwards. Well, I suppose it will come out all right in the end."

"But don't you think that the men are greatly to blame?" I asked.

"As soldiers certainly; but you see they're not real soldiers after all. Then again, it's hard even for a regular soldier to knuckle under when he has right on his side. It's curious what heart a man gets in him when he is sure of being in the right. Why, I've seen a fellow with the pluck of a mouse be brave then."

"But you're begging the question, Dick; you are arguing

from the wrong end. Because these men have the audacity to revolt, you judge that their cause must be a just one. That seems queer logic."

"I am not thinking of the men at all, but of the leaders," he said. "If the troops had been in the wrong, the rising would have been put down with a strong hand. What are these half measures for? Officers don't usually play with mutiny; they set to work and root it out. Why isn't that done here? I don't pretend to understand much of these high matters, but the reason seems clear enough to me: it's because the men have a right to claim their discharge."

"There is something in that," I admitted.

"Everything, Mr. Powell; but don't let us talk about it any more; it's a dismal topic for an old soldier. Besides, there is something to tell you. I have had some visitors—two Spaniards."

"Strangers?"

"One of them; the other was my old comrade Pedro. They shook my hand and smiled in a friendly way, but we didn't get on very fast in the talking line; Pedro's English doesn't go very far."

"What a pity!" I exclaimed, for it at once occurred to me that the second visitor was young Eizmendi; "I wish I had known. How did you manage?"

Dick's eyes twinkled. "It would have done you good to see us," he said; "half the patients in the ward nearly screwed their heads off trying to get a sight. Pedro was the showman and one of the actors. First, he brought a chair, and setting it down by me, said, 'Señor Powell, Pow-ell.' I nodded, and began to feel quite interested; it was like a new game."

"Charades," I suggested.

"Very likely; it was odd enough, anyway. However, the next move was to place an empty bottle close behind the chair. 'Vitoria,' he said, 'Vitoria,' and I nodded again, while my other visitor got out of the way carefully, so as not to interrupt the performance. Reaching a second bottle from the shelf above my bed, Pedro placed it some distance off, and dubbed it Bilbao. Then he came back to the chair, and motioning me to stand on one side, took his place on the other, and cracked his fingers like a whip. Away we went, post-haste for the bottle, 'Señor Powell' in the middle, I with my crutch, and Pedro keeping a sharp lookout for the enemy.

"'Good, good!' I cried; '*bueno, bueno!* don't smash the town, Pedro,' for one leg of the chair seemed likely to shiver our landmark into atoms.

"The excitement began to run high. Quite a crowd of orderlies, dressers, and invalids gathered round and chaffed me unmercifully. 'Bravo, Truscott! you'll get there first; keep up your pluck—the Don's weakening; two to one on the sergeant.' 'Hurrah! here's the sergeant practising a Spanish dance! Tuck up your coat, old man; you'll knock the bottle over.' 'That's what they dance on; it's what the Dons call the bottle dance; they're very clever at it.' 'Nonsense! it's a conjuring trick the sergeant's learning.' Oh, they had fine sport, I can tell you."

"It must have been funny," I said, shaking with laughter at my comrade's droll looks.

"It was," he answered, "for those who looked on. But we had only performed one act of the play. Pedro stopped, bent down, and made as if he was lifting something on the chair. 'Señorita,' he said, 'lady,' and stared at me hard. Then he whipped up again, and we all made a dash for the bottle, which I am sorry to say got broken. Still I understood what he was driving at, and told him so in good, plain English, at which he took me to the other Spaniard, and pointing to him, said, 'Señorita — fra. Lady—brother.'

"This one shook me by the hand again, and seemed as if he was going to make a speech; but just then Doctor Martin came up, and seeing our difficulty, offered to talk to my visitors in Spanish.

"Then it turned out that the young gentleman was the brother of the lady whom we picked up outside Bilbao, and he had come to thank me. After a bit he offered me a purse of money; but I shook my head, and asked the doctor to explain that I couldn't take it."

"Quite right, Dick," I interrupted approvingly; "you are not the man to turn a humane act into a monetary transaction."

"That's what I told the doctor, but the Don wouldn't take the purse back. The two had a little talk, and then Doctor Martin said, 'Men, Captain Alphonso Eizmendi of the Chapelgorris wishes me to keep this money, and buy some nice things for the sick comrades of the brave Sergeant Truscott.' Well, with that the captain wished me good-bye, and the boys didn't forget to cheer as he and Pedro left the room."

"It was very kind and thoughtful of him to come. Some day I will tell you about him and his sister; but now I must be going—the brigadier has some work waiting for me."

"Good-bye, sir; give my respects to Major Forrester, if you should see him; tell him that I shall soon be fit for duty."

"I shall most certainly inform him of your new accomplishment," I answered laughingly, as I took my leave.

During the next two or three weeks the agitation in the Legion increased, as the time was fast approaching when several hundreds of the men would claim their discharge.

To test the truth of their assertions, a court of inquiry was formed, of which General Shaw, who shortly afterwards resigned and went back to England, was appointed president.

Meanwhile, with the exception of an unsuccessful attack on the Ametza hill by the First Regiment, no offensive operations were undertaken, and the Carlists on their side were content to remain quiet.

In other parts of the country they were carrying on the most vigorous warfare, which made it necessary for the Christino general Cordova to withdraw a large part of the northern army in order to protect the interior.

From time to time information reached us in San Sebastian of the marvellous success attending the exploits of a

Carlist chief named Gomez. With a force consisting of barely seven thousand men, this daring leader, cutting himself off from the security of his mountain fastnesses, marched boldly into the interior of the country. Town after town yielded up its keys, and helped to swell his booty. His movements were made with such amazing rapidity that not even the capital was deemed safe. General after general was sent in pursuit of him, but he foiled them all. In the heart of a hostile district, surrounded by enemies, with armies far superior to his in number close on his track, he marched and countermarched, swooping down on a town here, sometimes scarcely half a day in front of his pursuers, and then vanishing no one knew whither.

Twice the news came that the destruction of his force was assured, that he could not possibly escape, that he had been driven into a corner and must capitulate; but later we learned that he had achieved the apparently impossible, and was levying contributions as gaily as of yore.

Thus, with the success of the Carlists in the south, the disorder in the Legion, and the continued illness of General Evans, matters wore a gloomy aspect; and several times I found myself wondering whether the whole enterprise would not end in disaster.

But the darkest night brightens into dawn, and the first gleam of light came to me when I heard that the Eighth Regiment, now once more in its right mind, was returning to San Sebastian.

CHAPTER XX.

THE BATTLE OF AMETZA.

BY this time Dick had thoroughly recovered from his wound, and eagerly took the opportunity of re-joining his regiment, where he was warmly welcomed by officers and men alike.

I spent an hour or two one evening with Pym and his brother officers, who expressed their satisfaction at the improvement in the Legion.

There was no longer any fear of mutiny; the most in-tractable of the malcontents had been drafted out, many of the one-year volunteers had extended their term of service, and every one looked forward to the future hopefully.

The youngsters amongst us, with the overweening con-fidence of youth, mapped out the plan of campaign, fought several brilliant if imaginary battles in which each of us gained distinction, ousted the Carlists from Fuenterrabia and Irun, drove them across the Ebro, cleared the northern provinces generally, and brought the war to a successful termination, just in time to spend Christmas in England.

Pym sat and listened with an amused smile; but when

we had finally reduced the country to a state of order, he said quietly, "What a pity it is that Evans doesn't resign, and give one of you a chance. As it is, I rather fancy that we shall eat our Christmas dinner in San Sebastian."

His words were greeted with a chorus of disapproval.

"You don't think it likely that we shall stay cooped up here all the autumn?" I suggested.

"What else can we do, if Cordova won't send reinforcements? We are not strong enough to hold a foot of ground more than we occupy. Suppose we marched out to-morrow, and drove the Carlists as far as Irun."

"That is just what we were proposing."

"In that case, we must abandon our present positions, which would immediately be seized by the enemy. We had a taste of that in July, when the Carlists captured the Ametza hill."

"But Cordova has resigned since then," urged one; "and they say that Espartero is to be the new general. He won't let the grass grow under his feet."

"We shall see," responded our mentor oracularly; "he hasn't done anything very brilliant yet. Besides, instead of sending more troops to San Sebastian, I hear that he is asking for help. No; whether we like it or not, until Espartero is able and willing to advance, we shall stay here."

"Then we must give up all idea of going home for Christmas, and I had been planning to have such a jolly time," said young Cotton dolefully.

"Put it off for a year," laughed one of his comrades;

"the pleasure will be all the keener when the time does come."

Poor fellow! how little any of us imagined that Christmastide would never again come for him!

Then the conversation turned upon the impending changes in the regiment, for Godfrey had been promoted to the rank of brigadier-general, and his place was to be taken by Colonel Apthorpe.

But the evening was growing late, and as I had some work to do, I reluctantly took leave of my genial comrades.

The next few weeks showed how much wiser than we Pym had been, since, with the exception of performing the ordinary routine work, we remained inactive.

Reports still came to hand of the marvellous exploits achieved by the daring Gomez, who appeared to be scouring the whole kingdom, while the Christino armies toiled after him in vain.

Full of subtlety and resource, hawk-eyed, swift-footed as the deer, confident in his own powers and the devotion of his little force, he marched and fought, plundered and retreated, laughed at the traps set for him by the Christinos, traversed mountains, crossed rivers, held to ransom the most opulent cities, and triumphantly displayed the flag of Don Carlos in every corner of the country.

The campaign in the north was ignored by the government, whose energies seemed exhausted by the efforts to catch the audacious Gomez; and it soon became clear that, until this was accomplished, we at San Sebastian must rely upon our own strength.

Still, this period of comparative idleness was not devoid of enjoyment. The weather kept beautifully fine; the men were in good health and spirits; General Evans had obtained a sum of money, which made it possible to secure for them a few trifling luxuries; and the work on the fortifications found them wholesome employment.

To me this month of September was the happiest time I had spent in Spain.

Dick and Pym were well, and the friendship which I had contracted with Alphonso Eizmendi brought me numerous invitations from the leading Spanish families in the town, with whom the youthful Chapelgorri was intimately acquainted.

But our round of pleasures was destined to be interrupted in the most unceremonious manner.

I had gone to bed about one o'clock on the morning of the first of October, and was awakened at daybreak by a loud hammering and a shout of "Get up, sir! you're wanted; General Chichester's waiting for you."

The hasty summons drove away all thoughts of sleep. I sprang out hurriedly, dressed in the dark, and ran down the stairs, almost tumbling over the brigadier.

"Have a care, Powell," he laughed; "don't break my neck before the fight begins. The Carlists are out, and by the sound of their guns they are in earnest."

"They are beginning early," I answered; "they might have given us another hour's sleep."

The alarm had roused the city. Doors slammed violently as the officers ran out; horses were being saddled and brought round to their owners; numerous questions were asked and answered; men ran hither and thither, some spurring furiously towards the gate; soldier-servants sought their masters—all was in confusion.

Our horses were at the door, and we leaped into the saddles.

The brigadier waited a moment, listening for the booming of the cannon.

"They are firing from the Ametza hill," he said. "Ah! there goes Evans with his staff. We must ride steeple-chase fashion, and take the hedges and ditches as they come. Look! the general doesn't mean to be last."

Down the street we clattered; past officers running, and finishing their toilets as they ran; out of the town, along the highroad, and then steering a straight course towards the brigade; while General Evans was riding hard to the picket nearest the Ametza hill.

The strength of the attack seemed to be directed against that spot, but gradually the firing extended along the whole line, and we could tell that our pickets were being driven in.

"Powell, tell Colonel Apthorpe to bring his regiment to the edge of yonder wood, and to halt there for further orders."

I saluted, and dashed off at a mad gallop; the fortunes of the day might hang upon a lost five minutes.

I passed young Cotton, who was running at full speed, and he gave me a bright smile of recognition as I sped by.

Poor lad! well was it for him that he could not foresee his share in the day's work.

But, perhaps happily, in the stress of battle the soldier

has little either of leisure or inclination for moralizing. Work has to be done, and—in the case of officers—work that absorbs every moment and every thought.

Young Cotton, as he ran there in the grey of the morning, was thinking not of himself at all, but of his men; and I, on my part, had but one idea—to convey my message as speedily as possible.

The ground where the fight raged the most furiously was held by the Third Regiment and the Rifles, while the Eighth occupied some houses about half a mile away.

The men had turned out promptly, and were drawn up, prepared to march. Colonel Apthorpe was at the head of the regiment, talking earnestly with Pym and Major Shields, while most of the remaining officers had by this time arrived.

I reined in my horse, and said, "Colonel Apthorpe, the Eighth will advance to the edge of the wood yonder, the instant you are ready. You will wait there, under cover, for further orders."

I passed a word with Pym, heard the colonel issue his instructions, and dashed off again, while the regimental band struck up the tune of "A' the blue bonnets."

All this time the Carlists were continuing the attack with the greatest energy, and while their infantry made charge after charge, the artillery posted on the Ametza hill was doing terrible execution.

Leaving the Eighth to advance almost in a straight line, under cover of a five feet embankment on their right, I rode up the lane, and so into the open field.

As my horse galloped forward I soon came within range of the firing, and a cannon ball, which ploughed a furrow in the ground scarcely a yard away, made it plain that I was in very unsafe quarters.

I did not know exactly where the brigadier would be found, but as it was generally safe to seek him where the bullets flew most thickly, I made straight for the picket-house of the Westminster Grenadiers.

As I drew nearer, Major Townley came towards me at a breakneck pace. Half turning in his saddle, he pointed in the direction of the building, cried, "Over there," and was gone.

Traces of the slaughter now became distinctly visible, and it was patent that both the Third Regiment and the Rifles had lost heavily.

But it was not until I had reported to the brigadier the advance of Colonel Apthorpe's regiment that I found leisure to look around more narrowly.

The house where the attack had begun was now a heap of ruins. Four cannon balls in succession had crashed through it, tearing off the roof, smashing the staircase, and killing some of the soldiers before they were fairly roused from sleep.

The survivors, about a score in number—bruised, wounded, stunned—rallying quickly from the confusion, had rushed into the courtyard, and there, behind the loop-holed walls, maintained an obstinate fight with a thousand Carlists, until the remainder of the Third could come up.

Here, where the fight began, was it the most vigorously

waged; but now Colonel Colquhoun was getting our artillery into position, and taking his observations.

He was standing well forward, fully exposed to view, when suddenly from one of the enemy's guns came a volume of smoke, and a huge ball crashing straight into our first piece of artillery rendered it useless.

Almost without intermission, a second and third fell in our midst, knocking over horses and riders, and causing consternation amongst the soldiers at the guns.

"That fellow knows his work," said Colquhoun, continuing to make his calculations with the utmost calmness.

A fourth shot missed another cannon by scarcely a foot breadth, skimmed lightly between two of the general's staff officers, and buried itself in our rear.

"That gunner is no Spaniard," exclaimed the chief emphatically; "Colquhoun, what do you make of him?"

"I think he does credit to his training in the British artillery," was the reply. "That fellow's one of our deserters, or I'm a Dutchman. However, we'll just speak a word with him;" and even while another ball came speeding on its way, he set about giving the needful instructions.

Three pieces were elevated for the Ametza hill, to each the match was applied; there came a deafening explosion, and when the smoke cleared away we perceived that the shells had spread disaster amidst the Carlist artillery.

"Faith, Colquhoun," said one of the staff, "you've made a mistake, and instead of a word have given them a sentence."

"I should call it a whole paragraph," remarked another.

"Finish the chapter then, Colquhoun," said General

Evans, as he galloped off to another part of the field; "it will keep them from annoying our infantry."

Meanwhile the Carlists on the south-west of the hill were pressing our troops hard, and I saw one of our chief's aides-de-camp suddenly dart from his leader's side and disappear behind a low hill.

In a few minutes the nature of his errand was explained. A cheer rose from the troops further in advance, was caught up by others, and I heard a shout of "The Lancers! the Lancers for ever!"

The regiment made a gallant show in its military finery, and I could but wish the daring fellows success in their desperate enterprise, for it was clear that they had been ordered to charge.

Colonel Wakefield, an officer distinguished for personal courage, rode at their head, well pleased at the opportunity of taking his regiment into action.

I stood up in my stirrups to get a better view, and gave them a cheer as they swept proudly past.

On they went, faster and faster, till they rushed almost at racing speed, riding, as the brigadier said, like men who meant to charge home.

Yet amidst their excitement they preserved the most faultless order. Every man knew his place and kept it; even the horses scarcely seemed to need guidance.

What would the Carlists do? Would they form square and endeavour to resist the shock? This was the first time that I had witnessed a cavalry charge, and I wondered how it would be met.

The active mountaineers did not keep us long in doubt. They fired a volley at long range, which did little damage, and then with a marvellous swiftness retreated behind their breastworks.

There I felt that they were safe; horse-soldiers could never surmount these obstacles.

Nevertheless the Lancers were in the humour to try. Without a moment's hesitation, they rode onward and upward after the flying foe. The excitement caused me to lose sight of my own danger. With a glass at my eye I watched anxiously, drawing a deep breath as the foremost files flung themselves against the stone walls.

For a few minutes the combatants were shrouded in smoke, the rattle of musketry made itself heard; then the cloud lifted, and I gave a heavy groan.

Riderless horses were galloping down the hillside; men on foot were running or walking, some limping in pain, some lying motionless on the ground; but those unhurt retained their matchless formation, and retreated as regularly as if on parade.

My eyes were still fixed on the dismal spectacle, when the brigadier touched me on the shoulder.

"Tell Colonel Ross to bring up the Sixth at once. Don't waste a moment. Let them form in the hollow to the west of where the Lancers are; then come to me."

The Sixth were on the extreme west, about two miles distant, and the ride would take me for a time out of the reach of bullets.

I settled myself in the saddle, dropped the reins lightly

on my horse's neck, and dashed off, not altogether sorry to be sent on the errand.

The Sixth and Seventh Regiments were guarding that end of the field, but the Carlists had not bothered them much, and did not appear likely to do so.

I gave Colonel Ross the brigadier's orders, and rode back by his side, answering the questions which he put, and describing the progress of the fight, as far as I had observed it.

Having led the regiment to the ground indicated by the brigadier, I sought out that officer, who with General Evans was watching the last ride of the Lancers up the hill.

"The Sixth is in position, sir."

"Ah, very good, Powell; very good. Colonel Ross has lost no time," then turning to the chief, he went on, as if resuming a conversation interrupted by my approach—"The Lancers are full of pluck, but they can't do it, sir; everything is against them."

This final charge of our cavalry was but a repetition of the first one, and soon the regiment came riding back baffled.

Just then Townley galloped up.

"Colonel Apthorpe is advancing, sir."

"Very well; let him support the Sixth," and the brigadier rode to where that regiment stood.

"Colonel Ross, you will take your men against those entrenchments.—Grenadiers, unless you wish to share the glory with the Highlanders, you will have to hurry. Don't fire; the work must be done with the bayonet."

A cheer greeted his little speech, and at the word of command the men marched out into the open as blithely as if no danger awaited them.

Yet they knew well how perilous was the task they were called upon to perform. They had watched the last gallant but futile charge of the Lancers; they saw the hill-slope dotted with the bodies of men and horses; but whatever their private feelings may have been, they exhibited no sign either of fear or faltering.

The Lancers, who were re-forming their shattered ranks, gave them a cheer as they pressed forward at the double; and well they deserved it.

As usual, the Carlists began firing the instant their opponents approached within range; but the Grenadiers kept on until they were only a few yards from the first wall.

Then the cheers of their officers were suddenly drowned in the rattle of musketry; a whole volley at close quarters was poured into the midst of the assailants, and when the smoke cleared away, we recognized sorrowfully that the attack had failed.

My attention was now diverted by the sight of the supporting regiment, and my heart leaped into my mouth as I beheld Pym's horse roll over. But my comrade was uninjured; he sprang to his feet, and, sword in hand, ran forward, Dick treading closely on his heels.

They reached the wall and received the Carlists' fire, but although suffering severely, they doggedly held their ground.

"Oh, good, good! bravo, Highlanders!" we shouted, as if our brave comrades could hear the words above the din of the strife.

A louder roar followed, as one of the Legion was seen to mount the wall and stand erect, waving his sword above his head.

"Who is he? who is he?" men asked each other excitedly; and peering through the glass I perceived that the daring fellow was young Cotton, who a little while before had gaily discussed the chances of being home at Christmas.

The glass nearly slipped through my trembling fingers as I watched what followed. It seemed as if a thousand muskets were levelled at him, and suddenly throwing up his arms, he tottered and fell at the feet of the enemy. At the same moment a body of Carlists rushed down from the second breastwork, and the Sixth were hurled back.

But some were there who would not leave the body of the fallen hero to the mercy of his foes. In the face of almost certain death Pym cleared the wall, so did Dick, and they were followed by nearly a score of noble fellows.

A solemn hush fell upon us, as in sickening suspense we waited for the result. So eagerly were our eyes fixed upon that one spot that we scarcely heeded what went on elsewhere.

I do not know how long the struggle lasted. Judging by my feelings, hours passed, but most probably it was all over in a few seconds.

We broke into a wild outburst of cheering as one by

one the daring band scrambled back, the more so as it was realized that Pym and Dick were bearing the body of the young officer.

The danger was still great, but we forgot that in our exultation, and the little body of rescuers descended the hill amidst tumultuous applause.

The brigadier spurred to meet them, and uncovered reverently in presence of the heroic dead.

"Highlanders," he said, with a touch of emotion, "you have lost a gallant officer, and one who did the regiment honour. I am proud that he belonged to my brigade; indeed, I am proud of you all. What you have just done will live in our memories long after this war is over."

The men saluted respectfully, and leaving poor Cotton's body, prepared to rejoin their regiment.

"All right, Arthur," Pym cried, as I turned after my chief; "not a scratch, and the sergeant has been just as lucky. Warm work, though, up there." And he pointed towards the Carlist entrenchments.

But the fight was nearly at an end, and the enemy had failed to gain an inch of our ground. Gradually the sounds of the firing died away, the cannon no longer thundered from the Ametza hill, and all was quiet in the direction of Alza, where for hours there had been an incessant cannonade.

As I have stated, we maintained our ground, and General Evans, for excellent reasons, did not desire to extend his lines, otherwise, I am convinced that we might have carried the Ametza hill.

Of my Spanish friend Eizmendi I had not heard any tidings during the day, so that it was with a feeling of pleasure I rode over to Alza, bearing a message to El Pastor.

Here the fighting had been unusually severe, but at length the Carlists, foiled in every attempt to storm the fortified positions, had sullenly retired.

Having delivered my message, I looked round for Eizmendi, and found him busily engaged attending to the wants of his men.

At sight of me his face lit up with a smile, and he came forward eagerly.

"I have been thinking of you," he said, "and wondering if you were safe. Have you seen Major Forrester?"

"Yes; he is uninjured, and has distinguished himself as usual. You have been making plenty of noise over here."

"Ah, the Carlists will remember your artillery. But are we not going to follow up our advantage?"

"I believe not. The general thinks it wiser to stay where we are."

"Perhaps he is right; yet it seems a pity, too—our men are full of fight."

Laughing at his impatience, I inquired after Pedro, and was sorry to learn that he had been wounded.

"It is not serious," my comrade hastened to assure me—"a bullet in his left arm; but the surgeon says he will soon be right again."

"Remember me to him. And now I must go back. I

shall be glad to get a little sleep; the Carlists cut my rest short last night."

Eizmendi laughed gaily.

"It was a change after our merry supper-party," he said; "but I don't think we shall be bothered again in a hurry."

I waved him an adieu, and rode off, glad at heart to be assured of his safety.

CHAPTER XXI.

WITH ESPARTERO AT BILBAO.

FOR several days succeeding the battle of Ametza the Legion remained in expectation of a further attack; but the Carlists had lost so heavily that they kept within their own lines, and things gradually settled down into their former state.

Lieutenant Cotton was buried with all the pomp and show of a military funeral; and when the ceremony was over, I made my way to the hospital of San Elmo, where Pedro had been taken.

My old ally plainly showed the pleasure which my visit afforded him. "You are very kind to me, señor," he said; "indeed, every one is alike. Captain Eizmendi has but just gone, and yesterday the sergeant sent a friendly message by one of my fellow-countrymen. Captain Eizmendi tells me that the Carlists were well beaten."

"That is correct. They lost all along the line, though they fought as stubbornly as ever."

"And they kept the hill?"

"Only because we didn't try to turn them out. General Evans is waiting for reinforcements from Espartero."

Pedro shook his head dubiously; he appeared to place little faith in the promises of the Spanish general, and when I was going he told me laughingly that his wound would be healed long before the Legion left San Sebastian.

Although the Carlists, in spite of superior numbers, failed to make any impression upon the northern army, it was far otherwise in various parts of the country, and we continued to receive the most gloomy reports.

In the east, Cabrera, the ablest if most cruel of the Carlist leaders, was gaining an almost uninterrupted series of successes; Gomez, laughing to scorn the feeble attempts of his Christino opponents to capture him, still harried the country; while the authorities at Madrid squabbled and wrangled amongst themselves, heedless of everything beyond mere self-aggrandizement.

Espartero had at last been made commander-in-chief, but had yet to justify his selection; while the other Christino generals, imitating the example set by the statesmen of Madrid, occupied their time in quarrelling with each other.

Yet it was well known to them that, without some assistance from the Spanish army, the Legion was unable to do more than protect San Sebastian from the enemy.

The delay was galling but imperative, and so the weeks crawled by, with nothing more exciting than an occasional trifling outpost affair.

Meanwhile winter was steadily approaching, and those of us who had endured the horrors of Vitoria did not view its advent with any feelings of pleasure.

Early in November we learned that the Carlists had again laid siege to Bilbao, and that Espartero was marching to its relief.

This information raised our expectations considerably, but for a time at least we were doomed to disappointment.

Other three weeks of dreary waiting passed, and then, through the men of the warships, we were informed that Espartero was at Castro with a force fourteen thousand strong.

But the Carlists were not in the humour to surrender their position without striking a blow, and under their energetic leader Villa Real, prepared to dispute the Christino advance on Portugalete, the little town at the mouth of the river Nervion, whence Espartero intended moving upon Bilbao.

In this dilemma the commander of the English squadron offered the use of his boats to transport the Christino army by sea to Portugalete, an offer which Espartero gladly accepted.

From this time the items of information which reached us at different times were of the most conflicting and contradictory character.

For three whole weeks Espartero advanced and retreated alternately, now driving the Carlists before him, again falling back in hot haste upon Portugalete.

One evening, shortly before Christmas, the brigadier told me that General Evans required an officer to carry a letter to Colonel Wylde, the British commissioner, who was with the Christino army, and asked if I would go.

Such a question could of course be answered only in one way, and before many minutes passed I was in the general's room receiving his instructions.

"Give the note to Colonel Wylde himself," he said, "and wait till he is able to send a definite reply. Most likely you will find him at Portugalete; but if Espartero has moved towards Bilbao, you must follow the army. I rely upon your prudence."

"I will do my best, sir; but how shall I get to Portugalete?"

"There is a brig called the *Olava* in the harbour; you had better go on board at once. Stay! I will write a note for the captain."

I returned to my room and put on my topcoat, as the weather seemed very threatening, and then called upon Pym.

"Going to Bilbao!" he exclaimed, when I had told him the news; "well, it is better than being cooped up here, but I am afraid that you will have anything but a pleasant journey."

"I shall be satisfied if it ends safely; these Spanish vessels are not much to my liking."

"Keep a stout heart, my boy. When you return, I shall expect to have a full account of what is happening at Bilbao; things seem very tangled so far."

The *Olava* proved to be a miserable-looking brig whose timbers creaked and groaned horribly even in the comparative smoothness of the harbour. What would happen when we got fairly into the open sea I did not care to contemplate.

The captain, a swarthy, seaman-like fellow, read the general's note, and very courteously offered me the use of his berth.

"We sail early in the morning, señor," he said. "I advise you to take a few hours' rest; the passage will be a stormy one."

I thanked him and turned in, feeling sure that there would be little chance of sleep when once we were under way.

In this surmise I was perfectly correct. It was quite dark when I roused myself, awakened by the shouts of the sailors, the creaking of timber, and the shrill whistle of the wind.

I had slept several hours; it was now morning, but by this time the prospect of fine weather with which the day had opened had utterly vanished.

I crept on deck, and was nearly hurled into the sea by the wind which swept fiercely across the bay. How the crazy little craft managed to live at all in that wild sea was more than I could imagine; it seemed as if each successive wave must crush in her side like an egg-shell.

The observations of a few minutes, however, made it plain that if any science or skill in seamanship could secure safety, we should weather the gale.

The master of the brig was a finished sailor—cool, prompt, and with a perfect knowledge of his art.

"Better stay below, señor; you will be washed overboard," he shouted, during a temporary lull in the storm; but to this I entertained a decided objection.

If the planks failed to hold together, my doom was certain in either way; but I had little liking to be drowned like a rat beneath decks, so I kept my place and held on tenaciously.

Once the captain coming near me shouted, "This can't last, señor; if the storm doesn't go down, we shall."

I nodded vigorously in reply, and steadied myself to meet the shock of the next mountain of water.

Still our craft, straining and creaking as if every single bolt were tearing itself from the woodwork, bounded forward, leaping in a mad race with the furious waves.

But the violence even of nature spends itself at length, and gradually but surely the gale moderated; tiny rifts appeared in the sullen clouds, and the sailors, crossing themselves devoutly, offered up a silent prayer of thanksgiving to the saints.

The danger was still great, but we had passed through the worst of it, and could face the rest with comparative serenity.

Later in the day, when it became possible for the captain to leave the deck, he and I went down into the cabin to get a little food.

"I see that you are something of a sailor, señor," he observed in a tone of approval; "so there is no need to tell you how close we have been to death during the last few hours."

"I am sailor enough to know that, under God, we all owe our lives to your skill."

He shook his head as if unwilling to accept the compli-

BRITISH
10 NO 97
MUSEUM

ment, but his bronzed face flushed with pleasure notwithstanding.

"Thirty years I have sailed these seas," he said; "but at one time this morning I thought I had made my last trip. And the bay will have me yet, like my father and his father before him," he added thoughtfully.

I told him of the wreck of the yacht and of my marvellous escape, by which he was much impressed, and then we went on deck together.

"The storm is over," he said, gazing aloft, where in places the blue sky was visible; "we ought to have a good passage to Portugalete," which as a matter of fact we had.

It was the afternoon of the twenty-fourth of December, and the snow was falling quickly, when I landed in the little port, now filled with Spanish soldiers.

From an officer of the English warship *Saracen* I learned that Colonel Wylde had accompanied Espartero to the post highest up the river, and that the latter had finally resolved upon a decisive engagement.

"High time too," added my informant; "he might have been in Bilbao a month ago."

When I asked what would be the best way of reaching them, he laughed and said, "My advice is to stay here and make yourself comfortable. Most likely Espartero will have another fit, and they will all come tumbling back in an hour or two. Our fellows spend the chief part of their time in pulling up the river and down again, or in building a bridge one day for him to burn the next."

"But my orders are to proceed straight to the commissioner."

"Well, there is a battalion just starting. Tell your errand to the officer in command; he will take you along."

After much difficulty, for the town and the bank of the river were crowded with troops, I made my way to the battalion in question, and discovered, alike to my surprise and pleasure, that the commanding officer was my old friend Don Philip.

We did not waste time in complimentary speeches; the fiery Spaniard was eager to push on, but while we marched along the river-side he explained the nature of the contemplated operations.

Espartero with eight companies was being towed up the river by the English sailors, and the Spanish leader hoped to capture the enemy's most advanced battery. Then a bridge of boats was to be placed across the stream for the passage of the main body, and an attempt immediately made to scale the heights in front.

Don Philip, as usual, was full of hope. "To-morrow we shall be in Bilbao," he said, "and then there will be time for a talk."

We plodded on amidst a blinding snow-storm, and had traversed a considerable distance, when Don Philip suddenly passed the word to halt.

A sound of firing came across the water, then a cheer, and we heard the sweep of oars as the English sailors rowed to our side of the river.

In a time so short that the Spaniards openly expressed

their wonder, the gallant British tars prepared the bridge of boats, and the battalion crossed over.

Another and another followed; and then, before the Carlists could gather their troops together, the heights were captured.

Again and again during the night the enemy returned to the attack, but their efforts were unavailing, and morning found the Christino army still in possession.

Now it was that Espartero proved his fitness for the post of leader. Whatever hesitation, whatever doubt or vacillation, he had previously displayed vanished. Thus far success had attended his last effort, but the scales of victory still hung trembling in the balance. The heights and fort of Banderas frowned down upon him; unless these were speedily secured, defeat was inevitable.

I saw him take his place at the head of two picked battalions and point upwards. What he said I did not hear, but his eyes flashed, his cheeks glowed, every line of his features was stamped with determination.

The Christinos responded to his brief address with an enthusiastic shout, and away they sped with bayonets fixed in the very teeth of the Carlist battery.

The contest was short; the Carlists, unable to resist the vigorous onset, wavered, gave way, and finally broke into flight, pursued by the victors.

At once the entire army was set in motion, and keeping by Don Philip's side, I marched with him to the very gates of Bilbao.

The rout was complete; and the citizens, with cries of

joy, came pouring out of the town to welcome their rescuers.

The evening arrived before I succeeded in delivering the letter to the British commissioner, who told me that he would write an answer on the following morning.

This gave me a little extra time, a part of which I used in seeking out my old friend the doctor, who, when he heard my name, remembered me perfectly.

"It is the generous Englishman who was so kind to the señorita," he cried; "you are heartily welcome, señor, to my poor dwelling. Have you heard news of my beautiful patient?"

"More than that, I have seen her; and whatever kindness I once did she has more than repaid. I, in turn, owe my life to her."

The doctor was loud in his expressions of surprise, and listened eagerly to the story of my capture and subsequent escape from the Carlists.

"Then you have learned the truth about the señorita?" he said.

"Yes; and more oddly still, have formed a friendship with her brother, who is a captain of the Chapelgorris."

My host sighed deeply. "Ah!" he said, "this terrible war, which splits up the members of one family into hostile groups—it is heartrending. But," he added more briskly, "the señorita is at least freed from one evil—Rubio, the robber chief, will not trouble her again."

"How?" I asked; "is he dead?"

"He was recognized last night as a Carlist agent, and

shot in the streets. He was a bad man and a traitor; he has bought and sold both sides."

"Well, I can't grieve at his fate. But why did he behave so badly to the señorita, seeing that they were both friends of Don Carlos?"

"The answer is simple, señor. Her father possessed great riches, and if Don Carlos becomes king—which even now many people think likely—the señorita will be a great heiress."

"Well?"

"In that case Rubio would have made her his wife, and taken possession of the property."

"Poor girl! it is a good thing she has escaped that fate."

I stayed with him a little longer while he told me about the siege and the privations of the citizens; then I took my leave, in order to spend a few hours with Don Philip.

The night was piercingly keen, the snow continued to fall thickly; but in their delight at the Carlist defeat, the inhabitants of Bilbao cared little for the inclemency of the weather.

There was, of course, a scarcity of provisions, but wine was plentiful, and the soldiers who for weeks had bivouacked in the snow revelled in the unwonted luxuries of light and warmth.

I found Don Philip with some other officers, one or two of whom I remembered having met at Vitoria.

The recent success had raised their spirits, and they were in high good-humour, laughing and chatting pleasantly about the conclusion of the war.

There was a pause in the conversation when I entered, and Don Philip introduced me as the Englishman who had been with him at the assault on Ovaro.

"And risked his life to save a wounded sergeant!" exclaimed one. "El Pastor wrote about it to Cordova.—Señor, you are heartily welcome."

"The English are a queer race; they kill you with one hand, and bring you to life with the other. My father used to say that an English soldier was both man and woman."

"That is a high compliment," I answered; "I wish it were always deserved."

"As it is in your case," responded Don Philip gallantly.

"And yet, señor, if I may say it without offence, the English are not popular," remarked the first speaker. "We Spaniards, for example, owe much to England; but I doubt if your countrymen are as well liked as the French, who have treated us so ill."

"The French tickle you with a rapier, the English knock you down with a bludgeon," said a young man who had hitherto been silent.

"Perhaps we lack polish," I interposed laughingly; "we care little for the shell if the kernel be sound."

"Which is a mistake, señor; a sound kernel is none the better for having an ugly covering. But let us change the subject. How have your troops fared at San Sebastian?"

They evinced a lively interest in my description of the doings there, asking numerous questions; and then in turn

Don Philip gave me an account of the campaign in the south.

On one thing they were all agreed—that the relief of Bilbao would prove the turning-point of the war; and when in the early morning I took my leave, it was in the full belief that we should soon meet again.

After breakfast I found Colonel Wylde, and received the letter for General Evans.

"A gunboat starts for San Sebastian in an hour or two," he said. "If you go down to Portugalete at once, the commander will take you with him."

The furious storm had ceased, but everything looked dreary and desolate, and the sight of the mountains covered with snow made Espartero's expected advance appear extremely problematical.

Fortunately the return journey was devoid of incident, and at night I found myself back in San Sebastian at the general's quarters.

"I fear that you have not had a very merry Christmas, Powell," he said kindly. "Did you give the commissioner my letter?"

"Yes, sir. I could not get to him before we entered Bilbao, and—"

"Bilbao! Then Espartero has raised the siege; that is good news. Where is the reply? Ah, thank you. Ask General Chichester to come to me."

I saluted and went out to give the brigadier the message.

"Back again, Powell!" said my chief; "I was just

wondering if you were at the bottom of the sea. What! Espartero in Bilbao! That's famous; we shall make a move. Going to look up Forrester, I suppose?"

"Yes, sir, if you can spare me for an hour or two."

"Oh, go and enjoy yourself, my boy; you've earned a good rest."

I found from Pym's servant that he had gone with a young Spanish officer—one of the Chapelgorris—to the house of Señor Escovedo.

"The major didn't know whether you would get back to-night, sir," the man added; "but if you did, I was to ask you to join him."

Señor Escovedo was giving a party, and the news of Espartero's exploit naturally caused much rejoicing amongst the guests.

As soon as I had given all the details known to me, I drew Eizmendi aside, and told him of Rubio's death in the streets of Bilbao.

"I am in debt to the citizens," he said; "but I hoped that the ruffian would fall by my hand. Still, my poor Juanita need fear him no longer. Ah, my brave friend, if only my sister were out of danger, I should be content. But this is not the time for sadness. Tell me of your adventures; the major was afraid that you would go down with the brig."

"That is just like the dear fellow. He fears for me, while he would laugh at the idea of danger for himself."

"I envy you his friendship," my comrade said; "I wish you two were always going to stay in Spain."

"Come back with us to England when we go," laughed Pym, who caught the last words—"that is, if the Carlists give us the opportunity."

Eizmendi sighed. "You forget my sister," he said; "I cannot leave her. It may chance that at some time she will want my help," and Pym agreed with him.

A little later, feeling tired and sleepy, I begged Pym to make my apologies to our host, and slipped away, glad of the chance to obtain a good night's rest.

The weather still continued unusually severe, but the troops were fairly well sheltered, and General Evans had considerately added a little extra money to the ordinary payment.

This, together with the generosity of many of the officers, enabled the men to indulge in several trifling luxuries, and in spite of the inclement season, the Christmas of 1836 passed merrily enough.

We were all cheered, too, by persistent rumours that the Christino leaders had formed a plan of campaign, and that the early months of 1837 would, at least in the northern provinces, witness the collapse of the Carlist cause.

But the days passed away—January came and went—and the promises of the Spaniards were still unfulfilled. The reinforcements from Espartero did not arrive, and without them General Evans was powerless.

February had well set in when five thousand Spaniards, among whom was my old friend Don Philip, landed at San Sebastian, having been brought round from Portugalete by the British warships.

Even then we were compelled to remain idle until Espartero was ready to march, and the snow still held him fast in the neighbourhood of Bilbao.

"The delay is vexing," Don Philip said one day, when Pym and I called upon him; "but I am content to wait. We are on the eve of striking a decisive blow. General Sarsfield is at Pamplona with fifteen thousand men, Espartero has twenty thousand at Bilbao, and directly the weather breaks up they will make a simultaneous attack upon the Carlist positions. At the same time, we shall advance in the centre, and the enemy will be driven back without a chance of rallying."

"Something ought to be done soon," Pym remarked thoughtfully. "Our men were only enlisted for two years, and their service comes to an end in June. My opinion is that we have wasted a month already. The difficulties were great, I admit, but they might have been got over."

Until my comrade spoke, it had hardly occurred to me that our engagement with the Spanish Government ended at any set time, and on our way back I asked Pym what he intended to do when the Legion was dissolved.

"We had better wait till the time comes, Arthur," he answered a little sadly; "perhaps before then the Carlists will have put it out of our power to choose," and somehow the reply filled me with misgivings.

CHAPTER XXII.

THE ATTACK ON THE VENTA.

ON the ninth of March 1837, the snow in the neighbourhood of San Sebastian covered the ground to the depth of more than a foot; but in spite of this, every one hailed with gladness the preparations for moving out. The vexatious delay was at an end; the campaign had been planned in detail by the responsible chiefs; within a fortnight the Carlists would be utterly crushed and the war in the north finished.

This was not a mere vain imagining, born in the brain of an ardent enthusiast, but that which, according to the sober calculations of experienced judges, was almost morally certain. General Evans had ten thousand men at his disposal, Espartero was advancing on the left with twenty thousand, Sarsfield on the right with fifteen thousand, so that only by a victorious engagement could the Carlists prevent themselves from being hemmed in.

In the morning the regiments were paraded and weeded of the invalids, two days' rations were served out, and a little money given to each man for the purpose of buying a few extras.

Later in the day the field-guns were brought close to the lines, and were followed by the mules laden with ammunition.

Then in the evening the soldiers made their purchases, ate their suppers, and lay down in their old quarters, as all fondly hoped for the last time.

Scarcely any one thought of sleeping. The men for the most part smoked in silence, or talked to each other in subdued whispers, while some occupied the time in scribbling a note to the loved ones at home, whom they might never see again.

About ten o'clock Pym and I, having spent an hour with Eizmendi, rode over to see Don Philip.

Our Spanish friend was infected by the excitement of the impending fight. His habitually grave and passive features were transformed; his eyes flashed; there was an air of recklessness about him that I did not like to see.

"You have come that we may wish each other God-speed," he said. "That is kind, and I thank you. I was hoping that we should be placed with your brigade."

"You will have plenty of work by the side of the Irish Brigade," I laughed; "but don't expose yourself without cause. Your life is too valuable to be lightly thrown away."

"Ah, my dear friend," he cried, "if you only understood how weary I am of it all! But we must banish sorrow at such a time as this. To-morrow we strike the first of the blows which will end the war. I will give you a toast, señors—'Success to the British Legion.'"

"And a prosperous reign to the little queen," I added.

"Arthur," said Pym, when, having bidden Don Philip adieu, we were riding back, "do you know the proverb about counting the chickens?"

"Yes; why?"

"It is a very unsatisfactory performance," he responded good-humouredly, at which we both laughed.

Leaving my comrade at the quarters of the Eighth Regiment, I rode on to meet General Chichester, who was returning from an interview with the chief.

"Well, Powell," he exclaimed cheerfully, "everything ready?"

"Yes, sir, the men only wait for the signal; they seem pleased at the prospect of doing something."

"There will be a tough fight; but if the queen's generals stick to their words, we are bound to win."

About one o'clock on the morning of the tenth, word was passed round quietly for the troops to fall in, and very soon Chichester's brigade—consisting of the Rifles, the Fourth, and the Eighth Regiments—was drawn up in close column behind the battery known as the Queen's.

Close at hand the Lancers were turning out, and various Spanish regiments marched past us to their appointed stations.

Leaving my horse behind, I walked to the battery with the brigadier, who was watching anxiously for the signal.

For a little time the soldiers continued their whispering, but gradually all sounds ceased, and were succeeded by a great hush of expectation.

Slowly the blackness gave place to a faint grey, the outlines of the adjacent hills showed up, and at last we discerned the signal which was to begin the fight.

General Chichester went back to the brigade and gave his orders. Almost immediately we were deafened by a tremendous roar from the big guns, and a blaze of fire leaped into the air—the artillery was at work.

Then, with the Rifles leading, we marched out, and were soon going forward at the double.

But the Irish Brigade, having a shorter distance to traverse, reached the hill first, and the Carlists, in obedience to orders, retired.

General Chichester at once directed his troops to ascend the hill on the north-west, upon which the Carlists abandoned the position, and the three regiments piled arms.

But although we were thus idle, the fight raged furiously both on our right and left. The Carlists, driven from their first line of defences, retired to several lofty heights near at hand, and here the fiercest fighting of the day took place.

One ridge in particular the enemy stuck to most resolutely. It commanded the road from Hernani, and its possession was therefore of the highest importance to both parties.

Four times in succession General Evans, sword in hand, led the Spanish regiments in a successful charge; but after each repulse the Carlists, as if invigorated by temporary defeat, returned and hurled the assailants from the heights.

Don Philip was engaged at this spot, and I trembled a thousand times for his safety.

Heedless of bullets, of bayonet-thrusts, or the play of swords, he rushed again and again up the slope, the first to reach the height, the last to leave it, and this reckless bravery inspired his troops with fresh courage.

"Arthur," said Pym sorrowfully, "our old friend is doomed; he can't keep up that kind of thing for ever."

I nodded, but did not speak; the same thought was running in my own mind.

Just then, however, Chichester sent me with a message to Brigadier-general Fitzgerald and on returning I beheld a grand and magnificent spectacle.

Nature, as if despising the efforts of the human combatants, treated us to a display of her power on a colossal scale.

The hills, from base to summit, were clothed—in some parts sparsely, in others thickly—with furze and brushwood, and this, towards the close of the day, caught fire.

Aided by a strong wind which now sprang up, the fire spread rapidly, leaping from height to height, from east to west, until the whole range of hills seemed in a glow.

Immense clouds of smoke ascended slowly, and through them pierced belt after belt of fire, bathing the very heavens in flame.

"Has Don Philip fallen?" I asked Pym, while we stood watching the terrible conflagration.

"No; he is across there to the left with his regiment. I wonder if any harm has happened to Eizmendi."

"He was with Jaureguy's brigade, which has captured San Marco."

"Then we have made a good start. I wonder what to-morrow's programme will be like."

"I expect Evans will wait for news of his colleagues; he can't do everything by himself."

"I don't like these divided commands," Pym remarked; "they almost always cause disaster. However, we must not begin to grumble yet."

The troops now prepared to camp for the night, and although a few found comfortable quarters in the neighbouring houses, the main body bivouacked on the hill-side.

The next day, as I anticipated, we simply kept our ground, and during the evening a letter was brought from Pamplona which rendered it necessary for Evans to change his plans.

The Spanish general Sarsfield, instead of adhering to the original arrangement, suddenly announced his intention of advancing, not towards our right, but on our left—a course which must inevitably end in the destruction of his army.

Eager to do anything that would prevent such a catastrophe, our chief ordered General Chichester to cross the Urimea with his brigade, and drive the Carlists from the village of Loyola, which was accordingly done on the morning of the twelfth, amidst a heavy downpour of rain.

As it was impossible to attempt anything further before the rest of the army came up, the men were quartered in the forsaken houses, while the sailors of the *Phœnix* threw a pontoon bridge across the river.

Unwilling to believe in the suicidal policy of his colleague, General Evans, hoping for fresh news, kept the army in Loyola; but on the morning of the fourteenth the arrival of a second letter removed any trace of doubt which might still have lingered in his mind.

Sarsfield was actually on his way, and every hour would bring him nearer to the formidable mountain positions of Lecumberi, where the Carlists had over fourteen thousand men, with a number of guns.

Many leaders would under such circumstances have probably remained inactive, at least until Espartero arrived; but the chief of the Legion resolved upon succouring the mistaken general to the best of his ability.

"We must advance, gentlemen," he said to those in his counsels; "an energetic attack upon the positions in front of us will very likely induce the Carlists to send a strong force from Lecumberi."

In other words, the army of San Sebastian was to rectify the Spaniard's error.

For the second day in succession the rain had poured down almost without a stop, and when about one o'clock the troops turned out, the soil was soaked.

The passage of the mules with the ammunition and light artillery rendered the ground a perfect quagmire, and we moved through the mud and water as best we could.

At one time sinking in the swamps, at another climbing barely accessible hills, or forcing a way through obstructing hedges, we kept on until the Carlist positions came into view.

Then the rockets blazed forth, and the guns, taken from the mules' backs, were discharged, while the infantry ran at the double.

All this time the rain continued to pour in torrents, and the enemy, finding themselves at a disadvantage, rapidly retreated.

The nature of the ground made pursuit out of the question, as the active mountaineers could easily go two miles for our one; but General Chichester ordered the Rifles forward, and to that regiment and the Fourth was assigned the duty of mounting pickets on the outposts during the night.

Thus far we had done extremely well, and even those who were acquainted with Sarsfield's communication felt little uneasiness concerning the ultimate result, at least with regard to the San Sebastian army.

The night was wild and stormy, but by good-luck I secured quarters in a house which evidently belonged to some Spanish nobleman, and in spite of the tempest raging outside, I slept comfortably for several hours.

The morning of the fifteenth opened as usual with rain, which, however, stopped towards noon, when all the regiments were paraded and the officers told what was expected of them.

I saw Don Philip for a few moments just before his battalion marched off the ground. He was still jubilant and excited, and declared that we should sleep in Hernani.

I smiled, and hoped that he would prove a true prophet, but at the same time I should have liked to hear something of Espartero and his twenty thousand men; how one army was going to accomplish the work of three, I did not exactly comprehend.

Happily, perhaps, for me, my sole duty lay in obeying, and while Don Philip still waited for his final instructions, I was galloping across the fields with an order to Colonel Fortescue of the Rifles.

The Carlists had opened fire with their heavy cannon, but the distance, as yet, was too great; and having delivered my message in safety, I cantered back to where the brigadier stood.

A little on the left, a body of Chapelgorris, perhaps two hundred strong, marched onwards with light, active steps, thinking nothing of the boggy ground.

I pulled up a minute to watch them, and then it was I recognized with joy that the officer leading was young Eizmendi.

At the same moment he caught sight of me, and raising his sword, uttered a cheery "*Viva,* Señor Powell!"

This was a pleasant meeting, the more especially as I had been uncertain if the dashing Chapelgorri still lived.

"We are about to begin the work," he cried exultingly, as I rode across; "I hope the enemy are tired of running."

"Good-luck to you and your brave lads!" I answered.

"*Viva,* Señor Inglese!" cried the band, and then to the "Forward!" of Eizmendi they swept past.

It was well that the successes of the previous days had

inspired the army with confidence, as the task now about to be undertaken was most assuredly of an exceedingly perilous nature.

Between us and Hernani towered the frowning hill of Oriamendi, or the Venta, as it was familiarly called. Almost impregnable by nature, the Carlists had strengthened it still further by a series of fortifications.

From base to summit the hill simply bristled with obstacles. Trenches had been cut, earthworks thrown up, walls stoutly built, while behind each line of defence stood the foe, musket in hand, prepared to fight with their usual dogged obstinacy.

The Venta was the key of the position; once we made ourselves masters of it, the town beyond seemed absolutely at our mercy.

The weather had now cleared, but the ground was still wet and slippery, making it difficult for the troops to march.

Unwelcome messengers from the Venta, in the shape of cannon balls, continued to fall short of us; but at length we advanced to a spot just out of range, and received an order to halt.

That moment had come, so full of suspense even to the bravest veteran—the brief interval before the actual beginning of the fight.

The elevation in front effectually screened us from the view of the Carlist gunners, but our shelter was only temporary; in a very few minutes we should be playing the part of living targets.

General Evans, accompanied by his staff, rode forward and promptly made his dispositions for the attack.

The Rifles, with the First Regiment and three battalions of Spaniards—one of these last commanded by Don Philip—moved out to the left; the Ninth and Tenth Regiments stayed to attack the centre, while the Eighth were ordered to advance in front.

"Find out where the Carlists are," said Chichester to Colonel Hogg, "but don't press them too closely;" and the Highlanders, scrambling across a wide ditch swollen with rain, entered a field of furze, amidst which they were half hidden.

"A capital place for an ambush," remarked Major Townley, as we watched intently for the first puff of smoke; "a whole battalion could lie concealed amongst that stuff."

"Perhaps they intend meeting us on the hill," I suggested.

"For the final struggle, but there is plenty to be done before we get there. Ah, I thought as much; look yonder."

Right away at the end of the furze rose up a volume of smoke, and we heard the whiz of the bullets, as they tore through the air, falling thickly amongst the men of the Eighth.

That volley was the signal for a general activity. Everywhere the bugles sounded the advance, and the brigadier turning to me, said, "Tell Colonel Hogg to clear the enemy out of that, and then wait for the artillery to get up."

I cleared the ditch, and making the best of my way through the furze, rode hard after the Eighth.

The Carlists, still firing, fell back to a thick wood, and Colonel Hogg, in obedience to his orders, drew up his regiment at a distance of about three hundred yards, under shelter of a ditch bank.

Meanwhile the other regiments advanced, and the marine artillery began to throw shot and shell into the wood, until the return volleys gradually slackened.

Seizing the opportunity, the brigadier ordered a further advance, and headed by the Eighth, we crossed the roadway into the wood.

Little by little we pushed the Carlists back on all sides to the Venta, where, as has been intimated, they had resolved upon making their final stand.

Everything depended upon the successful storming of the hill, and I will frankly acknowledge that the feat appeared to me little short of the impossible.

But the critical moment had arrived; the thunder of the artillery ceased, and with a loud yell the men, headed by their officers, dashed at the first barricade.

It is quite beyond my power accurately to describe what then took place. Over the heads of the charging regiments the artillery threw shot and shell; the rockets went hissing through the air; while the Carlists, undaunted, kept up an incessant musketry fire.

Then, too, the great guns at the top of the hill boomed out, but through it all the soldiers pressed on with fixed bayonets; and a great shout arose when Colonel Hogg, with Pym, Dick, and a handful of others, scrambled to the top of the huge barricade.

At this juncture I rode off with instructions for the artillery to cease firing, and from my new vantage-ground beheld those who were already over tearing down the barricade to make way for the rest.

Then re-forming under a heavy fire, the assailants pressed on until they were completely enwrapped by the heavy smoke.

For some time I continued to gaze, able to distinguish the progress of our troops only by the shouts and flashes of musketry.

But it soon became evident that the Carlists were in full retreat; the sounds of firing became less and less distinct, the mist partly cleared, and showed us that the Carlist flag was no longer flying over the battery at the summit.

We had paid dearly for it, but the stronghold was ours, even without the aid of Espartero and his big battalions.

We were unable to follow up our success before the morning, as darkness was rapidly drawing in, but according to every human probability we should be in Hernani ere the setting of another sun.

Meanwhile it was necessary that the soldiers should bivouac in the open fields, and during the next hour or two I was riding from one place to another with the various directions.

All along the range of heights the regiments were quartered, and very speedily a row of twinkling fires shone out, as the men applied a light to everything of the nature of wood which by any possibility could be induced to burn.

Some, who preferred sleep to warmth and chatter, made primitive bedsteads for themselves by lopping off branches of trees and laying them on the marshy ground.

The majority, however, sat round the fires, and talked about their recent deeds of daring, or boasted of the ease with which Hernani would be taken on the morrow.

But amongst the officers, with whom I sat for an hour, this feeling of confidence was not so marked, and curiously enough the one who most clearly perceived the danger of our position was Alphonso Eizmendi.

"I know my countrymen, and of what they are capable," he said. "While we rest here, the whole country-side is astir. By this time the news of our victory has penetrated into every corner of the province. Across every goat-track on the mountains swift runners are speeding to summon help. From the villages the peasants are pouring forth; every man for miles around will bring his musket, and stand to the last against us."

"A few thousand undisciplined peasants will make little difference," Pym remarked; "a couple of drilled battalions would work much more harm."

"You can count on half a score. If I know anything of the Carlist leaders, their troops are already on the way."

"They will arrive too late—that is, unless they possess the means of flying."

"Besides," said another speaker, "you are taking no notice of the queen's forces; you have forgotten both Espartero and Sarsfield."

Now, Eizmendi was a Biscayan, and had unbounded confidence in the superiority of his countrymen. According to his ideas, the finest soldiers in the world were the Chapelgorris, and next in order came their opponents the Carlists; the Spaniards from the south did not count.

"If Hernani falls to-morrow, it will be at our hands," he declared gravely; "we shall not be helped by a single extra bayonet."

This was far from a cheering opinion, but nevertheless the youthful Chapelgorri obstinately maintained it, and I noticed that Pym in particular seemed inclined to lean to his views.

Night, however, was closing in rapidly, and as under any circumstances a heavy day's work lay before us, we stretched ourselves in our comfortless quarters, and tried to sleep.

I do not know how it fared with others, but in my case the attempt was only partly successful. I closed my eyes, and endeavoured resolutely to banish all thoughts of a disagreeable character, but the vision conjured up by Eizmendi's words would not go away.

In my waking dream I stood on the mountain-top, and beheld at my feet regiment after regiment of active, lightly-armed Carlists pass by with long, swinging strides.

On the faces of all was a look of intense eagerness, and

the officers who marched at their head appeared to be listening for something—perhaps for the thunder of the guns.

Restlessly I turned and tossed from side to side, and once the nature of my dream was so vivid that I sprang up; but all was still, and nothing could be seen in the darkness of the night save the embers of the dying fires.

CHAPTER XXIII.

THE DEATH OF DON PHILIP.

DAY opened on a dreary, cheerless scene, and I rose from my wretched couch wellnigh overpowered by a sense of physical weariness.

The soldiers were already stirring, and eagerly swallowing the mouthful of *aguardienta* which, with a little biscuit, served as the morning meal.

I had just buckled on my sword and mounted my horse, when the heavy guns began the operations of the day by throwing a few shells into Hernani.

No news of Sarsfield had as yet come, and General Evans, afraid that his colleague was in desperate straits, resolved upon attacking the enemy at all costs.

In order to accomplish this object, it became necessary to extend the troops considerably, and very soon the different regiments were marching forward to take up their new ground.

Everything at first went well, and it appeared as if our exertions were to be rewarded by a further and perhaps decisive success.

The Carlists gave way, some of them retiring into the

town, while others retreated slowly to the rocky hill of Santa Barbara, which overhangs Hernani from the westward.

At this time it seemed probable that the engagement would closely resemble the contest of the previous day.

As far as I could judge, and the idea was shared by many others, the enemy intended making a stand on the height of Santa Barbara.

The ground on our extreme left, and far in advance of the main body, was held by the First Regiment, whose colonel, the brave and gallant De Lancy, had met his death on the preceding evening.

The two flank companies were posted at two houses near the river-side, and it was here that the first disaster of the day occurred.

A Spanish battalion was drawn up in support of the regiment, the Rifles were at some distance, and behind them again a battalion composed of the Third and Fourth Regiments.

As I have said, there seemed scarcely any likelihood of an attack; the enemy continued to retire, and our troops were marching to their appointed stations.

But within a few minutes the whole aspect of the battlefield was changed.

We had left the Eighth in the shelter of a hollow, and were riding towards the artillery, when I suddenly caught sight of the Spanish battalion in full retreat, and drew the brigadier's attention to the spectacle.

With an angry exclamation he spurred his horse to the

gallop, and attended by Major Townley and myself, dashed forward at a headlong pace.

Then, as we obtained a clearer view of what was taking place, I remembered Eizmendi's words, and realized that he had not spoken without reason.

The Carlist leader Moreno had achieved a feat which we deemed impracticable. Whether he had beaten or slipped past Sarsfield we had not the means of finding out, but here he was with his indomitable troops, having made a forced march of twelve leagues.

Wet, famishing, and foot-sore they were, but full of fight withal, as we were soon to learn. While they marched along the Hernani road in the direction of Astigarraga, they were screened from observation by the lofty ridge of Santa Barbara, and the ill-fated soldiers at the outposts were ignorant of their presence until they crossed the river.

The situation of the two advanced companies was appalling. The main body of their regiment could give them no help, the Spaniards were hurrying off, and they were literally surrounded by the victorious foe.

But they did not intend dying without striking a blow. Headed by their officers, they dashed with a loud "hurrah" at the enemy, and although many fell, a few succeeded in cutting a way through.

The Carlists, to the cry of "*Viva Carlos Quinto!*" pressed on, and the First, disconcerted by the startling suddenness of the attack and the flight of the Spanish battalion, wavered.

"Powell, tell Colonel Fortescue to throw his right wing

at them," and while the brigadier kept straight on, I turned aside towards the Rifles.

The task was full of peril, but the Rifles did not pause to reflect when the colonel gave his order.

Down the ravine in front of them they rushed with such a wild impetuosity that the nearest Carlist column, in spite of the bravery displayed by the leaders, broke up in momentary confusion.

But as I turned to go back, it became only too plain that we were surrounded and far outnumbered.

From left to right the whole line blazed with fire.

General Chichester, some distance up the field, was leading his men in person; but before I reached him I beheld a sight which filled me with the deepest grief.

Don Philip's battalion was excellently posted on a slight eminence, towards which a Carlist column approached, firing. I saw my old friend encouraging his men, exhorting them, probably, to stand fast. Suddenly the Carlists halted, poured in a destructive volley, and prepared to charge.

I could hardly keep from a cry of rage as I perceived the Spaniards, panic-stricken, turn and bolt, like rabbits scurrying to a warren.

But gallant fellows were there, too, who scorned to desert their heroic leader. Untouched by the hail of bullets, he sat his horse, looking at the oncoming host with a proud defiance; then, as if courting death, he dashed into the midst of their ranks, and was followed by about a hundred of his men.

His "*Viva Isabella!*" was almost drowned in the roar of "*Viva Carlos Quinto!*" as the Carlists swallowed up their victims.

But the officer who led that gallant little remnant was fighting not for life but death. It was the scene in the old inn played over again on a larger scale. Even at a distance I could mark his track through the crowded throng, as he forced his horse now this way, now that; and I noted, too, with a feeling of gratification, how nobly his men seconded his efforts.

With lightning-like movements his sword flashed here and there, and ever he guided his horse where the enemy clustered most thickly.

I looked round for any possible help, but none was forthcoming; in that part of the field there was not an idle bayonet.

My own duty called me elsewhere, but in the excitement I forgot the brigadier, and spurred forward furiously to the Don's aid.

What good could come of this mad ride I did not stop to consider, but I longed to do something for my gallant ally.

Alas! the hope was a vain one. Against such overwhelming odds the greatest valour, the most desperate energy, availed little. The *vivas* of the Christinos grew fainter and more faint, while those of their opponents increased in strength.

For a moment I lost sight of Don Philip in the *mêlée;* then he reappeared, and rising in his stirrups, the better to wield his sword, he urged on the survivors with a last "*Viva Isabella!*"

But the end was at hand. Maddened by their heavy losses, the Carlists sprang at him with a vindictive fury. They seized the bridle-rein of his horse, they surrounded him with a forest of bayonets, and bleeding from innumerable wounds, rider and steed sank slowly from sight.

At the fall of their leader, those of the Christinos who could manage to struggle from the press turned and fled, nor did I blame their action. Inspired by the spectacle of the Don's courage, they had fought valiantly and well, with the full knowledge that they must eventually be overpowered.

To stay longer was to die, and that to but little purpose. Therefore they ran towards their more cowardly comrades, who had viewed the death-struggle from afar; and the victorious column, giving tongue like a pack of fox-hounds, swept after them.

I knew that my old ally was dead, but rode on nevertheless to the spot where his body lay. His stiffened fingers still grasped the sword, and in spite of his violent death his features wore an air of peace.

I bared my head in reverent homage to the fallen hero, and turned sorrowfully away.

Meanwhile the enemy had been persistently following up their advantage in all quarters, and in spite of numerous individual deeds of heroism, of reckless bravery, of stern self-sacrifice, our troops were driven back.

Fresh from witnessing the death of Don Philip, I perceived Eizmendi with his Chapelgorris. Near them a body of Carlists had seized a height, and from that advantageous position they continued to pour volley after volley into the ranks of the Fourth, which was hotly engaged with another battalion.

Without waiting for orders, Eizmendi pointed to the hill-side and set off running. The Chapelgorris wanted no coaxing, no encouragement; their officer was in front, and that alone sufficed.

Away they sped, leaping like goats over the uneven ground. Military men, I suppose, would have censured their formation, or rather want of formation; but the result of the charge was none the less effective.

It was a case of the fleetest first, while all would be in time to do good service.

And of this band the swiftest of foot was young Eizmendi, who ran before the others as if engaged in a race.

Still foremost, he gained the hill, and without even one backward glance, went up. I could hardly bear to keep my eyes upon him, so deeply had the recent death of Don Philip impressed me.

But he stood alone only for an instant. The Chapelgorris, who worshipped their daring young leader, rushed forward, reached him, and almost without a pause hurled their opponents down the slope.

"Splendidly done!" exclaimed Chichester, whom I now joined.—"Powell, do you know the name of that officer?"

"Captain Eizmendi, sir."

"A brave fellow. Come on, Fourth, come on; we'll give them a taste of the bayonet."

The men, who had been exposed to a telling fire both in front and on the flanks, responded gladly; they felt it a relief to be moving, and with a thundering "hurrah" ran after us.

At the critical moment Eizmendi's band fired, and the Carlists, partially disconcerted, wavered. That one instant decided the affair. Before they could rally we were upon them, in their midst, and throwing them into utter disorder.

Elated by this success, many of our men ran in pursuit, upon seeing which the brigadier ordered the recall to be sounded, and sent me to bring them back.

We had ousted the Carlists from their position, but were too weak to do more.

Just previously to the charge the Eighth had come up, and now I darted an anxious glance at them. They had been in the thick of the fight only a short while, but had been roughly handled, and a groan rose to my lips when I discovered that Pym and Dick were missing.

If these my two trustiest friends had fallen, then indeed would this sixteenth of March be a black-letter day to me.

I longed to rush over and make inquiries—the suspense was sickening; but duty compelled me to sit my horse calmly amidst the whizzing of the bullets, and await the orders of the brigadier.

On our right, the Sixth were gradually being overpowered by the sheer weight of numbers; on our left, the Eighth,

Ninth, and Tenth were throwing their lives away in a vain endeavour to check the progress of the swarming columns.

Suddenly the brigadier, who had been peering anxiously through his glass, turned to me and said sharply, "Powell, do you see yonder wood? Major Forrester is holding it with a part of the Eighth. He must come back at once; the enemy are closing round him. Ride, my boy, ride; take the shortest course."

My heart gave a great leap as I bounded away. Pym still lived and was in danger. Should I be in time to save him? I fixed my eyes on the goal, and utterly indifferent to all else, urged my horse onwards. Bullets hissed past me, shot and shell flew screaming over my head, long fiery rockets went trailing in their snake-like paths; at one moment I was enveloped in clouds of smoke, at another, I became a clear target for a thousand Carlists.

Men shouted and cheered as they stood to receive the onset of the enemy, or in their turn rushed forward to the charge. The wounded lay groaning on the ground, or crawled towards their comrades; officers waved their swords, and urged their men to stand fast; bodies of troops advanced or retreated; but of all these things I was only dimly conscious—my senses were centered in that yet distant wood.

Should I be too late? That was all I could think of. I rode wildly, and my gallant horse, as if fully understanding the need of speed, literally flew over the ground.

The Eighth, guessing my errand, gave me a cheer as I swept by, and then making straight for the wood, I rode right across the head of a Carlist battalion. A mounted officer snatched at my bridle-rein, but a stroke from my sword sent him reeling.

A shower of bullets fell about me, so close that I marvelled at their missing; but still unchecked I rode on, until my horse's sides were bathed in perspiration.

And now it appeared that, whichever way I turned, death or capture, which was worse, stared me in the face. By this time I was actually in the rear of some of the Carlist regiments, and others were moving up, while round that part of the wood where Pym's detachment was posted stretched a belt of fire.

But duty and friendship alike impelled me to go on, and through the smoke and fire I dashed in a kind of frenzy.

The question which had been ringing in my ears was answered.

Too late? Yes, too late for life, but soon enough for death. We had faced it before together; we would do so again. My sole hope now was that I might reach my friends; death would lose half its terrors if Dick and Pym were by my side.

I cheered loudly as my horse carried me into the enclosure, and at the familiar sound Pym turned his head.

"You are to retire at once," I cried excitedly; "it is the brigadier's order."

He pointed to the Carlists massed on three sides and said, "Too late, Arthur; before we got twenty yards we should be cut down to a man.—My lads, shall we meet the enemy's bullets in front, or be pierced by their bayonets in the back?"

"We'll die here, major," they answered with a shout.

"Good-bye, Arthur," Pym said; "tell the brigadier how it was, and remember me to those at home."

"Good-bye, sir," cried Dick; "God bless you! Off you go; they're coming."

I sat still, gazing steadily at the approaching host. The sergeant seized my bridle-rein to turn the horse's head.

"No need, Dick—I'm not going," I said; "we three stand or fall together, my friend; it's your own teaching."

"Back, Arthur, back, for God's sake!" urged Pym passionately; "why should you die?"

"Let him be, major, let him be," said Dick.—"Boys, a cheer for the captain, who thinks our company good enough to die in."

The brave fellows, simple in many respects as children, responded with a rousing cheer which startled the Carlists, who halted a moment in order to learn the cause of such enthusiasm.

For the last time I pressed Pym's hand, smiled at Dick, and waited calmly for the onslaught.

"Steady, lads," said Pym; "keep your fire till the word is given, and then trust to the bayonet."

It was, as we all thoroughly believed, the last moment of our lives, yet I did not see a single man shrink. They stood up boldly, some pale, with lips sternly compressed, others red and excited, but all showing a gallant front to the foe.

Suddenly we heard a burst of the most glorious music —the bugles of the Lancers sounding the charge.

Pym's face shone with the light of a renewed hope, and instantly he wheeled his men to leave the ground clear.

As the leading files were nearly abreast of us he gave the order to fire, and many of the Carlists dropped.

Immediately after our volley the Lancers swept upon the disconcerted column and broke it, so little did the enemy dream of having to withstand a cavalry charge.

"Bravo!" we shouted; "cheers for the Lancers!" but the work was not yet done. Indeed the situation became more critical than ever. From behind a stone wall two fresh regiments unexpectedly sprang up; the Lancers were within an ace of annihilation.

But now a battery which had been hastily shifted from another position began to play upon the enemy, who scattered in all directions.

The Lancers' work was done, and they prepared to retire.

"Back, lads, with the cavalry!" shouted Pym; and so, with many of the men clinging to the Lancers' stirrups, the retreat began, while on both flanks the enemy continued firing.

Pym, whose horse had long ago been shot, was walking in the rear, and supporting a wounded man.

I looked round for Dick, secretly wondering that he was not with the major.

However, I soon discovered him a few yards away, kneeling on the ground over some dark object.

"Come, Dick; we are all behind," I cried, and rode towards him.

"That you, sir," he answered, as coolly as if we were in a Devonshire lane; "then it's all right. I was wondering how to get this fellow away; he can't move a step. If you'll just lend a hand, we'll stick him on the horse somehow, and I can hold him."

I looked at my old friend admiringly; his was the kind of courage that did not need the stimulus of the battle-shout to sustain it, and I rejoiced in the knowledge that this stout-hearted veteran considered me to be worthy of his friendship.

I leaped to the ground and helped to raise the fallen man.

"Gently, sir, gently; mind his leg. Ah!" as a groan escaped the sufferer, "there's plenty of life in him yet. He isn't much of a weight, that's one thing. Now you get up while I hold him. That's a good horse."

"And a good aim," I answered, as a bullet tore a hole through my cap.

"Yes," said my comrade reflectively, "there's some pretty fair marksmen in that crowd."

This, I felt, was a subject that might well stand over till a more convenient season. I had no desire to prove the truth of Dick's assertion at the expense of a bullet through my body, so bidding my comrade hold fast, I pushed on to overtake the rear.

Fortunately for us the bursting shells still kept the enemy back, and although the regiments on our flanks kept up their fire, they did not effect much more execution.

Outside the wood Pym re-formed his men, and by making a wide detour succeeded in rejoining the nearest regiment, which was, I believe, the Tenth.

In spite of all the Legion's efforts, the retreat had now become general, and the Carlists, making use of every available bayonet, pressed their victory home.

I was asking Colonel Wakefield of the Lancers if he had seen General Chichester, when an officer, whose name has escaped me, galloped up furiously with the news that the artillery were surrounded, and their retreat cut off.

The heavy guns had been taken from the main road and placed on an eminence, from which it was difficult to remove them.

This was unknown to me at the time; but when, in obedience to their colonel's orders, the Lancers rode off, I of course went with them.

Several times that day the Lancers had shown themselves capable of valiant deeds, but now they were called upon to surpass their most daring achievements.

On either side of the main road was wooded ground filled by the enemy, who, themselves unseen, could sweep the intervening space with their fire, while close to the battery thousands of Carlists were massed.

For many of us that ride was to be the last, but no one faltered. The honour of the Legion demanded that the guns should be brought back; while the sight of the heroic artillerymen, battling hand to hand with the foe, would have caused even a coward's sluggish blood to flow more swiftly.

When the retreat first set in, the gunners might have escaped as easily as the others if they had chosen to abandon the cannon. Life was theirs at the expense of honour, and the choice was made without hesitation.

They saw the foe surround them, their chance of escape cut off, death drawing nearer every moment; but, encouraged by the brave Maclaine and the equally valiant Colquhoun, they stood firm.

And the Carlists on their side advanced with a stubborn determination to have the guns at all costs. Shot and shell mowed them down, but the survivors pressed on until they got so close that it was no longer possible to fire.

Then the gunners, grasping their hand-spikes, stood at bay—a little knot of heroes, unconquerable save by death.

The charge was more dangerous than many a forlorn hope, but our countrymen were in need of assistance, and we gave it gladly. In spite of the terrible cross-fire which emptied many a saddle, we rode on, gathering speed at every stride, till, like a whirlwind, we burst upon the Carlists and bore them back a little way.

Swift as lightning the artillerymen seized advantage of the diversion, and working with a will, placed the guns on the road, while we with sword and lance kept the enemy back.

Then, when the safety of the battery was assured, we rode for the second time along the fire-swept road.

The army was now hurriedly falling back on the Venta,

which the Carlists in vain attempted to capture. Every assault was successfully repulsed, until about six o'clock in the evening orders were issued to retire to our old positions.

"What about Sarsfield?" I asked Major Townley, as the first regiment marched off. "Why are we going back? Our fellows can hold this hill easily enough."

"There is no need of it, my boy; Sarsfield is comfortably quartered in Pamplona. His messenger reached here between three and four o'clock, and his information makes the return to San Sebastian absolutely necessary. It appears that Sarsfield marched out and back again; a fall of snow prevented him from coming on."

I looked at the speaker in amazement, scarcely able to credit his statement, which, however, proved to be perfectly correct.

The Legion now withdrew to the Ayetté lines in admirable order and without further loss, as the Carlists made only a half-hearted effort to renew the conflict.

For several hours after the wearied soldiers had turned in I was occupied in various duties, but about midnight I lay down—not to sleep, but to mourn in silence the death of the heroic Don Philip.

CHAPTER XXIV.

VICTORY AND SORROW.

JUST at first I thought it likely that the enemy would follow up the recent success, but this did not prove to be the case, and towards the end of April a portion of Espartero's army, amounting to several thousand men, disembarked at San Sebastian.

The command at Pamplona was transferred from Sarsfield to a general named Irribarren, and it gradually began to be understood that a further attack on the Carlist strongholds would shortly be made.

In order to find accommodation for the new arrivals, it became necessary for General Evans to extend his ground; and, accordingly, on the fourth of May, the troops of the Legion crossed the Urimea, and after a slight skirmish occupied the houses and heights of Loyola.

I spent the night of the fifth of May in San Sebastian, but before daylight my servant came running to tell me that the Carlists were making an attack upon the village. To dress and mount my horse occupied little time, and I was soon riding out of the town towards the pontoon bridge which spanned the river.

The attack was well planned, and the Carlists, as usual, displayed the most undaunted courage, hurling themselves time and again on our foremost battery, but only to be repulsed with heavy slaughter, and shortly before nine o'clock they retired into their redoubts.

It was perhaps the failure of this assault which induced the Carlists to alter their tactics, a proceeding which General Evans learned on the night of the thirteenth, through the services of a trusty spy.

This man reported that the enemy had withdrawn all their artillery and the greater part of the troops, leaving only a few battalions to mask their movements and endeavour to delay our progress.

Espartero had joined us with the remainder of his army, and the two generals decided upon an immediate advance.

Having an inkling of what was coming, I snatched a few hours' sleep during the evening of the fourteenth, and it was well that I did so.

At midnight I was summoned to attend General Chichester, and by two o'clock the whole force was turned out.

The rain, of course, came down in torrents—most of our operations were conducted in the pouring rain—and by the time the march began we were thoroughly wet.

It soon became apparent that the spy had spoken the truth, as the Carlists showed up in inconsiderable force, and replied to our artillery fire only with volleys of musketry.

This running fight was kept up until we reached the Venta, and here the enemy with admirable pluck made a gallant stand, and it was only when they found themselves outflanked that they retreated towards Hernani.

While the Irish Brigade moved in the direction of the village, the Eighth, to which I had been sent, was ordered to take the strong position of Santa Barbara, which the Carlists seemed inclined to defend.

At the same time the Chapelgorris received a command to attack it in the front, and these indefatigable warriors advanced with their usual impetuosity.

Eizmendi, who carried his left arm in a sling—he had been wounded in March—gave me a cheery greeting as he passed; and I could not forbear thinking of that other gallant Spaniard who lost his life on the very field which we had just traversed.

Scant time, however, could be afforded to musing, as there was work to be done; and having watched the Eighth set off on their journey, I rode back to the brigadier.

Shortly after this the Carlists evacuated Hernani and Santa Barbara, while about four o'clock in the afternoon they were driven from the neighbouring village of Urineta, and the day's operations were concluded.

Our losses, compared with those of former engagements, were trifling; but the men, having been marching up and down wet, clayey hills since daybreak, were thoroughly exhausted.

Still the object of the expedition had thus far been satisfactorily accomplished; we had driven the enemy out of Hernani, and very few doubted that in a short time the road to the French frontier would be in our possession.

The next day was spent in getting ready for the forward movement, and early on the morning of the seventeenth, the Legion, together with two Spanish divisions, was again in motion.

Espartero stayed with the bulk of his army in Hernani, and two or three battalions, detached from our force, were placed at various points along the road.

The little villages through which we passed were deserted by all save the women and children, who crowded to the doors in order to catch a glimpse of the dreaded Ingleses.

At ten o'clock we arrived in front of Oyarzun, which after a slight skirmish opened its gates, and we resumed our march to Irun, about two miles distant.

On the brow of a hill, screened from the enemy's observation by tall trees, the troops were halted, and the generals rode on for the purpose of reconnoitring.

From this spot a good view of Irun could be obtained, and I gazed with absorbing interest at the preparations which the Carlists had made to receive us.

The town was a walled one, and every kind of defence which human ingenuity could devise had been called into service. Partly covering it stood the Fort del Parque, on a commanding height, and having eight large guns.

A few seconds convinced us that these last were not mounted for the sake of ornament. Almost at the instant of our appearance a cannon ball came crashing over our heads, smashing a tree directly behind us. A second and third, aimed with greater accuracy, covered us with mud, while a fourth knocked over the horse of a Spanish officer at my side.

But, preserving the utmost coolness, the generals went on making their observations, spying through their glasses, selecting positions, and all as if the enemy were a hundred miles away.

At last, and it must be owned greatly to my relief, the chief began to deliver his orders to the aides-de-camp, and these were soon riding in all directions.

I had scarcely spoken a dozen words to Pym during the last few days, and now I only saw him for an instant while on my way to the Rifle Corps.

His regiment had received instructions to march westward, while my duty took me to the east.

"Good-luck!" I cried, as I rode past, and he waved his sword in response.

I look across the years and see him still, with his martial bearing, and his brave, handsome face lit by a kindly smile.

By this time nearly every regiment was in motion, and some of them already under fire.

The Rifles, with whom I rode by the side of the brigadier, advanced close to the battery, from which a heavy fire was poured in, and then formed on a height under cover of a hill.

Beneath us were several buildings close to the town gates, and occupied by a number of Carlists.

"We must have those houses, my lads," exclaimed the brigadier, and at the word away we ran across the fields and into the road.

Men dropped fast, but we kept on; and the Carlists, saluting us with a final volley, fled into the town.

I shall not readily forget the scene which followed. The riflemen, wrought to the highest pitch of excitement, dashed forward madly, as if thinking to enter the town.

This, of course, they were unable to do, as the gates were fastened; and the brigadier, perceiving how perilous was the position, called to them to seek shelter in the adjoining buildings.

"Into the houses, riflemen!" he shouted; "quick! come back. Every man of you will be killed. Stop that bugler, some one"—the bugler was sounding the advance lustily—"Powell, drive those fellows back."

At the corner of the gate stood a massive house, the original strength of which had been materially increased. All the walls were loopholed, and at every hole gleamed the barrel of a musket. A heavy gun also was mounted, and pointed so as to command the space in front of the gates.

Our men, as I have said, were inflamed by passion, and did not stop to reflect upon what might result from their heedless rush.

The Carlists gladly availed themselves of this opportunity for slaughter, and opened fire from their heavy gun and scores of muskets upon the brave riflemen, who, brought to a halt at the gate, could not get forward, and were in little humour for retreat.

Chichester, whose cool bravery had long before won for him the admiration of all, ran through the bullets and the whizzing grape-shot, calling upon the riflemen to enter the houses.

Unwittingly the enemy did us effectual service, for they laid low the bugler who was so vigorously urging on his comrades.

Again and again the Carlists plied their gun, and every wall vomited forth smoke and flame and death-dealing bullets.

By degrees, however, we succeeded in withdrawing the riflemen, and housing them in the church and adjacent buildings, there to await fresh instructions.

Towards sunset, General Evans, always desirous of avoiding unnecessary bloodshed, sent Colonel Cottenor of his staff with a flag of truce, to offer the enemy terms if they would surrender.

For an hour the conflict was stayed, when, the negotiations having failed, the guns from the fort thundered out afresh, and were answered by our artillery.

Towards night the firing ceased, but at daybreak it began anew with the same fury.

The garrison, remembering the cruelties formerly practised upon prisoners from the Legion at this very place, and having no hope of victory, fought with a frenzy born of desperation.

They fully believed that we should massacre every prisoner in cold blood, and inspired by this idea they recklessly threw their lives away.

But in spite of their heroic resistance, the fortunes of the day were plainly going against them.

At our end of the town, some men of the Rifles and First Regiment escaladed the windows of a house close to the gates, and jumping into the street, drove the defenders back at the point of the bayonet. Then the gates were thrown open, and the rest of the two battalions rushed in.

My horse had been shot on the previous evening, but I ran on foot to the front, hoping that I might be able to restrain the passions of the soldiers.

The fight now became a house-to-house one, the Carlists holding each separate building with the utmost tenacity, and retreating only at the last instant.

The streets, too, were strongly barricaded and stoutly held; but our progress, though impeded, was not stopped. From house to house the active riflemen made their way, while the noise in other quarters of the town showed that our comrades were also advancing.

Borne ever backward by the irresistible rush, the Carlists sought their last rallying-place—the massive town-house in the square.

It was here that I witnessed a lamentable occurrence, the memory of which saddens me even now.

We had cleared the street, driving the Carlists before us to the square, in which they still held the strongly-fortified town-house and an adjacent line of buildings.

Conspicuous throughout the morning for his daring was a dashing young officer, who, but for his uniform and the fact that he fought against us, I should have thought was Captain Eizmendi.

Exposing himself freely, he had not once flinched before

our fiercest fire, but now with rifle, now with sword, had done far more than his share in the endeavour to support a sinking cause.

The bulk of his men, having been forced to the corner of the square, made a dash for the town-house; and the young officer, the last to retreat, as he had been all the morning, prepared to follow.

His undaunted courage, and the striking resemblance which he bore to Alphonso Eizmendi, aroused a deep interest in my breast, and I would gladly have given everything I possessed to see him gain shelter.

The Carlists, who in the excitement of the fight had probably forgotten their officer, reached the building; the doors were closed, and he stood outside, alone and wounded.

But the spirit which had hitherto sustained him still lived. He turned round and faced us proudly, standing there amidst the hail of bullets, unconquered and unconquerable.

Then baring his head, he waved his cap, and high above the din of musketry sounded his strong, clear voice.

"*Viva Carlos Quinto!*" he cried exultingly, "*Viva Carlos Quinto!*"

I should have shaded my eyes, but an astounding apparition compelled me to look on like one fascinated.

The Carlists, as I have said, retained possession of an adjacent line of buildings, and from one of these houses a girl now ran swiftly towards the very centre of the square.

I recognized her instantly—the beautiful maiden who had saved my life, the princess, as Pym jokingly called her.

Alas! the ending of the romance was to be far different from that which his imagination had pictured.

Straight across the line of fire she ran to where the wounded officer still stood.

"*Viva Carlos Quinto!*" he cried again in proud defiance, and fell when the girl was within a yard of him.

The stupor which had as it were held me spell-bound was now dispelled, and with a cry of despair I in my turn raced madly across the open.

Our men raised a cheer as I darted out; but the Carlists, ignorant of the nature of my errand, opened a vigorous fire.

The bullets hissed and sputtered past me as I ran; one tore through the collar of my coat, another struck my hat, but these unwelcome messengers only served to quicken my speed.

By this time the girl had sunk to the ground, whether in a faint or wounded was uncertain, but she lay motionless.

The Rifles gave another cheer when they beheld me reach the spot unhurt, and I suddenly became aware that several of the gallant fellows were running after me.

A single glance made it plain that the Carlist officer was dead; but the girl lived, although severely wounded.

"Poor thing!" said a voice at my elbow; "shall I go back for a stretcher, sir? I'd risk my life a thousand times to get the lady under cover. Her sweetheart I reckon; he was a plucky chap," and the rifleman who had come up jerked his arm towards the dead Carlist.

"We shall manage to carry her between us," I said. "Make for that corner house, and go gently."

The musketry fire continued as hot as before, but the bullets no longer came our way; the Carlists, I suppose, had divined our intention, or feared lest their shots should hit the señorita.

We laid her on the ground-floor of an empty house, and Dr. Duplex, the regimental surgeon, came in.

"Can she live?" I asked, and he shook his head despondently, saying,—

"No skill on earth can save her, my boy; she will be dead in an hour."

I thought of Eizmendi and groaned.

"If you see any of the Chapelgorris, tell them to send Captain Eizmendi here," I said; "the lady is his sister. Can we do anything for her?"

"Only let her die in peace;" and the surgeon went out.

How long the noise continued outside I do not know; my time was wholly occupied in watching the dying girl, and pitying her brother, unconscious as yet of his terrible bereavement.

He came in quietly, and it was only when he stooped to kiss the white cheeks of his sister that I perceived him.

Then I pressed his hand, and speaking in whispers, told him of what had occurred.

"My cousin Ignacio," he said, referring to the Carlist officer.

As if some potent charm lay in the word, the speaking of it brought a sudden flush to the face of the girl, and half opening her eyes, she murmured dreamily, "Ignacio, Ignacio."

The young man knelt, and raising her head, pressed her tenderly to him. I do not think she saw him—her eyes were closed again; but perhaps some subtile instinct told her who he was, and she said, "Alphonso, my Alphonso—enemies no more. Ah, now I am happy."

Eizmendi looked from her face to mine in dumb entreaty, but I shook my head sorrowfully. It was hard to speak the bitter words, yet truth was more merciful than suspense, and I told him what Duplex had said.

The sounds of the strife outside had ceased, and thinking that I might be able to secure the services of a woman for my heart-broken friend, I went out, after telling him my intentions.

The fight was at an end; the Carlists had surrendered, and were awaiting their fate, which most of them imagined would be speedy death.

But British readers will not expect me to dwell upon the humanity of a British general.

The bulk of the prisoners were placed in a position of security, and the first man I met was the brigadier running with a white flag, giving orders that every Carlist who surrendered should be granted quarter.

In one of the houses I found an old woman, who, on hearing my story, volunteered to go to Eizmendi's assistance; and she instantly set off, guarded by two riflemen.

Having discharged this duty, I hastened after the brigadier, who was still exerting himself to secure order.

I saw several men of the Eighth Regiment, but neither Pym nor Dick, and was shortly afterwards sent with a message to the Béhobia gate, at which we had entered in the morning.

Perhaps it was the death of Eizmendi's sister which gave a gloomy tinge to my thoughts, but whatever the cause, I went about my duties in a very despondent frame of mind, carrying messages to one quarter and another, but never in any direction where I was likely to hear news of Pym.

Within two hours of the capitulation the Royal Irish marched with colours flying along the road leading to Fuenterrabia, the last of the Carlist strongholds in the neighbourhood, and I had to bear my suspense as well as I was able.

Major Townley gave me a little comfort. "Don't look so glum, Powell," he said. "You may depend that your chum's all right. Evans has left a part of his force in Irun, and no doubt Forrester is amongst them. Anyway, we shall be back to-morrow. Fuenterrabia is not likely to hold out."

The enemy had broken down the bridge over the river, and while we halted for it to be rebuilt, I met Captain Peyton of the Sixth.

"Forrester!" he said, in reply to my question; "yes, he was alive this morning. I saw him at the attack on the fort. He was on the top of a ladder, and that sergeant of yours was close behind. Cheer up, Powell; I don't think he can be hurt, and I'll tell you why. Just as our fellows were swarming up to the assault, a Carlist brought us the keys of the gate, and the fighting was practically over. I suppose the garrison yonder will yield peaceably; I hear that Evans has offered them terms."

Peyton's information had the effect of making me a little more cheerful, yet I chafed at every delay, and was consumed by a passionate longing to be back again in Irun.

Duty, however, compelled me to go with the army, and in the morning we were in front of Fuenterrabia.

Here, in spite of the general's assurances, the garrison refused to believe that the lives of their comrades at Irun had been spared, and requested that two of their officers might be allowed to go and see for themselves.

Evans gave his permission, and when they returned with their report the garrison capitulated.

The gates were opened, the soldiers filed out slowly, depositing their arms on the glacis before the town, and the Sixth received instructions to enter.

Even in my deep distress I felt a glow of honest pride at the conduct of General Chichester—conduct worthy of a true English gentleman.

The Sixth had arrived within a hundred yards of the disarmed Carlists, when he asked Colonel Ross to halt the regiment.

"My brave lads," he said, "I am about to make a request which I am sure you will grant. In the fight you have behaved nobly; now that the hour of your triumph has come, respect the vanquished. Don't hurt their feelings by cheering or by any sign of exultation."

"Never fear, sir," they responded, and marched on

quietly, unostentatiously—gallant soldiers under a gallant leader.

The work so long held in view was accomplished. Throughout the northern provinces the Carlists were broken up, their strongholds captured; the land right to the French frontier was in our possession.

I was standing amidst a group of officers who were congratulating each other on the success of the expedition, when Major Townley came up and drew me on one side.

"My dear boy," he said gravely, "I have sad news. Forrester is hurt, and I am afraid seriously. Hamilton saw him fall. If you like you can take my horse. There is nothing more to be done here, and I will make it right with Chichester."

Barely staying to thank him, I mounted his horse and galloped off at full speed.

Pym hurt—dying—perhaps dead! Ah! that must be the meaning of Townley's solemn face. Pym was dead, and I had been absent from his side.

The horse flew along the road, and yet the pace was not swift enough; lightning would have seemed too slow.

Pym dead! killed by almost the last shot! What did Townley say? Hurt seriously. Of course people always said that. How foolish of me not to have seen through it at first!

I pulled up my horse in the square of the town, and proceeded more slowly towards the temporary hospital. Now that the truth was so close at hand, I dreaded to face it.

"Looking for Forrester?" exclaimed a friendly voice; "come this way. They carried him into a house near the fort, and I would not have him moved."

The speaker was Murphy, the surgeon, and I jumped down, saying excitedly, "Is he dead?"

"No, but he soon will be if you go tearing in on him like that."

"Oh, I'll be quiet enough when we get there," and slipping one arm through my bridle-rein, I took hold of the surgeon with the other.

"Will he live?" I asked, as we approached the house.

"Can't say yet; but there is a chance, though a slight one. Hush! don't speak loudly; the less noise, the better for him."

I tossed the reins to a soldier outside, and entered, treading softly.

A man moved noiselessly across the room, and I recognized Dick.

"Thank God, you've come!" the trusty fellow whispered. "I began to fancy you were down too."

I bent over the bed and gazed sadly into my old friend's face. He lay with closed eyes; there was a flush on his cheeks, but the lips were bloodless.

"The bullet just missed the lung," Murphy explained; "if we can beat the fever, he'll pull through yet. Has he been pretty quiet, sergeant?"

"Yes, sir, but wandering in his mind."

"Ah, that is to be expected. Will you stay with him, Powell?"

"Certainly."

"Then the sergeant had better go back to his regiment. I'll call again this evening. Keep his forehead cool, and if he gets violent send for me; there are some people up-stairs."

"How did it happen, Dick?" I asked, when Murphy had gone out.

"Simplest thing in the world, sir. He was on the top of the ladder, calling to the men, when some one shouted that the gates were open. I looked down, and sure enough there were some of our fellows inside. 'The game's up, major,' I said; 'they've opened the gates.' 'Very glad, Dick, I'm sure,' said he, 'especially as the poor beggars have no earthly chance of winning.' With that there was a flash from the house opposite, and I only just stopped him from tumbling over. 'They've done for me, Dick,' he said; 'tell Arthur.' Some of the men helped to carry him here, and I fixed him up on this bed, while Corporal Jackson went for Murphy. Now I must get back to the regiment, but you'll let me know if—if—"

"Yes," I said, swallowing the lump in my throat that threatened to choke me; and Dick, after another look at his beloved officer, crept softly away.

For several hours I sat by the bedside while the sufferer remained in a state between sleep and insensibility, but towards the evening he became restless and his eyes opened.

I could not tell by their expression if he was sensible; but the fingers of the hand nearest me closed on mine, and gave it a barely perceptible pressure.

My heart overflowed with gladness as I placed my face to his.

"You mustn't try to speak, old fellow," I whispered. "You have been hit badly; but Murphy says you have only to be careful, and everything will come right."

The pressure of my hand was repeated, and with a sigh which sounded like one of relief, Pym lay back.

CHAPTER XXV.

HOME AGAIN.

FOR me the interest of the few weeks succeeding the triumphant battles of the Legion was centered in Pym's fight with death.

He had been removed to San Sebastian with the army, and mainly owing to the surgeon's skill and tender care, had suffered little from the journey.

Every minute not occupied in military duty I spent at his side, where Dick was also a privileged visitor, and always when we left we told each other that he was surely getting better.

What Espartero's plans were I do not know, but for a whole week the army remained in a state of inaction around San Sebastian, and the evening of the twenty-eighth of May arrived before I received orders to attend General Chichester on the march towards Pamplona.

It was for the most part merely a military promenade, unworthy of chronicling, only that it involved a separation of some days from Pym.

Murphy, however, solemnly assured me that, whatever might be the ultimate result, there was no prospect of immediate danger; and relieved by his words, I resolved to banish my fears.

"You will find him alive on your return, and you won't have to go away again," he said. "In a fortnight the Legion will be disbanded."

We turned the Carlists out of Andoain without much trouble, and while the troops were halted there, I saw my former comrade Pedro for the last time.

"Well, old friend," I said, "I suppose that we are not likely to meet again. You are going south, while I, in a few weeks, am returning to England."

"I am sorry, señor, though for your sake I ought to be glad," he replied. "I can only wish you many years of happiness."

"The same to you, Pedro; and a speedy ending to this cruel war."

The bugles now sounded the advance, and with a respectful salute the Spaniard stepped into his place, nor has it been my fate ever to meet with him since.

Some distance beyond Andoain the army broke up into two divisions, and while the major portion marched southward with Espartero, the soldiers of the Legion returned to San Sebastian.

"That," remarked one of the officers, as we began to retrace our steps, "I am thankful to say, ends our share in the war."

"We'll come out again in twenty years' time and see the finish," laughed a comrade.

"The government could stop the fighting in a month, if

it went the right way to work," a third declared. "Give these Biscayans their ancient privileges, and they would hunt Carlos from the mountains."

"What about the new Legion? The Spaniards are making desperate efforts to induce the men to re-enlist."

"I can't give you the Spanish rendering," responded the young officer, whose name was Key; "but at home we used to say, 'If a man cheat me once, shame on him; if twice, shame on me,' and that, I think, sums the matter up pretty fairly. I wonder our fellows didn't kick the traces over long ago."

"The men will follow the chief's lead; if he goes back they will."

"That's all settled; Evans has declined a fresh command. What will you do, Powell?"

"I haven't made up my mind."

"Then take my advice, and come back with us. By the way, how is Forrester?"

"He was better when I left him on Sunday, but not out of danger."

"He'll pull through right enough; never fear."

"Key is an authority on surgery," laughed Major Townley; "he once drew a man's tooth out with a piece of string.

"And a sound one too, which made the feat all the harder."

"It's all very well for you fellows to chaff," growled Key; "but I happen to know about Forrester. Murphy told me himself that he felt sure of his recovery, and old Murphy doesn't make mistakes."

"He didn't tell me that," I said dubiously.

"He wouldn't raise your hopes too high in case the unexpected happened, but all the same he believes that Forrester will get better. What became of that girl at Irun, Powell?"

"Died," I answered curtly, and rode forward in a reverie induced by the question.

I had not met Eizmendi since the affecting scene in Irun, but Duplex had told me of his sister's death, and I brooded sorrowfully over her tragic fate.

However, we had barely entered San Sebastian when the sight of Dick, with a bright smiling face, drove all thoughts of the Chapelgorri and his sister from my mind.

Directly he saw me at liberty he came across.

"You bring good news, Dick," I cried joyously.

"Ay, sir; I couldn't bring better. The major's got the turn. I went this afternoon, and he knew me at once. He asked after you, and I reckon he's counting the minutes till you get there."

"Then I'll go at once;" and leaving Dick, who had to return to his duties, I hurried away.

It was as the sergeant said. The delirium of fever was past, and as I approached the bed Pym stretched out his hand in welcome.

"Thank God for this, my dear fellow!" I cried, and then stopped; my heart was too full as yet for much speech.

"I expect it has been a stiff bout, Arthur," he said, after a while; "I feel as weak as a child. Do the folk at home know?"

"Not how bad you really were. I wrote and told them of your injury, but worded the letter so that they should not lose hope."

"That was a good fellow," he said gratefully, and then lay silent.

Fearful of overtaxing his puny strength, I soon took my leave, but with a promise to look in early on the following day.

Then finding that General Chichester did not need me, I went to my room and spent the next hour in writing a cheerful letter to England.

"There," I exclaimed, when the last word was written and the paper folded, "that will carry joy into one household at least," and placing it in my pocket, I went to bed.

"Well, Powell," said the brigadier at the breakfast-table, "have you seen enough soldiering, or will you stay with the new Legion? I hear that your friend Forrester is recovering."

"Yes, but he is still very weak, and I am going to take him to England as soon as he can travel."

"Quite right. There's no place like home for an invalid.—How does the recruiting go on, Townley?"

"Rather slowly, I believe. The men are beginning to want something besides promises."

"Well, we have done our best and can do no more," said the brigadier as he left the table.

Taking my cap, I went out with the intention of visiting Pym, but had only proceeded a few yards when I met Eizmendi.

Neither of us spoke for an instant; the unexpected meeting brought to our memories the last occasion on which we had seen each other.

Eizmendi broke the silence, and suggested that we should enter an adjoining café.

"I intended calling upon you," he said; "but it is scarcely worth while going farther now. I have only to thank you for all your kindness, and say good-bye. We start for Durango this evening, and our return is uncertain."

"You will come and see Forrester," I urged; "he will be sorry at having missed you."

Eizmendi shook his head. "I would rather not. Have you told him—"

"Not yet," I interrupted hastily.

"They lie in one grave. The priest was very kind, and buried them with the rites of the church. I knew it would please her. But my heart is broken, Arturo, and I care not to talk of it. That is why I do not wish to visit Señor Forrester."

For a moment I thought that he would break down, but the iron will of the man sustained him.

We had ordered some wine, but it remained untasted; and now, standing up, Eizmendi gave me his hand.

"Farewell, my friend," he said, with just a trace of emotion; "perhaps in the days to come you will give a thought to the unhappy Alphonso Eizmendi; and if no news of me ever reaches your peaceful English home, you will know that I have fallen in the service of my country."

Alas! poor fellow! Looking into his face, it was easy to

realize that the Alphonso Eizmendi of former days was already dead. The freshness and vivacity of his youth were gone, and though he still smiled, the light in his eyes was devoid of life; it was like the cold and cheerless ray of a wintry sun.

Time, perhaps, would be merciful to him as to others, but I knew full well that he would not give it the chance. Erelong, on some hotly-contested field, he would fling his life away, and the house of Eizmendi would live only in the memory of its former glories.

We parted at the corner of the street, and I continued to watch him until he disappeared amidst the throng.

I said nothing to Pym that day of my farewell interview with Eizmendi, as I felt that it would be unwise in his weak state to make any mention of the death of the princess.

We talked, instead, of the homeward voyage, and the sick man seemed positively to gather strength from the thought of the happy days to come.

"But we must not go just yet, Arthur," he said; "the little mother would break her heart if she saw me like this," and he laid one wasted hand on the coverlet.

"Suspense will do her more harm than a knowledge of the truth," I urged. "When she learns that the others have returned, she will imagine all sorts of dreadful things."

"Perhaps so," he said; and then after a pause, "Yes, you are right, Arthur; we will hear what the doctor says, and abide by his decision. Dick was here this morning talking about the new Legion. They want him to join, but I told him that he must not desert us."

"Quite right," I said quickly; "we will go back together. Three we came, and by God's grace three we will return."

"Ah, there is Doctor Alcock.—Doctor, how long before I shall be fit for a sea-voyage?"

"In other three weeks, major, perhaps less, if you continue improving, but you mustn't be in too great a hurry."

"I think," said Pym reflectively, "that the smell of the Devonshire fields would make me well."

"All in good time, my dear fellow; but remember the homely proverb, 'The more haste, the less speed.' As it is, you are doing remarkably well."

"Yes, I ought not to complain; I have had a marvellous escape."

"Honestly, I would not have given much for your chances when you were brought here," responded the doctor, snapping his fingers; "but it is time for the mixture, and I want to see you sleeping—your face is too flushed."

Pym smiled faintly. "Keep out of the doctors' hands, Arthur," he said, as I bade him adieu; "they are regular tyrants. I thought we were going to have a nice long chat."

On the tenth of June, the day when the Legion was formally disbanded, Pym sat up for half an hour, and from that time he began to make rapid progress towards recovery.

From time to time several of his old comrades in arms dropped in to see him before they sailed for England, and many were the exclamations of delight at the improvement in his health.

"Get him away as soon as you can," said young Key, with a laugh, "or he'll be accepting a commission in the new Legion;" but from this Pym strongly dissented.

At last the day came when, in company with some other officers, we were to leave Spain, probably for ever. Most of the men were still in San Sebastian waiting for means of transport, and several of the Eighth clustered round their former officer, showing both by looks and words their pleasure at his recovery.

"A pleasant voyage, sir," cried one, shaking his hand; "and I hope the old country will soon set you right again."

"Ay, so do I; we'll never have a better officer."

"That's a true word, Jack, if ever there was one.—Boys, let's send the major off with a parting cheer. Three cheers for Major Forrester—hip-hip-hurrah!" and the crowd joined right heartily.

The act was so spontaneous, and above all so sincere, that Pym's face flushed with a glow of genuine pleasure.

"Thank you, my lads," he said warmly; "and in return, let me wish all of you good-luck. We have been through a good deal together, and I am glad that we part as friends."

I perceived that the excitement was becoming too much for him, and felt quite relieved when we reached the ship, where, on the deck, the captain had rigged up a comfortable awning.

The men on shore waved us a last good-bye, to which we responded by taking off our hats; the sailors sang merrily while getting up the anchor; the ship began to move through the water, and we were fairly started on the voyage home.

"After all," said Pym thoughtfully, "I do not regret my two years in Spain. It is a goodly land, and now that the ideas of tolerance and freedom are taking firm root, it should begin to see a new era of prosperity."

"What have you to say about it, Dick?" I asked.

"Plenty of kicks, and very few ha'pence," was the reply of the philosopher, delivered amidst a chorus of approvals from the bystanders.

"Bravo, sergeant! that hits the bull's-eye. A short and pithy statement that a plain man can understand. I'll put it down."

"I can answer for the scarcity of the coppers," remarked another. "My pay is twelve months in arrears at present. I suppose I must write it off as a bad debt."

"Stevens of the Rifles has declined to leave San Sebastian till they have paid up to the last farthing. I told him yesterday he would be buried there."

"How do you feel now?" I asked Pym, under cover of the conversation.

"Better, old fellow. Every motion of the ship gives me new strength. I wonder if any of them will be at Plymouth?"

"All of them, sir, down to the little missy," said Dick. "Sir Nicholas will be marching up and down the Hoe with a spy-glass to-morrow morning, asking why the ship's not in sight."

"Hardly as soon as that," Pym laughed, but Dick stuck to his assertion, and we learned later that he was not far wrong.

What a glorious sensation is that of being homeward-bound! And above all, when the first tiny speck of the dear old land rises out of the ocean, how fast the heart beats, how the cheeks flush and the eyes sparkle!

On that morning when we sighted the English shores I saw strong men who had risked their lives on many a battle-field, who had stood unmoved amidst the hail of bullets, fairly break down.

We clustered on the deck, but not to talk. We leaned over the vessel's side, and drawing deep breaths, gazed fixedly on the bold cliffs as if they were the outworks of an enchanted land.

And to us it was a land of enchantment, for it was England.

The very breath of heaven seemed to understand and appreciate our eagerness. The wind carried the good ship along right merrily, until we dropped anchor in Plymouth Sound.

How can I do justice to the scene which followed?—how describe the leave-takings, the merry jest, the sigh of regret, as we parted from those who had been our trusty comrades in the stirring times past? Or that other scene, when we found ourselves surrounded by Pym's family, from his father down, as Dick had truly prophesied, to the little missy herself?

How they laughed and cried over us! How, after Mrs. Forrester had kissed Pym to her heart's content, she hugged me to her bosom, and murmured, "My other son!"

And Dick, the philosopher, the "Cast-iron man," how curiously his eyes blinked when the little missy, clambering into his arms, kissed him on the mouth, "for being so good to bruvver Pym!"

Ah! the pen may write of these things freely enough, and yet how little of the reality it can convey! Only those who have lived through such a scene can understand its inner significance. Even after this lapse of time, when many of the actors have been carried to their long rest, I cannot recall it without emotion.

Then, again, I love to dwell upon our reception in the little village, almost within sound of the sea, where Pym's father dwelt.

From the veriest toddler to the old grandsire with white locks and rounded shoulders, the villagers turned out to welcome the young squire and his comrades.

And what a welcome they gave us! What hearty cheering and waving of caps! what thronging round the carriage, as we drove slowly through the long, straggling street to the Hall!

"One would think we were conquering heroes," said Pym, laughing, but well pleased, nevertheless, "instead of only bruised and battered soldiers." And then, as we

BRITISH
10 NO 97
MUSEUM

drove through the gates of the pretty lodge, he added, "Ah, Arthur, my boy, it is good to be home again."

And here the story of our adventures with the British Legion comes to an end. The years that have passed since have not been devoid of incidents, but they cannot be chronicled in these pages.

Concerning this period of our lives nothing remains to be written; I have but reluctantly to trace the last word—FAREWELL.

THE END.

Young Lady's Library.

The Heiress of Wylmington. By EVELYN EVERETT-GREEN, Author of "True to the Last," etc. Crown 8vo, cloth extra, gilt edges. Price 5s. *Cheaper Edition*, 4s.

"There are some remarks in its pages with which sensible people of every creed and every shade of opinion can scarcely fail to sympathize....It is pleasantly and prettily told."—SATURDAY REVIEW.

Temple's Trial; or, For Life or Death. By EVELYN EVERETT-GREEN, Author of "The Heiress of Wylmington," etc. Crown 8vo, cloth extra, gilt edges. Price 5s. *Cheaper Edition*, 4s.

An interesting study of character, going mainly to show the beauty of a quiet, manly Christian life; on the other hand the terrible moral degradation to which selfishness unchecked may lead.

Winning the Victory; or, Di Pennington's Reward. A Tale. By EVELYN EVERETT-GREEN, Author of "The Heiress of Wylmington," etc. Post 8vo, cloth extra. 3s. 6d.

A very interesting tale for young people. The charm of a thoroughly unselfish character is displayed, and in one of an opposite description the idol Self is at last dethroned.

Rinaultrie. By Mrs. MILNE-RAE, Author of "Morag: A Story of Highland Life," etc. Crown 8vo, gilt top. Price 5s. *Cheaper Edition*, 4s.

"We heartily commend this fresh, healthy, and carefully-written tale, with its truthful and vivid pictures of Scottish life."—ABERDEEN FREE PRESS.

On Angels' Wings; or, The Story of Little Violet of Edelsheim. By the Hon. Mrs. GREENE, Author of "The Grey House on the Hill," etc. Crown 8vo, gilt edges. Price 5s. *Cheaper Edition*, 4s.

"Is interesting from the intensity of human feeling and sympathy it develops."—LITERARY WORLD.

Mine Own People. By LOUISA M. GRAY, Author of "Nelly's Teachers," etc. Crown 8vo. Price 5s. *Cheaper Edition*, 4s.

It is a work of great human interest, and all the more is it human because it recognizes the supreme human interest—namely, that of religion, and the strength, purity, and gladness which religion brings to them who receive it in its simplicity and power. A wholesome, suggestive, and wisely-stimulating book for young women.

Nelly's Teachers, and what they Learned. By LOUISA M. GRAY, Author of "Ada and Gerty," etc. Post 8vo, cl. ex., gilt ed. 3s.

A tale for the young. Alice and Lina while themselves children, trying to teach on Sunday evenings a very young and ignorant child, become learners also in the best sense of the word.

Ada and Gerty; or, Hand in Hand Heavenward. A Story of School Life. By LOUISA M. GRAY, Author of "Dunalton," etc. Post 8vo, cloth extra, gilt edges. 3s.

A touching story of two girls, giving an interesting account of their education and school experiences.

The Children of Abbotsmuir Manse. A Tale for the Young. By LOUISA M. GRAY, Author of "Nelly's Teachers," etc. Post 8vo, cloth extra, gilt edges. 3s.

"This is a book we should like to see in the hands of children. It will help them to be both happy and good."—DAILY REVIEW.

Dunalton. The Story of Jack and his Guardians. By LOUISA M. GRAY, Author of "Nelly's Teachers," "Ada and Gerty," etc. Illustrated. Post 8vo, cloth extra, gilt edges. Price 3s.

"A well-conceived, well-told, and deeply interesting story."—PRESBYTERIAN MESSENGER.

T. NELSON AND SONS, LONDON, EDINBURGH, AND NEW YORK.

Library of Historical Tales.

Dorothy Arden. A Story of England and France Two Hundred Years Ago. By J. M. CALLWELL. Crown 8vo, cloth extra. Price 4s.

A story of the dragonnades in France in the time of Louis XIV. Also of the persecutions in England under James II., the Monmouth rebellion, the Bloody Assize, and the Revolution.

How they Kept the Faith. A Tale of the Huguenots of Languedoc. By GRACE RAYMOND. Crown 8vo, cloth extra. Price 4s.

"No finer, more touchingly realistic, and truthfully accurate picture of the Languedoc Huguenots have we met."—ABERDEEN FREE PRESS.

The Lost Ring. A Romance of Scottish History in the Days of King James and Andrew Melville. Crown 8vo, cloth extra. 4s.

"The plot of the romance is skilfully constructed, the dialogue is admirable, and the principal actors in the history are portrayed with great ability."—U.P. MISSIONARY RECORD.

The City and the Castle. A Story of the Reformation in Switzerland. By ANNIE LUCAS, Author of "Leonie," etc. Crown 8vo, cloth extra. Price 4s.

Faithfully portrays the state and character of society at the time of the Reformation (in Switzerland).

Leonie; or, Light out of Darkness: and **Within Iron Walls,** a Tale of the Siege of Paris. Twin-Stories of the Franco-German War. By ANNIE LUCAS. Crown 8vo, cloth extra. Price 4s.

Two tales, the first connected with the second. One, of country life in France during the war; the other, life within the besieged capital.

Under the Southern Cross. A Tale of the New World. By the Author of "The Spanish Brothers," etc. Crown 8vo, cl. ex. 4s.

A thrilling and fascinating story.

Alison Walsh. A Study of To-Day. By CONSTANCE EVELYN. Crown 8vo, cloth extra. Price 4s.

La Rochelle; or, The Refugees. A Story of the Huguenots. By Mrs. E. C. WILSON. Crown 8vo, cloth extra. Price 4s.

Wenzel's Inheritance; or, Faithful unto Death. A Tale of Bohemia in the Fifteenth Century. By ANNIE LUCAS. Crown 8vo, cloth extra. Price 4s.

Presents a vivid picture of the religious and social condition of Bohemia in the fifteenth century.

Helena's Household. A Tale of Rome in the First Century. With Frontispiece. Crown 8vo, cloth extra. Price 4s.

The Spanish Brothers. A Tale of the Sixteenth Century. By the Author of "The Dark Year of Dundee." Crown 8vo, cloth extra. Price 4s.

The Czar. A Tale of the Time of the First Napoleon. By the Author of "The Spanish Brothers," etc. Crown 8vo, cloth extra. Price 4s.

An interesting tale of the great Franco-Russian war in 1812–13; the characters partly French, partly Russian.

Arthur Erskine's Story. A Tale of the Days of Knox. By the Author of "The Spanish Brothers," etc. Crown 8vo, cloth extra. Price 4s.

The object of the writer of this tale is to portray the life of the people in the days of Knox.

Pendower. A Story of Cornwall in the Reign of Henry the Eighth. By M. FILLEUL. Crown 8vo. cloth extra. Price 4s.

A tale illustrating in fiction that stirring period of English history previous to the Reformation.

T. NELSON AND SONS, LONDON. EDINBURGH, AND NEW YORK.

Lightning Source UK Ltd.
Milton Keynes UK
UKHW030726050521
383174UK00009B/666